THE POWER OF SILENCE

THE POWER OF SILENCE
Silent Communication
in Daily Life

Colum Kenny

KARNAC

First published in 2011 by
Karnac Books Ltd
118 Finchley Road
London NW3 5HT

British Library Cataloguing in Publication Data

A C.I.P. for this book is available from the British Library

ISBN-13: 978-1-85575-841-4

Typeset by Vikatan Publishing Solutions (P) Ltd., Chennai, India

Printed in Great Britain

www.karnacbooks.com

For my sons

And some of us who have already begun to break the silence of the night have found that the calling to speak is often a vocation of agony, ...

—Martin Luther King

CONTENTS

FOREWORD

Silence is useful. Falling silent can be a means of learning about the world around us, or a powerful way of letting someone know what we feel. Silence is also a space in which to cultivate peace of mind and body. It is a defence against intrusion.

But silence may also be deadly. A long silence in marriage is sometimes fatal to the relationship. Political silences kill.

Silence is effective. Without measured silence music would be cacophony. An astute broadcaster falls silent to entice the interviewee to open up; an analyst to invite interpretation; a business executive to wrongfoot those with whom he or she negotiates.

Silence is refreshing. The meditator is quiet in order to settle the senses and to enhance perception; a monk to listen for the word of the Lord; the exhausted worker to embrace relaxation and recuperation. Silence may have secular or spiritual significance.

Clearly, silence has an important place in our lives. Yet, just as it is increasingly difficult to escape artificial lighting at night, so we have accepted noise or constant sound as a price worth paying for contemporary conveniences.

The author of this book set out to discover why silence matters, and to discern how being silent is an intrinsic feature of being human. We need some silence in our lives, and silent spaces in society.

Drawing from the wells of literature and science, among other sources, we are reminded of what the wise and the not so wise have said about the pleasures and perplexities of silence.

Words, music, and ambient sounds are the meteors, planets, and stars of silence. Silence also has its black holes, seeming absences that are, on closer inspection, significant presences. These include the silences of people who choose not to speak, and of people who are unable or who are not allowed to express themselves.

Silence even has its "Big Bang" debates. For just as scientists differ on the origin of the universe, and many people believe that God created matter, so some philosophers discern in cosmic silence a benign Presence. Others find only abysmal absence. If we listen hard, can we hear anything other than our own plaintive voices echoing across the universe? And which came first, sound or silence?

We are variously acting, breathing, choosing, desiring, excreting, feeling, hearing, meditating, playing, remembering, seeing, speaking, thinking persons. Our loving and our consuming are not separate from these manisfestations of life. Both may involve (for example) choosing, desiring, and feeling. Nor, for its part, is being silent a separate state.

To be or to fall silent is a way of enhancing other ways of being, especially that of hearing. Silence is a necessary precondition of speech and music: without it there would be continuous noise. Silence is related to communication in general. There is some silence in even the busiest life.

We can actively or passively fall silent. In other words, we may either choose to avoid speech or simply fail to respond. We may even be garrulously silent, concealing the self quietly within a carapace of speech.

There is no intransitive verb corresponding to the adjective "silent". One can "act" or "breathe" but one cannot "silence" without an object. The object may be oneself, as in "I silenced myself", or another, as in (usually with some force) "I silenced her/him". Silencing is seldom experienced pleasantly by the person who is silenced.

Falling silent may be the precursor of fresh insights or creativity. It can be a means of manipulation or resistance. Pausing for thought and saying nothing are not necessarily the same things. Silence is seldom an end in itself, unless perhaps the silence of the grave.

Thus, silence is not merely the absence or opposite of speaking or sound. Nor is it identical to solitude or to stillness, although there appears at times to be a seamless connection between such states and silence.

Silence is not a realm that we access outside everyday experiences and phenomena. It is embedded, relatively, in and between the moments of daily life. It is powerful. By understanding its uses we enhance our appreciation and enjoyment of the physical, psychological, and spiritual dimensions of existence.

* * *

Something in silence summoned me and I wrote this book. When I was a child, my mother once suggested in a kindly but exasperated way that I sometimes asked too many questions. She was probably right. We were sitting in a bus as it made its way down O'Connell Street, and I had been interrogating her about the various statues and buildings along Dublin's main thoroughfare. For all of us, as for my mother on that day, there comes a point when we exhaust our capacity or desire to explain the world. Silence is an option.

This book on silence speaks for itself. Silences of various kinds have long seemed to me to be significant, and worthy of investigation. There are, not least in families or relationships, facts that remain noisily unmentioned and feelings that stay unexpressed. There is, beyond that, a social consensus that may tend to smother diversity. However, there is also the calming retreat, an elected silence that sings to us of a balanced and happy state.

Silence is evidently as intrinsic to human existence as is speech, and is also complex. Silence and sound are interdependent, and open-ended. When exploring various areas or domains in which the significance of silence is evident, in which it is in a sense experienced, our observations may be refracted through the prism of theory. I have not attempted to enclose each field of silence that is considered below within a neat philosophical frame. However, some familiarity with relevant theories that have been developed enhances our understanding of particular silences. Accordingly, one chapter below is especially devoted to the work of Max Picard, George Steiner, Deborah Tannen, Adam Jaworski, and others. In charting the course of silence through areas of everyday life, those who have recourse to theory at any point will gain insights into the nature of their experiences. Yet the power of silence lies ultimately in its capacity to transcend our best efforts to define or defy it. Silence waits patiently for sound to fade out.

Towards the end of her life, I returned with my mother to sit quietly among the rose bushes in Dublin's Botanic Gardens where she had played with her sister when they were children, and where she had brought me when I was a boy. Subsequently, on a warm summer evening, we strolled slowly and alone among the little lawns and manicured ruins of Mellifont Abbey in Co. Louth. On such occasions, one can almost hear time passing. Silence is bitter-sweet.

* * *

Among those who have encouraged or helped me in some way in the preparation of this book were Patrick Brereton, Brother Gregory Cavalier, Anthony Curran, John and Wendy Ferré, Fr Laurence Freeman, Mary Kenny, Colm Keane, Tom Lawrence, Patricia Macken, Sara Maitland, Stephanie McBride, Dave McMahon, Pantelis Michelakis, Jolyon Mitchell, Marie Murphy, Louis O'Dea, Linda Tucker, and Max Underwood.

For their hospitality and assistance, I owe a debt of gratitude not only to the community of the Trappist Abbey of Gethsemani, near Bardstown in Kentucky, but also to those of the Cistercian Abbey of Notre-Dame de Sénanque, near Gordes in Provence, and Kagyu Samye Ling monastery, near Lockerbie in Scotland.

I am indebted to the librarians of Bray Public Library, Co. Wicklow; the British Library; Dublin City University; National Library of Ireland; King's Inns, Dublin; New College, University of Edinburgh; St Deiniol's Library, Wales; the University of Louisville, KY; Thomas Merton Center, Bellarmine University, KY; and Trinity College Dublin.

A number of authors and publishers have kindly given me permission to quote from their works. Thanks are due to Dedalus Press for permission to reproduce lines translated by Kevin O'Rourke from the original Korean by Chong-Ju in *Tilting the Jar, Spilling the Moon*

(Dublin: Dedalus, 1993); Maria Mazziotti Gillan for permission to include her striking poem about the experiences of a migrant family, "Public School No. 18: Paterson, New Jersey": this originally appeared in *Winter Light* (Midland Park, NJ: Chantry Press, 1985) and was republished in *Where I Come From* (Toronto: Guernica Editions, 1995); Adrienne Rich and W. W. Norton & Company for permission to include Part 1 of "Cartographies of Silence" (© 2002 by Adrienne Rich, © 1978 by W. W. Norton & Company, Inc.), and also to include lines from Poem IX of "Twenty-One Love Poems" (© 2002 by Adrienne Rich, © 1978 by W. W. Norton & Company, Inc.), from *The Fact of a Doorframe: Selected Poems 1950–2001* by Adrienne Rich; and Li-Young Lee, for "A Story" from *Book of My Nights* (© 2001 by Li-Young Lee, reprinted with the permission of BOA Editions Ltd., www.boaeditions.org); Heidi Levitt and Taylor & Francis Ltd., http://www.informaworld.com, for extracts from "The unsaid in the psychotherapy narrative: voicing the unvoiced" (*Counselling Psychology Quarterly*, 2002).

Mary Beth Baker, managing editor, Regnery Publishing, Washington, DC, helped me to locate the current copyright holder of Max Picard's *World of Silence*. Extracts from that work are by kind permission of Eighth Day Press, Wichita, KS, which published a paperback edition in 2002. Dr Andrea Sabbadini's work on silence and psychotherapy, published in the *British Journal of Psychotherapy*, is quoted by his kind permission; extracts from Vanda Scott and David Lester, "Listening to silence: a column from Befrienders International", are with permission from *Crisis: Vol. 19* (3), 1998 © by Hogrefe & Huber Publishers (Seattle, Toronto, Göttingen, Bern); and Takie Sugiyama Lebra's article, "The cultural significance of silence in Japanese communication", published in 1987 in *Multilingua*, 6 (4): 343–357 (also available at http://www.reference-global.com/), is quoted with permission from De Gruyter. I am grateful to Faber & Faber for permisison to include extracts from their editions of George Steiner's *Language and Silence*, and for Marianne Moore's poem "Silence".

Thanks to ICS Publications for some passages from *The Collected Works of St. Teresa of Avila, Volumes 1–3*, translated by Kieran Kavanaugh and Otilio Rodriguez (© 1976 & 1980), and from *The Collected Works of St. John of the Cross*, translated by Kieran Kavanaugh and Otilio Rodriguez (© 1964, 1979 & 1991), all by Washington Province of Discalced Carmelites, ICS Publications, 2131 Lincoln Road, NE, Washington, DC 20002-1199, USA (www.icspublications.org).

Thanks to Wim Haan of the University of Amsterdam for his thoughts on the relative place of silence in Africa and America. Extracts from Pepe Choong's thesis relating to Chinese women in New Zealand are by kind permission of that author.

But thanks most of all to my wife Catherine Curran and to our sons Oisín, Conor, and Samuel for reminding me that silence is a relative phenomenon, and for helping in various other ways with my work and life.

It was Catherine, a social worker and psychotherapist, who suggested to me that Karnac Books might well be interested in this exploration of silence. That Karnac were indeed interested and welcoming means that a long exploration of silence has borne fruit in the pages that follow.

ABOUT THE AUTHOR

Born in Ireland in 1951, **Professor Colum Kenny**, BCL, PhD, barrister-at-law, is chair of the Masters in Journalism programme at the School of Communications, Dublin City University. He also co-ordinates an interdisciplinary module entitled Belief & Communication. A board member of the Broadcasting Authority of Ireland and of the EU Media Desk in Dublin, Kenny contributes frequently to public debates about culture and society. The author of eight books, he is married with three sons and lives in Bray, Co. Wicklow.

CHAPTER ONE

Silent types

Not everyone thinks highly of silence. Shakespeare, in the *Merchant of Venice* (Act I, sc. 1, lines 111–112), has Gratiano declare that,

> Silence is only commendable
> In a neat's [cow's] tongue dried and a maid not vendible [marketable].

Yet it remains true that many people believe silence to be "commendable" in more cases than Gratiano was willing to admit—or sometimes so, at least. Asking "Is it good in general to practise silence?", Basil of Caesarea (c329–379) answered that question as follows: "The good of silence is dependent on the time and the person, as we are taught by the God-inspired Scripture" (Silvas, p. 387).

Some people practise reticence or silence so habitually that they become known as "the silent type". They are, to use an unusual and even archaic word, "silentious". Various types of silence will be considered here, although not all are mutually exclusive. More than one may be manifest in a particular person at the same or different times. Nor is this classification necessarily exhaustive. It is, however,

1

sufficient to illustrate the truth of a statement made in the Book of Ecclesiastes (3:7) that there is "a time to keep silence".

Understanding the functions of silence in daily life can help us to deal with its challenges. François, Duc de La Rochefoucauld, (1613–1680), advised that,

> We should observe the place, the occasion, the temper in which we find the person who listens to us for if there is much art in speaking to the purpose, there is no less in knowing when to be silent. There is an eloquent silence which serves to approve or to condemn, there is a silence of discretion and of respect. In a word, there is a tone, an air, a manner, which renders everything in conversation agreeable or disagreeable, refined or vulgar (Willis-Bund & Friswell, p. 93).

Likewise, Henry David Thoreau (1817–1862) observed that, "Silence is of various depths and fertility, like soil. Now it is a Sahara, where men perish of hunger and thirst, now a fertile bottom, or prairie, of the west" (Torrey, vol. 2, p. 472).

There are quite mundane reasons for remaining silent. For example, in the scriptures commended above by Basil, Abraham's servant gazes in silence at Rebekah to gauge from her reaction if certain words that he has spoken to her have the consequence that he hopes they will (Genesis 24:21). On occasion, silence is simply a form of good manners or common sense. Thus, elsewhere in those same scriptures, the Book of Proverbs advises that, "Whoever belittles another lacks sense, but an intelligent person remains silent" (11:12). We should be willing to fall silent while a friend helps us to understand how we have gone wrong (Job 6:24), to be silent and ponder our problems rather than distract ourselves (Psalms 4:4), and to keep silent when people have something to say that is worth hearing (Acts 15:12 and 19:33). Job kept silent about his sins because he feared the contempt of others (31:34).

Sacred as well as secular sources point to other forms of silence. In the New Testament, some of the disciples are silent with embarrassment or shame when Jesus discovers them arguing with one another about which among them is the greatest (Mark 9:33–35). Not all would agree, although some still do, that "A silent wife is a gift from the Lord, and nothing is so precious as her self-discipline"

(Sirach 26:14). Even then, scribes and prophets recognized that silence might be forced on people punitively (Isaiah 47:5; Lamentations 2:10), a phenomenon that will be considered later in some detail.

It is quite evident to the author of the apocryphal Book of Sirach (also known as Ecclesiasticus) that there are different kinds of everyday silence:

> Some people keep silent and are thought to be wise,
>   while others are detested for being talkative.
> Some people keep silent because they have nothing to say,
>   while others keep silent because they know when to speak.
> The wise remain silent until the right moment
>   but a boasting fool misses the right moment.
> Whoever talks too much is detested,
>   and whoever pretends to authority is hated (Sirach 20:5–8).

One man with a reputation for talking at length, if not too much, was the English historian Thomas Babington Macaulay (1800–1859). It was said of him, perhaps quite waspishly,

> There are no limits to his knowledge, on small subjects as well as great; he is like a book in breeches .... Yes, I agree, he is certainly more agreeable since his return from India. His enemies might perhaps have said before (though I never did so) that he talked rather too much; but now he has occasional flashes of silence that make his conversation perfectly delightful (Holland, p. 234).

An English chancellor, Francis Bacon (1561–1626) addressed the topic of "loquacity" within a range of "examples of the colours of good and evil, both simple and comparative" (Spedding, Ellis & Heath, vol. 4, pp. 484–485). He advanced arguments both for and against silence. In favour are his assertions that silence is "the sleep which nourishes wisdom"; it is "the style of wisdom" and "aspires after truth"; it is "the fermentation of thought" and "gives to words both grace and authority". His first assertion in favour echoes Pliny's *Epistles* where it is said (book 9, ep. 36) that, *"Mire enim silentio et tenebris animus alitur"* (For in silence and darkness the mind is wonderfully nourished). Bacon's arguments against silence include the opinions that, "He that is silent betrays want of confidence either in others or himself" and that, "Silence, like night, is convenient for treacheries". More oddly perhaps, he also stacked against it the fact that, "Silence is a kind of solitude". He appears to have taken a dim view of solitude, as did Dr Johnson—whose views on the matter will be considered later.

If Bacon saw the colours of silence metaphorically, they appear almost real for Hodgken. The latter finds that "a drab silence" is made generally by a company of tired men and women, "busy with countless cares, dusty with worries, each wrapped in his own thoughts, bearing his own burdens, unmindful of his neighbours except to criticise them"; but "a blue silence" is "the silence that is found often out of doors, sometimes during simple services on shipboard, far away at sea …. For this deep blue is the creative silence in the world of thought" (pp. 217–218).

One of the great Victorian admirers of silence was Thomas Carlyle (1795–1881). He is believed to have been the first person to write in English the phrases "Speech is silvern, silence is golden", doing so when in his *Sartor Resartus* of 1836 he translated from German an inscription found on doorways in Switzerland (p. 172). Given that the observation that "silence is golden" is now common, and was even the title of a very popular song recorded in the 1960s by The Tremeloes, it is surprising to learn of its relatively recent migration into English.

Carlyle was a prolific writer and made so many fond references to silence that Augustine Birrell, later the United Kingdom's chief secretary for Ireland, was led to remark that,

> No man talked against talk or broke silence to praise it more eloquently than he, but unfortunately none of it is in evidence. All that is given us is a sort of Commination Service writ large. We soon weary of it. Man does not live by curses alone (pp. 108–109).

The Commination Service is a Church of England liturgy for Ash Wednesday (a day marking for Christians the start of the penitential season of Lent) that includes strong warnings to impenitent sinners.

Indeed, silent people themselves can irritate others by their very silence. William Hazlitt (1778–1830) thought that at least some of those who pride themselves on their restraint are merely manifesting a national characteristic rather than a moral one. He says of the English that, "We compliment ourselves on our national reserve and taciturnity by abusing the loquacity and frivolity of the French" (Hazlitt & Horne, p. 68). Carlyle too made a comparison of that nature, although not with the French. Referring to "the Saxon British" (of 1840!), he wrote in the context of political reform that, "With this strong silent people have the noisy vehement Irish now at length got common cause made" (1840, p. 30). Given Carlyle's very favourable views on silence, there is in his statement an implicit negative judgement on the Irish.

A more explicit judgement is evident in the lines of one Irish political refugee who made his home in America. John Boyle O'Reilly (1844–1890) was a journalist and a Fenian activist, transported by the British from Ireland to Australia. He escaped from prison and made his way to the United States, where he became such an influential public figure in Boston that local people later erected a statue in his memory. In an "aphorism in rhyme", delivered on 1 February 1890, O'Reilly said,

> I judged a man by his speaking;
> His nature I could not tell;
> I judged him by his silence,
> And then I knew him well (Roche, p. 343).

O'Reilly did not enumerate particular kinds of silence by which one might know a man or woman. However, for her part, Saville-Troike attempted a broad functional classification. She identified 20 or so types of silence, and clustered these into the institutionally-determined, group-determined, non-interactive, and individually-determined or negotiated (pp. 16–17). Even then, she maintained, these types require further amplification and refinement. Such an elaborate taxonomy is useful for some purposes, but the types of silence that will be considered here below are more simply defined. They are broad enough to encompass many daily experiences of the phenomenon, being,

- Wise or virtuous
- Modest
- Cunning or calculating
- Eloquent
- Dumbfounded
- Culpable
- Strong
- Weak
- Ceremonial
- Satisfied
- Idle
- Dead.

The wise or virtuous silent

This is a quiet and gentle silence. It does not arise from a sense of superiority and is one of the signs of compassion. It reflects an unwillingness to pass judgement harshly or definitively, or to hold oneself out as purporting to understand the nature of reality in any way that is arrogant. It arises from being aware that what we put into words frequently fails to express truth adequately and may be regretted.

This type of silence is acknowledged by old sayings in many cultures. For example, adages attributed to the Chinese sage known as Lao-Tse include (sections 1 and 56 respectively),

> The name that can be named
> is not the enduring and unchanging name.

> and

> He who knows (the Tao) does not (care to) speak (about it);
> He who is (ever ready to) speak about it does not know it.
> He (who knows it) will keep his mouth shut and close the
> portals ...

The Italians say, "*Ci più sa, meno parla*", the French, "*Qui plus sait, plus se tait*" and the Spanish, "*Quien mas sabe, mas calla*", all meaning that the person who knows most speaks least. Sometimes wisdom lies simply in knowing that one does not know, and sparing others an opinion that is mere bluster. For, as one ancient Jewish writer has it (Ecclesiastes 10:14), "A fool multiplies words, though no man know what is to be, and who can tell him what will be after him?"

This is also the wisdom of Socrates who, as Plato tells the story in the *Apologia*, was regarded as being the wisest because he knew what he did not know, and did not have an opinion on everything. Hebrew texts indicate that there are times when it is prudent and wise, in particular, to refrain from expressing moral disapproval of others (Amos 5:13; Sirach 20:1). Similarly, in his fifth "Nemean Ode", Pindar (c520–438 BC) recognised that silence might be the best course, when he wrote, as translated,

> 'Tis not for every truth to show
> Its undisguised and open brow –
> Oft the best prudence of the wise
> In silent meditation lies (p. 183, lines 35–38).

The Romans had a saying: "*Indictum sit*" (Let it stay unspoken). That was the course taken by Jesus when faced with interrogation by the Roman governor Pilate. His silence then was enigmatic and complex. While, at one level, this perhaps led some people to believe that Jesus had consented to the charge that he claimed to be the son of God, his silence may also be seen as marking a moment when the underlying truth of an encounter could no longer be encompassed within language. Accounts of his entire life are distinguished by enigmatic silences, including that concerning his years before the age of 30 and that of the 40 days and 40 nights that he later spent on retreat in the desert. Indeed, the parables that Jesus used to tell sometimes baffled even his own followers (Matthew 13:10–17). His parables conveyed more meaning than the words themselves literally signified. As Funk observes, this was a use of language that brought the kingdom of God nearer. In this respect the parables are akin to some poetry. Funk adds that St Paul's letters also are "a language gesture", in that the language used and its form "likewise evidence traces of the silence that surrounds language" (p. 237).

The most eloquent way to communicate wisdom may be through one's way of life and not one's words. In a popular Jewish compilation known as "Pirque Aboth" (also "Pirqei Avot") which formed part of the Mishnah by the end of the second century, it is reported that,

> Shime'on his son said, All my days I have grown up amongst
> the wise, and have not found aught good for a man but silence;
> not learning but doing is the groundwork; and whoso multi-
> plies words occasions sin (Taylor, pp. 24–25).

This Shime'on, or Simeon, is himself thought to have lived in the
first century after Christ. Much later, Philip Sydney (1554–1586),
courtier and poet, and eldest son of the lord deputy of Ireland, preferred silence to sound, "Nightingales seldom sing, the [mag]pie still
chattereth …. Shallow brooks murmur most, deep silent [brooks]
slide away …" (p. 52). Also in the 16th century, at Avila in Spain,
a certain nun wrote of the great good that lies in staying quiet and
not excusing oneself even when blamed without good reason, notwithstanding her concession that, "… at times it is lawful to give an
excuse and it would be wrong not to do so":

> Indeed, it calls for great humility to be silent at seeing oneself
> condemned without fault. This is a wonderful way to imitate
> the Lord who took away all our faults. So, I ask you to take great
> care about this practice; it brings with it great benefits. I see no
> reason at all for us to try to excuse ourselves, unless as I say, in
> some cases where not telling the truth would cause anger or
> scandal …. The truly humble person must in fact desire to be
> held in little esteem, persecuted, and condemned without fault
> even in serious matters. If she desires to imitate the Lord, in
> what better way can she do so? (Teresa, vol. 2, p. 91)

Teresa of Avila (1515–1582) found also that, when she had to make
journeys with her colleagues, the "quiet way of arriving" was the
most fitting (Teresa, vol. 3, p. 271), "for if we begin discussing opinions, the devil disturbs everything; even though he cannot gain, he
stirs unrest". Her co-founder of the Discalced Carmelite order, the
man later known as St John of the Cross (1542–1591), believed that
spiritual self-examination and the doubt that accompanies it (the
"dark night of the soul" in existential suffering) brings humility,
and with it the realization that it is best to maintain where possible
a charitable silence about neighbours. He advised, "do not judge
them" (p. 389).

Three hundred years after John of the Cross, in an essay entitled "Intellect", Ralph Waldo Emerson (1803–1882) waxed eloquent about wise silence. He noted that,

> The waters of the great deep have ingress and egress to the soul. But if I speak, I define, I confine, and am less. When Socrates speaks, Lysis and Menexenus are afflicted by no shame that they do not speak. They also are good. He likewise defers to them, loves them, whilst he speaks. Because a true and natural man contains and is the same truth which an eloquent man articulates: but in the eloquent man, because he can articulate it, it seems something the less to reside, and he turns to these silent beautiful with the more inclination and respect. The ancient sentence said, Let us be silent, for so are the gods. Silence is a solvent that destroys personality, and gives us leave to be great and universal (p. 426).

Thomas Hardy (1840–1928) translated such insight into the everyday language of one of his novels, *Under the Greenwood Tree*, writing through his characters,

> "Ye never find out what's in that man [Geoffrey Day]: never. Silent? Ah, he is silent! He can keep silence well. That man's silence is wonderful to listen to."
>
> "There's so much sense in it. Every moment of it is brimming over with sound understanding."
>
> "A [He] can keep a very clever silence—very clever truly," echoed Leaf. "A looks at me as if 'a could see my thoughts running round like the works of a clock."
>
> "Well, all will agree that the man can pause well in conversation, be it a long time or be it a short time" (p. 91).

In 1912, Hardy removed the words "silent" and "silence" in this passage and substituted in some cases "close" and "dumbness" among other changes. Tim Dolin believes that, "The result is a more precise sense of Day's reserve, one that is linked more forcefully with his money" (pp. 71 and 207). Perhaps so, but the original is striking.

Wise silence must be distinguished from the posed wisdom of a person who simply tries to appear knowing, and from the silence of sheer ignorance. In respect of the latter, it has been observed that, "Even a fool who keeps silent is considered wise; when he closes his lips he is deemed intelligent" (Proverbs 17:28). For that reason, perhaps, the English chancellor, Francis Bacon (1561–1626), ostensibly citing an apophthegm of Simonides, warned in *De dignitate* against silence,

> *Silentium stultorum virtus: Itaque recte illi silent. Si prudens est, stultus es: si stultus, prudens.* (Silence is the virtue of a fool. And therefore it was well said to a man that would not speak, "If you are wise you are a fool; if you are a fool, you are wise") (p. 498).

In the same vein, Dr Samuel Johnson did not entirely agree with his friend James Boswell about the merits of silence. One day in 1775, writes Boswell the diarist,

> We talked of publick speaking—JOHNSON. "We must not estimate a man's powers by his being able, or not able to deliver his sentiments in publick. Isaac Hawkins Browne, one of the first wits of this country, got into Parliament, and never opened his mouth. For my own part, I think it is more disgraceful never to try to speak, than to try it and fail; as it is more disgraceful not to fight, than to fight and be beaten." This argument appeared to me fallacious; for if a man has not spoken, it may be said that he would have done very well if he had tried; whereas, if he has tried and failed, there is nothing to be said for him. "Why then, (I asked,) is it thought disgraceful for a man not to fight, and not disgraceful not to speak in publick?": JOHNSON. "Because there may be other reasons for a man's not speaking in publick than want of resolution: he may have nothing to say, (laughing.) Whereas, Sir, you know courage is reckoned the greatest of all virtues; because, unless a man has that virtue, he has no security for preserving any other" (vol. 2, pp. 339–340).

Johnson's own talking was said by one of his close acquaintances to have "had commonly the complexion of arrogance, his silence of superciliousness" (Piozzi, p. 233).

In Japan, it is believed that, "Any clown can tell the difference between wise talk and foolish talk; but it takes a good master to distinguish between wise silence and foolish silence" (Johnston, p. 56). While not denying that there is such a phenomenon as wise silence, Hazlitt too was suspicious of those people who were reluctant to join in discussions, believing that, "We may give more offence by our silence than even by impertinence" (Hazlitt and Horne, p. 38). He went further:

> The most silent people are generally those who think most highly of themselves. They fancy themselves superior to every one else; and not being sure of making good their secret pretensions, decline entering the lists altogether. They thus "lay the flattering unction to their souls", that they could have said better things than others, or that the conversation was beneath them (ibid., p. 67).

Perhaps for this very reason, their superiors have long advised Christian monks that their silence in the presence of guests is not to be haughty or cold. As Wathen explains, "It is a silence that must be formed by charity and humility ... that expresses concern and interest and a deep faith" (pp. 56–57). The importance of charitably and humbly listening to the other person in communicative exchanges has been underscored also by the work of the feminist theologian Nelle Morton (1905–1987), and by her concept of "hearing to speech". She has observed that, "Speaking first to be heard is power-over. Hearing to bring forth speech is empowering" (p. 210). Our way of listening to others has a further ethical dimension in that such listening should be open and ongoing. We ought not to assume that either we or they can fully and definitively express everything that there is to be said, every aspect of reality for any party to the conversation, in a particular form of words or at a particular time.

The French psychoanalyst Jacques Lacan (1901–1981) understood the enigmatic subtlety of silences and the need for the analyst to be reticent. He saw silence not simply as a technical device for allowing space to others to express themselves but as an invitation to being in its fullness. Referring to Leonardo da Vinci's curious painting of St John, semi-naked and gesturing towards the heavens, Lacan asked, "What silence must the analyst now impose upon himself if he is to make out, rising above this bog, the raised finger of

Leonardo's 'St. John the Baptist', if interpretation is to find anew the forsaken horizon of being in which its allusive virtue must be deployed?" (p. 536).

And if one characteristic of wise silence is a reluctance to impose imperfect opinions on people, another is the willingness to listen and learn for our own benefit. Such learning may contribute to an increase in one's own virtue, or be valued mundanely for material reasons. It is not known to which end precisely a piece of doggerel, said to have hung in his home but reproduced in slightly varying versions in the absence of the original, was meant to direct the mind of the 30th president of the United States, Calvin Coolidge (1872–1933):

> A wise old owl lived in [or sat on] an oak;
> The more he saw the less he spoke.
> The less he spoke the more he heard.
> Why can't [or aren't] we be [or all be] like that wise old bird?

Simpler and less ambiguous was the advice of Max Ehrmann (1872–1945), who wrote the well known and frequently published American prose poem, "Desiderata". It begins,

> Go placidly amid the noise and haste,
> And remember what peace there may be in silence.

The modest silent

One may keep silent simply out of modesty, and not necessarily because one is particularly wise or is thought to be wise. Popular sayings such as "Fools rush in where angels fear to tread", and "Least said, soonest mended", remind us that there is no virtue in speech for its own sake. The Egyptian author of the "Book of Ptahhotep" (sometimes called "the oldest book in the world") advises:

> Do not repeat any extravagance of language; do not listen to
> it; it is a thing which has escaped from a hasty mouth. If it is
> repeated, look, without hearing it, toward the earth; say noth-
> ing in regard to it (Horne, p. 70).

The Book of Sirach advises,

> If you have understanding, answer your neighbour;
> but if not, put your hand on your mouth,
> Glory and dishonour come from speaking,
> and a man's tongue is his downfall (Sirach 5:12–13).

The ancient Jewish sage Bar Kapara is said to have taught that "Silence is seemly for the wise, all the more so for fools" (*Balylonian Talmud*, "Pesachim", 99a). In his "Enchiridion", the late-Stoic philosopher Epictetus (c55–135) advised his followers to adopt a moral code, as follows,

> Immediately prescribe some character and form of conduct to yourself, which you may keep both alone and in company. Be for the most part silent, or speak merely what is necessary, and in few words. We may, however, enter, though sparingly, into discourse sometimes when occasion calls for it, but not on any of the common subjects, of gladiators, or horse races, or athletic champions, or feasts, the vulgar topics of conversation; but principally not of men, so as either to blame, or praise, or make comparisons. If you are able, then, by your own conversation bring over that of your company to proper subjects; but, if you happen to be taken among strangers, be silent (vol. 2, p. 318).

Yet, even still, his appears to be a more moderate form of silence than that which had been prescribed for the students of Pythagoras and which will be considered in a later chapter.

In the same spirit as the advice of Epictetus is a maxim sometimes attributed to Seneca ("Moral Maxims", no. 34) but possibly written by a Christian living in Gaul. It enjoyed wide circulation by the eighth century: "*Magna res est vocis et silentii temperamentum*" (Moderation is a great thing in both speech and silence). Such moral advice later found favour during the Renaissance and the Protestant Reformation when there was a flowering of texts intended to improve civil society through education. Thus, for example, in 1523 in Basel, the Protestant reformer Ulrich Zwingli (1484–1531) composed a tract to be used in the formation of young men. Zwingli's particular objective was to teach "the mystery of the Gospel". In "Education of youth", he wrote that the young man who finds Christ "will know that in all his acts and counsels, so far as human frailty allows, he must venture to manifest some part of the virtues of Christ":

> He will learn of Christ both in speech and in silence, each at the proper time. In early youth, he will be ashamed to speak those things which are more fitting in adults, for he will note that Christ did not begin to preach until about his thirtieth year. It is true that when he was only twelve he attracted the attention of the doctors of the law, but from this instance we do not learn to rush in hastily, but from early youth to exert ourselves in the high matters which are worthy of God.
>
> For as silence is always the greatest adornment of a wife, so nothing is more becoming to youth than to try to be silent for a time, so that mind and tongue may be instructed both individually and together, and thus learn to co-operate with each other. It is not my intention to enfore a five years' silence, like that which Pythagoras demanded of his disciples, but to warn against a too great readiness in speech. And I forbid a young man to speak at all unless he has something useful and necessary to say (Bromiley, pp. 105 and 109–110).

In England, in 1546, John Heywood (c1497–c1580) published a collection of proverbs that included this caution for the orally impulsive, "It is good to have a hatch before the door" (p. 32). Some 50 years later, in *The Merchant of Venice*, Shakespeare's Lorenzo declares,

> How every fool can play upon the word! I think the
> best grace of wit will shortly turn into silence,
> and discourse grow commendable in none only but
> parrots (Act III, sc. 5, lines 39–42).

Francis Bacon (1561–1626), who was Shakespeare's contemporary, wrote approvingly in "An advertisement touching the controversies of the Church of England" that, "… if we but did know the virtue of silence and slowness to speak, commended by St James, our controversies of themselves would close up and grow together" (Vickers, p. 2). Meanwhile, in France, Michel de Montaigne (1533–1592) had also been singing the virtues of restraint in speech, particularly for young men. He thought that,

> Silence and modesty are very good qualities for social intercourse [*"la conversation"*]. This boy will be trained to be sparing and thrifty with his ability when he has acquired it; not to take exception to the stupid things and wild tales that will be told in his presence, for it is uncivil and annoying to hit at everything that is not to our taste (p. 113).

A modest silence might even be the best way to deal with lies and slander. In 1642, at the outset of his "Apology for Smectymnuus", John Milton wrote that, "I will not deny but that the best apology [defence] against false accusers is silence and sufferance, and honest deeds set against dishonest words." Adopting such a course of inaction is not always easy, as becomes clear from reading the advice of Edmund Burke in February 1796. He first appears to share Milton's opinion but, as his letter to "a noble lord" (the fourth Earl Fitzwilliam) proceeds, things seem less clear-cut:

> Loose libels ought to be passed by in silence and contempt. By me they have been so always. I knew that as long as I remained in publick, I should live down the calumnies of malice, and the judgments of ignorance. If I happened to be now and then in the wrong, as who is not, like all other men, I must bear the consequence of my faults and my mistakes. The libels of the present day are just of the same stuff as the libels of the past. But they derive an importance from the rank of the persons they come from, and the gravity of the place where they were uttered. In some way or other I ought to take some notice of them. To assert myself thus traduced is not vanity or arrogance. It is a demand of justice (1887, vol. 5, p. 177).

Nevertheless, to Burke's mind, the demands of justice were not always reason enough for assertion. Thus, convincing himself that Catholics who suffered discrimination and desired greater political freedom had the sympathy of the most powerful and talented Protestants in Parliament, that they were indeed supported by "every Protestant (I believe with very few exceptions) who is really a Christian", he counselled Catholics to remain quiet. Despite his own proclivity to speak out and not to hold his tongue, he felt that the best course for Catholics then was a public silence. Ever the intellectual, Burke acknowledged the "difficult and delicate" dilemma in which Catholic leaders might find themselves as a result of such modesty. On 18 May 1795, he wrote to Rev Dr Thomas Hussey, a former chaplain to the Spanish ambassador in London and the first president of the Catholic seminary at Maynooth, Co Kildare:

> If the better part lies by in a sullen silence they still cannot hinder the more factious part both from speaking and from writing; and the sentiments of those who are silent will be judged by the effusions of the people who do not wish to conceal thoughts that the sober part of mankind would not approve. On the other hand, if the better and more temperate part come forward to disclaim the others, they instantly make a breach in their own party, of which a malignant enemy will take advantage to crush them all. They [the enemy] will praise the sober part, but they will grant them nothing they shall desire; nay they will make use of their submission [and former silence] as a proof that sober men are perfectly satisfied in remaining prostrate under their oppressive hands. These are dreadful dilemmas ... (1857, vol. 2, pp. 488–489).

"Burke's dilemma", as one may call it, will be familiar to many political pressure groups that have been promised progress by the powerful in return for moderation, only to find promises broken when the passion of a particular period has passed. They never can be sure if they would have gained more by being more or less assertive of their rights. Such issues of silence and silencing in politics will be considered further below.

Meanwhile, the merits of a modest silence in everyday encounters remain and are not least appreciated by those who have endured the long-winded or bombastic person. An exasperated Job declares to those offering him advice, "Oh that you would keep silent, and it would be your wisdom!" (Job 13:5). In his tract on garrulity, Plutarch (c45–120) observes that,

> ... when a fool, full of noise and talk, enters into any room where friends and acquaintance are met to discourse or else to

feast and be merry, all people are hushed of a sudden, as afraid
of giving him any occasion to set his tongue upon the career.
But if he once begin to open his mouth, up they rise and away
they trip, like seamen foreseeing a sudden storm and rolling of
the waves, when they hear "the north wind begin to whistle
from some adjoining promontory", and hastening into harbour
(W. Goodwin, vol. 4, pp. 221–222).

Eighteen hundred years later, George Eliot wrote,

> Blessed is the man who, having nothing to say, abstains from
> giving us wordy evidence of the fact—from calling on us to look
> through a heap of millet-seed in order to be sure that there is no
> pearl in it (1879, p. 97).

The cunning silent

In the face of adversity, it can be difficult to keep quiet. "My heart
is beating wildly; I cannot keep silent; for I hear the sound of the
trumpet, the alarm of war," cries out a prophet in the Old Testament
(Jeremiah 4:19). However, faced with danger or even simply with
disfavour, it is perhaps more common for people to keep their heads
down and mouths shut for as long as possible. The Book of Proverbs
advises that, "He who guards his mouth preserves his life; he who
opens wide his lips comes to ruin" (Proverbs 13:3 and 21:23).

"Say nothing" (or "Indictum sit" as the Latin proverb had it) is
advice often given to those risking conflict with the powerful. The
old Italian version is, "He that speaks doth sow, he that holds his
peace doth reap" (Ray, p. 19). The more one speaks, the more one is
inviting attention and perhaps an unfavourable or even dangerous
response. As noted earlier, "Least said, soonest mended" has long
been a popular expression in English. Menander (342–291 BC) had
urged that, "When on the verge of action say not one word before-
hand to anybody. All things, save silence alone, bring repentance to
a man" (Allinson, p. 535). Horace (65–8 BC) touched on the benefits
of not sounding off, in lines that were to be often quoted (and that
are translated here by the present author):

Sed tacitus pasci si posset corvus haberet
Plus dapis et rixae multo minus invidiaeque.

But if the raven could have fed in silence, he'd have had
More of a meal and far less envious quarrelling (*Epistles*, I, 17,
line 50).

Writing about AD 30, Valerius Maximus proclaimed in his *Memorable Deeds and Sayings*,

> *Quid Xenocratis responsum, quam laudabile! cum maledico quorun-*
> *dam sermoni summo silentio interesset, uno ex his quaerente cur solus*
> *linguam suam cohiberet, "quia dixisse me" inquit "aliquando paeni-*
> *tuit, tacuisse numquam".*

> That response of Xenocrates, how praiseworthy! When some
> men were speaking maliciously he stayed completely silent.
> One of them asking why he was holding his tongue, he
> answered, "Because I have sometimes regretted speaking, but
> never regretted staying silent" (Book. 7, ch. 2).

In *Thyestes*, a Roman drama of the first century after Christ by Seneca the Younger (c4 BC–AD 65), the character Atreus has to decide whom he will inform about his murderous intentions. He decides not to tell his own sons, partly on the grounds that young men find it difficult to be discreet. He declares that, "*tacere multis discitur vitae malis*" (One learns to be silent through life's many sufferings) (pp. 258–259, line 319). The silence thus learnt is one of calculation or cunning and is not the same as that forbearance from speech of John of the Cross who, in 1590, advised a nun suffering from scruples, "When something distasteful or unpleasant comes your way, remember Christ crucified and be silent" (p. 756, also p. 762).

In an essay "On the art of discussion", Montaigne (1533–1592) advises rulers to recognize the value of saying nothing. He writes, "As they promise more, so they owe more; and therefore silence is for them a bearing not only decorous and grave, but often also profitable and economical" (p. 712). One man, who was born in the same year as Montaigne, practised this virtue so assiduously that he became widely known as "William the Silent". It is said that in 1559 Henry II of France revealed his plans for a massacre of Protestants to William, Prince of Orange, believing the latter to be sympathetic. Motley writes that, "The Prince, although horror-struck and indignant at the royal revelations, held his peace and kept his countenance" (pp. 68–69), and subsequently took steps to counter the planned massacre. One is reminded of what Shakespeare's Richard Plantagenet, Duke of York, is advised by his uncle, Mortimer, in 1 *Henry VI*: "With silence, nephew, be thou politic" (Act 5, sc. 5, line 101), or of what Cressida proclaims to Troilus:

> Sweet, bid me hold my tongue,
> For in this rapture I shall surely speak
> The thing I shall repent. See, see, your silence,
> Cunning in dumbness, from my weakness draws
> My very soul of counsel! Stop my mouth (Act 3, sc. 2, lines
> 122–126).

A work attributed to the English jurist John Selden (1584–1654) advises that,

> Wise Men say nothing in dangerous times. The Lion, you know, called the Sheep, to ask if his Breath smelt: she said, Aye; he bit off her Head for a Fool. He called the Wolf, and asked him: he said, no; he tore him in pieces for a Flatterer. At last he called the Fox, and asked him: truly he had got a Cold and could not smell. King James was pictured, &c. (p. 151).

In his tale of "The bear and the amateur garden", La Fontaine's moral is that, "*Il est bon de parler, et meilleur de se taire, Mais tous deux sont mauvais alors qu'ils sont outrés*" (It is good to speak, and better to be quiet, But both are bad when overdone) (*Fables*, book 8, no. 10).

Writing his lines "On Poetry, a Rhapsody", Jonathan Swift (1667–1745) had some words of advice for the poet who receives a bad review, words that recognized the capacity of political activists to sense when to stay quiet in one's own interest,

> And if you find the general vogue
> Pronounces you a stupid rogue,
> Damn all your thoughts as low and little,
> Sit still, and swallow all your spittle;
> Be silent as a politician,
> For talking may beget suspicion;

Silence is a refuge for those who stand to gain, or at least not to lose, by being mute. Their reasons could vary from guilt to shyness to fear. La Rochefoucauld (1613–1680) writes in his 79th maxim that, "Silence is best resolve for him who distrusts himself" (Willis-Bund & Friswell, p. 12). Indeed, a somewhat crude old agricultural adage had it that, "The silent pig is the best feeder." About which Haliburton observed, "but it remains a pig still and hastens its death by growing too fat"! He continued, "Now the talking travel-ler feeds his mind as well as his body, and soon finds the less he pampers his appetite the clearer his head is and the better his spirit" (vol. 1, p. 201).

By the end of the 19th century, the biblical verse that tells us, "Even a fool who keeps silent is considered wise, when he closes his lips, he is deemed intelligent" (Psalms 17:28) had a secular counter-part: "It is better to remain silent and be thought a fool, than open one's mouth and remove all doubt." This saying has been attributed variously to Samuel Johnson, Mark Twain, and Abraham Lincoln, but it is unclear who coined it.

John Boyle O'Reilly echoed Menander by advising, in his poem "Rules of the Road", "Be silent and safe—silence never betrays you" (Roche, p. 533). An Apache respondent told Basso,

> When someone gets mad at you and starts yelling, then just don't do anything to make him get worse. Don't try to quiet him down because he won't know why you are doing it. If you try to do that, he may just get worse and try to hurt you (p. 77).

Nevertheless, notwithstanding such a line of authorities in favour of calculating silence, the cautious or browbeaten silence of the poor and downtrodden may come to be regarded by a dominant class as sullenness or even stupidity. In a curious work published in 1918, Kirk discusses the "silent mind" of British soldiers at the front with little or no reference to the appalling carnage that they had just wit-nessed or to its numbing effect on their senses. The author, a former London secretary of the Student Christian Movement, cites a memo-randum that had been privately circulated relating to "educational experiments with troops in the field" (pp. 25 and 153–154). This memorandum concluded,

> A vast majority of our troops—representing the entire body
> of unskilled labour before the war and a great part of the
> irresponsible skilled workmen (thus excluding foremen,
> managers, clerks and others in responsible positions)—do not
> think at all.

Kirk describes seeing men idle, lazing about or staring vacantly. He abhors such apparent passivity, "For the silent mind is a danger; and it is a waste". It is a danger because it is prey to temptation, and a waste "because its possibilities for good, be they small or great, lie dormant and untouched". As well as glossing over the reality of shell-shock, or what today might be called post-traumatic stress, the author never seems to allow for the fact that the soldiers may have had many thoughts that they were not inclined to articulate openly. Perhaps their lives were less unexamined than he thought. Their reticence may have been due to a sense of powerlessness or to a fear of the consequences of saying what they felt, or due to either contempt for or deference to their social superiors who had dropped them in the mess of trenches. One is reminded of the declaration of the chorus leader in Aeschylus's *Agamemnon*, performed half a millennium before Christ, that "I have long found silence to be an antidote to harm" (line 548), and of a statement in the "Tractate Berakot" that, "… a charm against suffering is silence and prayer" (*Babylonian Talmud*, p. 410).

It is worth recognizing, as Farrar has written, that, "… what is called the silence of ignorance may sometimes be the silence of repudiation, sometimes even the reticence of scorn" (p. 29). As one of the characters in R. D. Blackmore's *The Maid of Sker* puts it,

> That Parson Chowne should dare to think that I would swallow
> such stuff as that, made me angry with myself for not having
> contradicted him. But all this time I was very wise, and had no
> call to reproach myself. Seldom need any man repent for not
> having said more than he did … (p. 216).

There are of course times when cunning silence simply does not work, as Mordechai warned Esther when he told her that she must not think that she could keep silent about a threat to the Jews and so escape imminent slaughter along with the rest of her people (Esther 4:14). There are also times when people will repent of their silence. Cowardly and culpable silences are considered later below.

The eloquent silent

Emotions such as deep gratitude, intense anxiety, or heartfelt love are rarely expressed adequately in words. The term "pregnant silence" is used to refer to a complete silence that is filled with the brooding presence of thoughts or feelings that one has not expressed. Some politicians like to believe that they can understand the desires and wishes of "the silent majority" of voters who make no public fuss about their opinions yet still manage to communicate their sentiments. Silence sometimes expresses disapproval, and the "silent treatment" may even be used deliberately as a form of punishment.

Ignatius of Antioch (c50–c107) believed that silence spoke for itself. In his epistle to the Ephesians, he commended to the Philadelphians the retiring disposition of their bishop and wrote that, "If a bishop is silent, he only deserves the more reverence" (Lightfoot, ii, 45–46, and iii, 24, para. 6). He thought explicitly that, "silence is more eloquent than speech" (ibid., para. 1). Ignatius's opinion was formed against the background of a Greek rhetorical culture in which, writes Maier, "rightly timed speaking and controlled speech are the measure of a man":

> Ancient authors regularly praised silence as a virtue of self-control in speaking, arising out of the disciplining of natural inclinations towards talkativeness and other vices associated with speech (p. 503).

Another kind of reluctance to speak, that of the envious who are unwilling to offer congratulations, is an eloquent form of tribute. Thus, Terence (c190–158 BC) has a character in one of his plays remark memorably, "*tacent: sati[s] laudant*" (they are silent; they praise enough) (*Eunuchus*, Act 3, sc. 2, line 476).

Shakespeare fully appreciated the eloquence of silence. Posthumus Leonatus declares, "O Imogen, I'll speak to thee in silence" (*Cymbaline*, Act 5, sc. 4, line 29). Claudio, on learning that Hero is permitted to marry him, manages to proclaim happily that, "Silence is the perfectest herald of joy: I were but little happy if I could say how much" (*Much Ado*, Act 2, sc. 1, lines 292–293). Duke Frederick tells Celia,

> She is too subtle for thee, and her smoothness,
> Her very silence, and her patience
> Speak to the people, and they pity her (*As You Like It*, Act 1,
> sc. 3, lines 80–83).

Theseus assures Hippolyta,

> Trust me, sweet,
> Out of this silence yet I pick'd a welcome;
> And in the modesty of fearful duty
> I read as much as from the rattling tongue
> Of saucy and audacious eloquence.
> Love, therefore, and tongue-tied simplicity
> In least speak most, to my capacity (*A Midsummer Night's
> Dream*, Act 5, sc. 1, lines 104–110).

Echoing this sentiment are some lines by the Californian poet Joaquin Miller (c1837–1913). In his poem "Sunset and Dawn in San Diego", he wrote that,

> Why, know you not, soul speaks to soul?
> I say the use of words shall pass.
> Words are but fragments of the glass:
> But silence is the perfect whole (p. 277).

In 1791, 290 deputies in the French National Assembly decided that they would continue to "sit along with those who have raised a misshapen republic upon the ruins of monarchy", but added that, "From this moment the most profound silence, on whatever shall not relate to this subject [the king and his authority], shall express our deep regret, and at the same time our invariable opposition, to every decree that may be passed" (*Annual Register*, p. 171). They told their constituents that they would no longer speak on any subject before the assembly. Edmund Burke wrote soon afterwards that, "this silence in the royal party carried a force and meaning that was not lost either there or throughout the kingdom, and that contributed as much, if not more, perhaps, than any argument, to the preservation of monarchy in France" (ibid., p. 192).

Referring to a biography of Sir Walter Scott, that great Scottish novelist and poet, his fellow Scot Thomas Carlyle (1795–1881) describes as "astonishing" a suggestion that Scott's biographer, John Gibson Lockhart, "at heart has a dislike to [sic] Scott". Carlyle says, "Of *that* astonishing hypothesis, let expressive silence be the only answer" (1860a, vol. 4, p. 196).

In respect of intense emotions, Jacob points out that, "The inability to express them is itself expressive." He recalls those whom he has seen leaving their native land perhaps forever, and who stand on deck watching it recede from view. They sit in silence, he says, "not merely because they do not care to speak, but because the thoughts of their hearts cannot be put into language" (pp. 2–3). Today, such thoughts of separation may still be silent beneath a sea of sound as the traveller retreats into a world of recorded music or in-flight "entertainment".

Later we shall consider silent prayer and the silences of meditation. Among those who have regarded such silences as not only receptive but also expressive was James Thomson (1700–1748), a Scottish poet who frequently chose the deep silence of night as his time for composition. In "A hymn", he wrote that, "I lose myself in Him, in light ineffable; Come then, expressive silence, muse his praise" (pp. 32 and 244).

But what does the silence of a person who is questioned and who declines to answer signify? May it be taken as assent, especially when one is accused of a serious offence? Sophocles (c496–406 BC) appears to have believed that such an assumption was reasonable, morally if not legally. He has the chorus in *Trachiniae* ("Women of Trachis", lines 812–813) ask Deianira why she is leaving in silence. Does she not know that silence pleads for her accuser? And Cicero (106–43 BC), in a letter to Cataline, assumes that the silence of certain senators could be taken to express their approval: *"De te autem, Catilina, cum quiescunt, probant, cum patiuntur, decernunt, cum tacent, clamant"* [They shout or cry aloud through their silence] (*In Catilinam*, 1, s. 21). That he was not alone in such assumptions is clear from the currency of a Roman saying, *Qui tacet, consentire* [*vedetur*], meaning, "The person who remains silent appears to have consented". Indeed, even in law, a person who remains silent may be found in some circumstances to have concurred with a particular course of action. The test is one of reasonableness. A judge may deem silence, or a failure to act, to amount to consent where a reasonable person would speak up if he or she objected. However, Thomas More (1478–1535), chancellor of England and scholarly "man for all seasons", unsuccessfully evoked this Latin maxim in his defence when accused by prosecutors of indicating malice by not having answered expressly the lords of the council who examined him as to whether or not he accepted that King Henry VIII was supreme head of the Church in England (C. More, pp. 259–260).

Burton Stevenson, a great collector of proverbs and famous phrases whose work has been of assistance to the present author, found many assertions that silence may be construed as consent (*Proverbs*, p. 2112). Yet, in the common law countries, there is also a long tradition of accused persons enjoying "the right to silence". An arresting police officer is expected to caution such persons that, "You have a right to remain silent …", and inferences will be drawn from such silence only in exceptional circumstances in criminal cases. The idea behind this principle is similar to that expressed two thousand years ago by Seneca the Younger (c4 BC–AD 65) when he asked, "If silence is not allowed, what is anyone allowed?"

Creon

Allow me silence. Can any smaller freedom be requested from a king?

Oedipus

Often the freedom of silence is more dangerous than speech to king and kingdom.

Creon

If silence is not allowed, what is anyone allowed? [*Ubi non licet tacere, quid cuiquam licet?*]

Oedipus

One who is silent when bidden to speak undermines authority (*Oedipus*, pp. 62–65).

Following the attack on New York City on 11 September 2001, there was a heated debate in the United States about the right of prisoners to remain silent. Alan Dershowitz of Harvard Law School argued that coercive interrogations—even when they amount to torture—can be ethically acceptable when used to prevent a crime, especially a terrorist attack, so long as the fruits of such interrogations are not prejudicially introduced into evidence at the criminal trial of the coerced person himself or herself. His critics were appalled by what appeared to them to be an argument in favour of torture.

One should distinguish the eloquent silence discussed so far from silences that are accompanied by gestures or signs such as those of the character Jacques Baptiste, in *The Son of the Wolf* by Jack London (1876–1916): "The Frenchman in Baptiste shrugged his shoulders, but the Indian in him was silent. Nevertheless, it was an eloquent shrug, pregnant with prophecy" (p. 43). Many gestures will be far less obvious than such a shrug, being perhaps just a raised eyebrow or a down-turned lip. When we know someone well, the slightest glance may express her or his wishes without words being necessary—as Oscar Wilde exclaims in his poem *"Silentium amoris"* ("The Silence of Love"),

> But surely unto Thee mine eyes did show
> Why I am silent, and my lute unstrung;

Circus clowns, or mime artists such as Marcel Marceau, may be silent but their bodies or faces can be simultaneously very expressive. The fact that gestures may speak as loudly as voices, and are not entirely silent in a communicative sense, was recognized in the third quarter of the 20th century when the Cistercian order relaxed its rule about talking in monasteries. Moreover, besides significant gesture and sign there is movement in its own right, which may be a means of expressing ourselves. Bruce believes that "silent movement" can facilitate deeper concentration and expand spontaneously into appropriate sounds:

> There is in such movement a purity, and in sharing another's
> rhythms a frankness …. Sound often comes spontaneously in
> children as they make movement effort. They may grunt, sigh
> or whistle …. One should encourage such sound (pp. 45–46).

There are also expressive symbolical silences such as the minutes of silence that commemorate certain deaths on public occasions.

In 2003, a thousand cyclists were reported to have participated in a "Ride of Silence" at White Rock Lake in Dallas, Texas. The event was organized after a local cyclist was killed when hit by a school bus mirror. It was emulated elsewhere (Durnan).

Eloquent silence has recently received some close scrutiny by Ephratt who believes that philosophers have always been concerned with it and that, "Contrary to its subordinate position in linguistic studies, eloquent silence has become central to research projects and investigations in various non-linguistic disciplines" (p. 1933).

Expressive silences may even be discerned in or projected onto nature. Following the early death of a close friend, Arthur Henry Hallam, and his subsequent burial at Clevedon, North Somerset, by the estuary of the great river that separates England from Wales, Alfred Tennyson (1809–1892) wrote that,

> There twice a day the Severn fills;
> The salt sea-water passes by,
> And hushes half the babbling Wye,
> And makes a silence in the hills ("In Memoriam A.H.H.", xix).

It is said that another tidal river was generally so quiet that it became known to the ancient Irish as *abha na bailbhe*, signifying "dumb" or "silent" river, whence today the Anglicized name River Barrow (O'Donovan, p. 4).

On a winter's night in the United States, in January 1853, Henry Thoreau was thrilled while walking from a village to the woods nearby. He wrote, "I wish to hear the silence of the night, for the silence is something positive and to be heard …. A fertile and eloquent silence…. I listen from time to time to hear the hounds of Silence baying the Moon…. I hark the goddess Diana. The silence rings: it is musical and thrills me. A night in which the silence was audible. I hear the unspeakable" (Torrey, vol. 4, pp. 472–473). Poets sometimes feel that their verses echo such silent ringing. John Boyle O'Reilly wrote in his poem "Songs That Are Not Sung" that,

> From the silence, from the twilight, wordless but complete they come.
> Songs were born before the singer: like white souls awaiting birth,
> They abide the chosen bringer of their melody to earth.

> Only sometime he may sing it, using speech as twere a bell,
> Not to read the song but ring it, like the sea-tone from a
> shell.
> Sometimes, too, it comes and lingers round the strings all
> still and mute,
> Till some lover's trembling fingers draw it living from the
> lute.
> Still, our best is but a vision which a lightning-flash illumes,
> Just a gleam of life elysian flung across the voiceless glooms
> (Roche, p. 447).

Deep waters were the subject of Jacques Cousteau's first film documentary to win an academy award. *Le Monde du Silence* ("The Silent World", 1956) was based on his book of the same name and he used underwater photography to show people places that they would never otherwise see. These places spoke silently to many viewers of the complexity of nature, albeit with a supportive voiceover!

Patrick Leigh Fermor has written that "elegiac sadness overhangs the rock monasteries of Cappadocia". And when he visits the ruined monasteries of England, he thinks that, "It is as though some tremendous Gregorian chant had been interrupted hundreds of years ago to hang there petrified at its climax ever since" (pp. 8–9). Those who have found themselves standing alone in the remains of a "famine village" in Ireland, deserted since the mid-19th century, will understand the force of such evocative contexts and the expressive silences of place.

The dumbfounded (lost for words) and dumbstruck

We may be lost for words when awed by great beauty or by wisdom or even by terror. The wise words of Jesus are said to have confounded those trying to entrap him (Matthew 22:34; Mark 3:4; Luke 14:4 and 20:26), and also to have silenced an unclean spirit in a man (Mark 1:25; Luke 4:35). His apostle Peter too had the capacity to silence critics by the sheer quality of his speech (Acts 11:18). And Peter, John, and James "kept silent" after seeing Elijah and Moses appear alongside Jesus and hearing a divine voice in a cloud that enveloped them (Luke 9:36; Mark 9:10).

Thomas Aquinas (c1226–1274), one of Christianity's greatest philosophers, had a spiritual insight in later life that resulted in him not writing for months. He proclaimed,

> All that I have hitherto written seems to me nothing but straw ... compared to what I have seen and has been revealed to me (Pieper, pp. 39–40).

Pieper describes this setting aside of writing by Aquinas as not being the silence of resignation, still less of despair, but of reverence. The silence lasted all winter. Yet, Aquinas remained committed to intellectual endeavour, believing that, "The man who does not use his reason will never get to the boundary beyond which reason really fails" (ibid., p. 38). He thought that, "... all our knowledge can only be the cause of new questions, and every finding only the start of a new search" (ibid., p. 41). Thus, the silence of Aquinas ultimately complemented rather than contradicted his words.

Dante (1265–1321), too, could find himself lost for words that might adequately match his experience or idea of paradise:

> Shorter henceforward will my language fall
> Of what I yet remember, than an infant's
> Who still his tongue doth moisten at the breast.

> O how all speech is feeble and falls short
> Of my conceit, and this to what I saw
> Is such, 't is not enough to call it little (*Paradiso* I, Canto 33, lines 106–108).

In "Tears Wept at the Grave of Sir Albertus Morton", Henry Wotton (1568–1639) lamented the death of an acquainatnce by declaring,

> Silence, in truth, would speak my sorrow best,
> For deepest wounds can least their feelings tell;

It may also be the case that humility results in us falling silent, as we recognize our own failings. Jacob writes that, "... the sinner is dumb before his God. What can he say? Can he give utterance to the overwhelming sense of personal demerit, or express the depth of humiliation in the convicted soul?" (p. 5). Or we may be overwhelmed by beauty, like Oscar Wilde in his *"Silentium amoris"* ("The Silence of Love"):

> As oftentimes the too resplendent sun
> Hurries the pallid and reluctant moon
> Back to her sombre cave, ere she hath won
> A single ballad from the nightingale,
> So doth thy Beauty make my lips to fail,
> And all my sweetest singing out of tune.
>
> … my too stormy passions work me wrong,
> And for excess of Love my Love is dumb.

We may be dumbstruck with embarrassment, too, as when a child is put on the spot in public by being asked a question by some adult. Even some adults themselves are reluctant to express their feelings, as Lebra saw in Japan. She wrote that, "I am not talking about the silence of the tired old couple with nothing to say to each other, such couples being abundant in Japan and elsewhere. I am referring to the husband and wife who are in love but who are too embarrassed to express their feelings in speech" (p. 349). It is common in Western societies today to hear couples being encouraged to express themselves to one another—to "get in touch" with their emotions and to communicate about these. Couples might pity their parents or grandparents, whom they perceive to have been tongue-tied or emotionally repressed. However, whether or not we agree that any trend towards articulation is itself a good thing, we may be mistaken if we assume that emotional silence between couples is necessarily an entirely negative phenomenon. Lebra points out that a Japanese explanation for conjugal embarrassment is that husband and wife are perceived as *isshin dotai* (one mind and body). It is, therefore, embarrassing to express love for oneself. For a similar reason, as an expression of humility, Japanese husbands and wives will denigrate rather than praise one another in speaking to a third person. Furthermore, post-coital silences in any culture mark the fact that there is sometimes nothing more to be said at particular points in a relationship.

Of course, in Japan as elsewhere, there can be darker reasons for conjugal silences and we shall return below to the phenomenon of silencing by one spouse of another. Children, too, may be dumbstruck in their powerlessness and misery. As one 11-year-old silent witness told a researcher, "I was scared of my dad. When he hit my mother I was scared that he would hit me and that is why I did not get involved to stop him" (M. Patel, p. 92).

But sons and fathers who love one another also encounter the "boundary beyond which reason really fails", as Aquinas put it, when words do not add up to reality. In "A Story", Li-Young Lee grapples with the "emotional equation" in which silence and need are matched:

Sad is the man who is asked for a story
and can't come up with one.

His five-year-old son waits in his lap.
Not the same story, Baba. A new one.
The man rubs his chin, scratches his ear.

In a room full of books in a world
of stories, he can recall
not one, and soon, he thinks, the boy
will give up on his father.

Already the man lives far ahead, he sees
the day this boy will go. *Don't go!*
Hear the alligator story! The angel story once more!
You love the spider story. You laugh at the spider.
Let me tell it!

But the boy is packing his shirts,
he is looking for his keys. *Are you a god,*
the man screams, *that I sit mute before you?*
Am I a god that I should never disappoint?

But the boy is here. *Please, Baba, a story?*
It is an emotional rather than logical equation,
an earthly rather than heavenly one,
which posits that a boy's supplications
and a father's love add up to silence.

The culpable silent

Menander (342–291 BC), as we have seen, thought that, "All things, save silence alone, bring repentance to a man." Likewise, discussing

"Talkativeness", the Greek historian Plutarch (c46–120) urged his readers, "Remember what Simonides said, that he never repented that he had held his tongue, but often that he had spoken" (p. 237). Then, in the third or fourth century after Christ, Dionysius Cato wrote in his *Disticha*, *"Nam nulli tacuisse nocet, nocet esse locutum"* (For being silent harms nobody, it is speaking that does harm) (bk. 1, no. 12).

However, others long ago acknowledged that there are times when silence may, in fact, result in harm, and when we are morally obliged to speak out. The author of the Egyptian "Book of Ptah-hotep" wrote that one should,

> Cause him who speaks to you to know what is just, even him
> who provokes to injustice; cause that which is just to be done,
> cause it to triumph. As for that which is hateful according to the
> law, condemn it by unveiling it (Horne, p. 70).

And, in "The prophecies of Neferti" of the 18th Egyptian dynasty, one also finds this exhortation,

> Stir, my heart,
> Bewail this land from which you have sprung.
> When there is silence before evil,
> And when what should be chided is feared,
> Then the great man is overthrown in the land of your birth
> (Lichtheim, 1975, p. 139).

The psalmists call on us to confess our sins to God rather than fail to admit them and remain silent. They also recognize that silence may be misconstrued as approval of immoral behaviour (Psalms 32:3–5, 39:1–2 and 50:21). However, it sometimes takes courage to speak up. At Corinth, Paul encountered resistance from some of the Jews but he is said to have had a vision in which Jesus told him, "Do not be afraid, but speak and do not be silent" (Acts 18:9).

An expression used in Greek by Aristotle and recorded in its Latin form by Erasmus, *"Turpe silere"* ("Shame to be mute" or "It is disgraceful to be silent"), clearly recognizes that there are culpable silences (Mynors, pp. 4–5). Bland explains this by saying, among other things,

> When a man is conscious that he is capable of instructing his
> fellow citizens, or those with whom he is connected, in any art
> that might be beneficial to them, it is disgraceful, or perhaps
> criminal, to withhold it (vol. 2, p. 214).

There are times when it is morally justified for all members of a
crowd to clamour. Some Pharisees wanted Jesus to rebuke his followers and to stop them praising God with a loud voice "for all the
deeds of power that they had seen, saying 'Blessed is the king who
comes in the name of the Lord!'" But Jesus replied that, "if these
were silent, the very stones would cry out" (Luke 19:37–39).

Pomerius, a fifth century contemplative bishop, recognized that
silence may be a retreat from responsibility or action. This is so
when one is morally obliged to speak out about immoral behaviour.
He wrote of priests that,

> He who has the commission of dispensing the word, however
> holy the life he lives, if he is either embarrassed or afraid to rep-
> rimand those who live wickedly, perishes with all who are lost
> through his silence (p. 42).

The reforming Czech priest Jan Hus (1371–1415) condemned people
who "participate in simony [trading a sacred object or making a church
appointment in return for temporal advantage] by non-correction or
silence", which silence he thought to be a common failing of "princes,
prelates and masters". He himself was silenced two years later by
being burnt at the stake as a heretic (Spinka, p. 265).

Edmund Burke, as we have seen, advised Irish politicians to tone
down their protests. Yet he had no problem rationalizing on moral
grounds his own "vituperative" prosecution of the impeachment
of Warren Hastings, late governor-general of Bengal, in the House
of Lords (*Oxford Dictionary of National Biography*, at Hastings). The
Lords later found Hastings not guilty. Speaking on the sixth article
of charge, on 5 May 1789, Burke said,

> My Lords, since I had last the honor of standing in this place
> before your Lordships, an event has happened upon which it
> is difficult to speak and impossible to be silent (1887, vol. 10,
> pp. 306–307).

In his "Reflections on the revolution in France", Burke also said that, "If the prudence of reserve and decorum dictates silence in some circumstances, in others prudence of a higher order may justify us in speaking our thoughts' (1887, vol. 3, p. 243). But Burke appears *not* to have said words that are frequently attributed to him, that, "It is necessary only for good men to do [or, say] nothing for evil to triumph" (Porter). It is not clear who did say this first.

The originator of another maxim, frequently quoted and often misattributed to Abraham Lincoln (Schwartz), is known. It was Ella Wheeler Wilcox (1850–1919). In her poem of 1914, entitled "Protest", she wrote that,

> To sin by silence, when we should protest,
> Makes cowards out of men (Wilcox, pp. 154–155).

John Boyle O'Reilly, the Irish emigrant and poet, accused the clergy in Ireland of culpable silence in the face of misery. In critical verses, "The Priests of Ireland", he wrote,

> You have stood with folded arms until twas asked—Why do they wait?
> By the fever and the famine you have seen your flocks grow thin,
> Till the whisper hissed through Ireland that your silence was a sin.
> You have looked with tearless eyes on fleets of exile-laden ships,
> And the hands that stretched toward Ireland brought no tremor to your lips; (Roche, p. 471).

Although silence is woven through the work of Samuel Beckett, he himself could never have kept silent. Deirdre Bair has recorded that he said, over and over again to her and to others, that, "I couldn't have done it otherwise. Gone on, I mean. I could not have gone through the awful wretched mess of life without having left a stain upon the silence" (pp. 640 and 723).

Addressing the subordination of women in history, Andrea Dworkin has quoted approvingly the words of the Russian writer Nadezhda Mandelstam (1899–1980) who struggled through the

Stalinist era and who wrote, "If nothing else is left, one must scream. Silence is the real crime against humanity" (p. 32). Another survivor, in this case of the Nazi Holocaust, was Elie Wiesel. On 10 December 1986, he delivered a speech accepting the Nobel Peace Prize and proclaiming,

> I swore never to be silent whenever and wherever human beings endure suffering and humiliation. We must take sides. Neutrality helps the oppressor, never the victim. Silence encourages the tormentor, never the tormented.

In 2009, Wiesel visited with US president Barack Obama and German chancellor Angela Merkel the former death camp at Buchenwald where Wiesel himself had once been interned. He has defended Obama against some Jewish critics who questioned the strength of his support for the state of Israel. But, ironically, Wiesel himself has been criticized for not objecting strongly to the violation of Palestinian rights.

Silences take many forms. Friedrich Nietzsche (1844–1900) accusingly wrote of the great German writer Goethe (1749–1832) that it was not possible to know what he really thought about the Germans, because "about many things around him he never spoke explicitly, and all his life he knew how to keep an astute silence" (p. 244). One "astute" or ambiguous silence that has aroused much comment was that of the philosopher Martin Heidegger (1889–1976), appointed rector of the University of Freiburg in 1933. He seemed ambivalent about, or even approving of, certain aspects of Nazism. Heidegger himself refers to occasions "when man speaks by being silent" (Krell, p. 357), so his own reluctance to comment on "The Jewish Question" more explicitly than he did even after the war is pointed. He was reproached for it because, as Lang writes in this context, "silence may represent a decision not to say what else one would be obliged to say if one spoke at all—contrasted then with the silence of indifference or silence that attests only that the speaker who might have been heard knows too little to say anything about a particular subject" (p. 15).

The negative power of silence as it is found in situations where truthful speech is morally demanded was identified in a hit song, "The Sound of Silence", written in 1964 by Paul Simon: "Silence like a cancer grows", his lyrics remind us. The song is a stimulus to people to ask always if there are those who suffer because they or their problems are not being discussed as they ought to be, and whether such failure results from fear or prejudice or even mere discomfort. Chow, for example, argues that an ideological polarization in US public discourse about abortion has meant that women who had abortions there and who feel a certain sense of loss, though not necessarily the loss of a "baby", become unaccounted for in their society because their reaction to abortion fails to comply with the usual pro-life or pro-choice perceptions. She believes that this "has caused a lack of objective, widespread response to post-abortion grief in America, as opposed to Japan" (p. 73).

The strong silent type ("tall dark stranger")

Determined men of few or no words: these are respected. They are presumed to be strong. Leaders defer to them. They are also the heroes, or anti-heroes, of Sergio Leone's westerns.

Against the backdrop of vast desert landscapes and open skies, set to the haunting soundtracks of Ennio Morricone, Leone's men step up to face a bleak world. They are played by Clint Eastwood or Charles Bronson, actors whom audiences have come to trust as characters who will ultimately do what is needed to put things right. Not so much virtuous as resolute, they move through scenes that are sometimes all but silent, our sense of expectation heightened by the merest creak of wood or squeak of a hinge (Frayling, p. 168). Their habitat is the Wild West, and their foes men of dark demeanour. Yet this Wild West is also, in words from the cinematic trailer for *Once Upon a Time in the West* (1969), "the promised land". Charles Bronson's character is there described as "the man in search of a name". His harmonica is more eloquent than his voice. Likewise, the trilogy of Sergio Leone westerns entitled *A Fistful of Dollars* (1964), *For a Few Dollars More* (1965), and *The Good, the Bad and the Ugly* (1966), was marketed in a video/DVD box set on which their lead character, played by Clint Eastwood, was described as "The man with no name". Although characterized by critics as morally ambiguous, and not necessarily either wise or virtuous, his nameless gunslinger of few words never harms the innocent. If moral rectitude is not necessarily his hallmark, the exacting of revenge for some injustice is his motivation. Our hero may be wrapped in existential if not contemplative quietness but he also trails a whiff of cordite. He is a coiled spring of violence, indifferent to social mores and unike the purer heroes of conventional earlier westerns.

A woman of no words has been proverbially admired in some cultures. A man of few words has been respected or feared. But where the silence of women is today interpreted by some critics as having been a sign of their social weakness, the taciturnity of men continues to be regarded by many as a sign of inner strength.

Not only gunslingers but also administrators may be silently strong. The ancient Egyptian "Papyrus Prisse", in the Bibliothèque Nationale in Paris, was composed at least 1800 years before Jesus was born. In it, a court official called Kagemni is instructed as follows,

> The respectful man prospers,
> Praised is the modest one,
> The tent is open to the silent [or, the quiet, modest person is well-liked],
> The seat of the quiet is spacious [i.e. the quiet person is well-received].
> Do not chatter! (Lichtheim, 1975, pp. 59 and 61)

Additional practical advice is found elsewhere in ancient Egyptian texts, as in this "Instruction of Ptahhotep", from the Middle Kingdom:

> If you meet a disputant in action
> Who is your equal on your level,
> You will make your worth exceed his by silence,
> While he is speaking evilly,
> There will be much talk by the hearers,
> Your name will be good in the mind of the magistrates (ibid., pp. 64 and 70).

Thus, the strong, silent type is sometimes seen as sensitive rather than proud or threatening. When a Clint Eastwood character helps someone vulnerable, remembering a past injustice that he himself has suffered, he may be thought to echo the words of Aeschylus in his *Prometheus*:

> No, do not think it is from pride or even from wilfulness that
> I am silent. Painful thoughts devour my heart as I behold myself
> maltreated in this way (line 436).

And so his type remains silent, and such silence reflects the outlook
expressed five years before the birth of Christ by the Roman poet
Ovid, in his *"Remedia amoris"* ("Love's Remedy"): "Don't say what
grieves you; but grieve secretly .... He who is silent is strong" (line
697). While those last six words have often been quoted, what is
seldom noted is their context. Ovid is in fact advising a man who
wishes to break up with a woman!

> *Nec dic, quid doleas: clam tamen usque dole.*
> *Nec peccata refer, ne diluat: ipse favebis,*
> *Ut melior causa causa sit illa tua.*
> *Qui silet, est firmus;*
>
> Don't say what grieves you; but grieve secretly.
> Don't refer to her faults, lest she dilute them. Do yourself a
> favour,
> So that your case will be better than hers.
> He who is silent is strong. [This author's translation.]

The gender tables are turned in sonnet 35 of "Modern Love" by George
Meredith (1828–1909), an English poet whose wife deserted him.
He laments his lady's "secretive" nature: "O have a care of natures
that are mute! They punish you in acts: their steps are brief".

Silence itself allows observers to project their subjective ideas,
positive and negative, onto a strong, silent man. One example of this
dual possibility concerns Oliver Cromwell (1599–1658), "lord pro-
tector" of England, Scotland, and Ireland. Commenting on the fact
that Ignatius of Antioch praised a taciturn bishop, the 19th-century
editor of the former's epistles noted by way of favourable comparison what Thomas Carlyle wrote about Cromwell: "His words—still
more his silences and unconscious instincts, when you have spelt
and lovingly deciphered these also out of his words—will in several ways reward the study of an earnest man" (Lightfoot, vol. 2,
p. 252, n. 4; Carlyle, *Cromwell*, vol. 1, pp. 14 and 74). Yet for some of
those who decipher his brooding presence in the light of his bloody
actions in Ireland, Cromwell's silences appear less than lovely. They

may instead conjure up La Fonatine's fable of the torrent and the river which teaches that, *"Les gens sans bruit sont dangereux"* (Silent people are dangerous). Dr Thomas Fuller later rendered the same adage as, in 1732, "Silent men, like still waters, are deep and dangerous" (p. 178, no. 4163).

There is an air of danger and even the smell of sulphur about Sergio Leone's anti-heroes. The fallen angels in Milton's *Paradise Lost* had, after all, been punished for their disobedience by being wrapped eternally in silence:

> For strength from Truth divided and from Just,
> Illaudable, naught merits but dispraise
> And ignominie, yet to glorie aspires
> Vain glorious, and through infamie seeks fame:
> Therfore Eternal silence be thir doome (Book 6, lines 381–385).

The Italian Leone was perhaps influenced by an old Italian drama when he directed his dark westerns. For there is a line at the end of the first scene of Vittorio Alfieri's tragedy, *La Congiura de' Pazzi* (c1779): *"Alta vendetta, D'alto silenzio è figlia"* (Deep vengeance is the daughter of deep silence).

The weak silent

In classical times, they used to say that someone who felt unable to speak had "an ox on the tongue". The envisaged "ox" may have been a certain coin or, even more figuratively, the animal itself. We say today, when someone whom we have expected to talk holds back, that "the cat has her/his tongue". The older saying appears to have had more of a sense of oppression about it than ours does (Barker, pp. 7 and 103–104).

The belief that silence befits a woman in the presence of men was frequently expressed in ancient Greece. This is clear from a reading of the context in which Ajax rebuked Tecmessa, in words by Sophocles (c496–406 BC) that are often quoted: "Silence is a woman's ornament" (*Ajax*, line 293). Tecmessa herself prefaces her account of Ajax's rebuke with the observation that the phrase, even then, was a well-worn one. However, Sophocles qualifies its force by acknowledging that the opinions of women might be valued in practice. Thus, he depicts Ajax as being beside himself with torment when dismissing Tecmessa's attempts to make him see sense; but as soon as Ajax returns shortly afterwards from his forays, in a state of emotional collapse, he himself falls silent and eventually asks Tecmessa to explain what had happened (*Ajax*, lines 290–320). Sophocles thus treats somewhat ironically the silence that men expect of women, recognizing that women may in fact know better. Aristophanes (c448–385 BC) goes further in his *Lysistrata* and is quite mocking about such imposed silences. Lysistrata having been asked by the magistrate to explain why some women are meddling in matters of state, Aristophanes puts into her mouth the following words (as translated by Jack Lindsay):

> Be calm then and I'll go ahead.
> All the long years when the hopeless war dragged along we, unassuming, forgotten in quiet,
> Endured without question, endured in our loneliness all your incessant child's antics and riot.
> Our lips we kept tied, though aching with silence, though well all the while in our silence we knew
> How wretchedly everything still was progressing by listening dumbly the day long to you.
> For always at home you continued discussing the war and its politics loudly, and we
> Sometimes would ask you, our hearts deep with sorrowing though we spoke lightly, though happy to see,
> "What's to be inscribed on the side of the Treaty-stone;
> What, dear, was said in the Assembly today?"
> "Mind your own business," he'd answer me growlingly
> "hold your tongue, woman, or else go away."
> And so I would hold it.
>
> WOMEN
>
> I'd not be silent for any man living on earth, no, not I!

There are strong hints in these passages that silence itself may constitute a form of rhetoric, and cannot merely be assumed to signify mute obedience. However, the fact that men who thought that women ought to remain silent were mocked did not put an end to the suppression of women's voices. Menander (c342–290 BC) later wrote that, "A marriageable daughter, even if she utters never a word, by her very silence says most of all about herself" (Allinson, p. 517). Bushnell points out that it is unclear whether women were even allowed to be present in the audience at Greek plays to observe their fictionalized representation (2005, p. 246).

Within the early Christian Church, as shall be discussed later, there were debates about the limits of women's participation. Theologians today still disagree about the meaning of advice given by Paul in his letter to the Corinthians, advice that seems fairly clear: "As in all the churches of the saints, the women should keep silent in the churches. For they are not permitted to speak, but should be subordinate, as even the law says" (1 Corinthians 14:34).

Down the centuries there echoed that same well-worn phrase heard in Greek theatres. For example, Erasmus (c1466–1536) included among his adages the Latin version, "*Mulierem ornat silentium*" (Baker, p. 358), while the Protestant reformer Zwingli (1484–1531) enthusiastically declared that, "… silence is always the greatest adornment of a wife …" (Bromiley, pp. 105 and 110). One proverb even had it that, "An eloquent woman is never chaste" (Labalme, p. 139).

In his *Monument of Matrones* published in 1582, Thomas Bentley stated that, "There is nothing becometh a maid better than sobernes[s], silence, shamefastnes[s] and chastitie, both of bodie & mind. For these things being once lost, shee is no more a maid, but a strumpet in the sight of God" (cited Hull, p. 142). Shakespeare discerned a certain power in such silence, as in the "prone and speechless dialect, Such as move men" that Claudio perceives in his sister's youthful femininity (*Measure for Measure*, Act I, sc. 3, lines 174–175). Likewise, in 1631, Richard Brathwait wrote in his *English Gentlewoman* that, "Silence in a woman is a moving rhetoricke, winning most, when in words it wooeth least." Referring to this statement in the course of her study of silent women in early modern England, Christina Luckyj argues (p. 1) that the idea of such a potent silence itself destabilizes any intention on the part of Brathwait to equate feminine silence with the "modesty" that he otherwise recommends.

Luckyj's study demonstrates clearly the persistent attraction of silent women to some men, although by 1732 Fuller was recording a twist to the old adage. Among his "collection of such remarkable sentences and sayings as are usual and useful in conversation and business" was this: "Silence is a fine jewel for a woman; but it's little worn". Perhaps somewhat wistfully, he added another saying, "Silence is not the greatest vice of a woman" (p. 178, nos 4166 and 4168). And if women do speak up, what is a man to do except patronize them? In the mid 17th century, one of the characters in William Davenport's *News from Plymouth* advised that, "Silence becomes men best, when women talk" (Act I, sc. 1).

Whether or not Thoreau was, in 1839, expressing a judgement on the respective silencing powers of men and women, is difficult to know. His enigmatic statement of 9 February that year is frequently quoted: "It takes a man to make a room silent" (Torrey, vol. 1, p. 73). Those nine words were all that he wrote in his journal on the day. They stand devoid of context. Had he been present during some dramatic entrance by a strong male personality, such as he had never seen made by a woman? Had he perhaps committed or witnessed a *faux pas*, something said or done by a man that stopped all conversation, in circumstances where he felt that a woman might never have been so awkward or undiplomatic? Was he simply sitting alone, brooding? Or did he really think that only a man can successfully call on a roomful of people to fall silent? We cannot be sure.

The process of silencing the weak or socially inferior is the subject of a later chapter below.

The ceremonially silent

Long ago, an Egyptian called Any, who worked at the palace of Queen Nefertari, included this advice for "the average man" among certain "instructions of the scribe" that he has left us:

> Do not raise your voice in the house of god,
> He abhors shouting;
> Pray by yourself with a loving heart,
> Whose every word is hidden.
> He will grant your needs,
> He will hear your words ... (Lichtheim, 1976, pp. 135 and 137).

The functions of silence in liturgical, contemplative, and meditative contexts will be discussed in Chapter Eight. Indeed, as we shall see, those who do not consider themselves to be religious in any conventional sense may too appreciate the need for silent spaces in our secular and noisy world.

The satisfied silent

People fall silent because they are physically content. We may be fortunate enough to feel balanced and well and in harmony with the world around and, at least for a short time, disinclined to disrupt what is a palpable silence—what Dante Gabriel Rossetti (1828–1882) calls, as we shall see in Chapter Six, the "visible silence" of which two lovers are a part on a summer afternoon in "sun-searched" countryside.

The idle silent

Most uses of silence, even in meditation, may be said to be purposeful. The wise person refrains from speech for the benefit of those with whom he or she is in contact, the monk or nun is silent for penitential purposes or to hear God better, and even the dumbfounded are leaving spaces within which their thoughts may gather so that they once again can respond to the world around them. However, there are people who appear to be silent for no reason, whose very silence may be considered by some to be an abdication of responsibility. St Ambrose was exercised about "idle silence" (*Catholic Encyclopaedia* (1912, xiii, p. 790), and we have seen above how one observer was frustrated by the silence of front-line troops in war and construed or misconstrued it as a kind of idleness. Yet, it is possible to rationalize even apparently pointless silence as being somehow consciously or unconsciously therapeutic, as a healing break that is necessary in our daily round. Thus, for example, William Penn exhorted his children,

> Love silence, even in the mind; for thoughts are to that as words [are] to the body, troublesome; much speaking, as much thinking, spends, & in many thoughts, as well as words, there is sin. True silence is the rest of the mind; and it is to the spirit, what sleep is to the body, nourishment and refreshment. It is a great virtue; it covers folly, keeps secrets, avoids disputes, and

> prevents sin. See Job 13.5. Prov. 10.19, c. 12.13, c. 13.3, c. 18, 6–7,
> c. 17.28 (pp. 47–48).

Silence is a balm. For many, the enjoyment of silence is a precondition
of spiritual and mental health. Indeed, the cessation of noise may
bring simple physical relief. This is reflected in a somewhat cranky
poem about an irritating organ grinder, written in 1836 by a relatively young Oliver Wendell Holmes (1809–1894). The best-known
lines of "The Music-Grinders" are,

> And silence, like a poultice, comes
> To heal the blows of sound.

More recently, a Welsh poet and sometime tramp, William Henry
Davies (1871–1940) asked in his poem "Leisure",

> WHAT is this life if, full of care,
> We have no time to stand and stare?
>
> No time to stand beneath the boughs,
> And stare as long as sheep and cows.

He added,

> A poor life this if, full of care,
> We have no time to stand and stare.

There is a thin line between such lolling, on the one hand, and a stillness that is guided by meditative techniques, on the other. For one
hears experienced spiritual guides warn against seeking rewards or
expecting "results" from sitting in meditation. Nevertheless, both
forms, ostensibly mindless or mindful, may bring psychological and
physical benefits.

It is also possible that there are silences that are entirely pointless.
As has been exclaimed jocularly in a declaration found on posters and
elsewhere, "Sometimes I sits and thinks—and sometimes I just sits."

The dead silent

A New York poet, Adelaide Crapsey (1878–1914) wrote a cinquain,
called "Triad":

These be
Three silent things:
The falling snow ... the hour
Before the dawn ... the mouth of one
Just dead.

There is nothing quite as powerfully silent as a loved one who has just passed away. There dawns an awful realization that one may talk to the deceased as much as one wishes but there will never be an answer in the normal way. As Hamlet observes at the close of Shakespeare's tragedy, "The rest is silence ..." (Act 5, sc. 2).

One speaks fittingly in English of "dead silence", in reference to absolute silence. Zoroastrians removed corpses to structures that became known to colonialists as "towers of silence". We even honour the celebrated dead by responding with one or more minute's communal silence of our own. Popular expressions include "silent as the dead", "dumb as death" or "still as the grave". The memorable title of Rachel Carson's powerful and prescient book about the potentially deadly consequences for birds and people of mankind's use of pesticides, published in 1962, was *Silent Spring*.

Ancient Jewish authorities wrote of the need for silence on occasions of mourning, when it was regarded as inopportune in particular to expound teachings (*Babylonian Talmud*, p. 31). In a well-known passage in the Old Testament it is said that there is "a time to keep silence and a time to speak" (Ecclesiastes 3:7), and in a commentary on that text we learn that,

> The wife of R[abbi] Mana died in Sepphoris. R. Abun went up to visit him, and said to him, "Would the master care to expound something of the Torah to us?" He replied, Behold the time mentioned by the Torah has come when one should keep silent and give preference to silence (*Midrash Rabbah: Ecclesiastes*, p. 80).

The Jewish psalms refer to the future state of death and to the impossibility of praising God when we have passed away. There is little in them that suggests celestial choirs, as envisaged in later religious writings; their silence of the grave seems final. It is to "the land of silence" (Sheol, also given in the ancient Greek Septuagint as "Hades") that one goes when dead, where no one is singing the Lord's praises (Psalms 17, 94, and 115).

The US poet Henry Longfellow (1807–1882) has drawn attention to the silence that delimits our lives. In "The Theologian's Tale: Elizabeth" (part 4), he wrote memorably of,

> Ships that pass in the night, and speak each other in passing,
> Only a signal shown and a distant voice in the darkness;
> So on the ocean of life we pass and speak one another,
> Only a look and a voice, then darkness again and a silence.

Responding in some anti-romantic lines, an exasperated Aldous Huxley amusingly harumphed, "If only the rest were silence! What joy if the rest of Wordsworth had been silence, the rest of Coleridge, the rest of Shelley!" (p. 187). But silence was less amusing for those like Siegfried Sassoon who, during the Great War of 1914–1918, were haunted by memories while "summering safe at home" in England. In "Repression of war experience", he wrote,

> You sit and gnaw your nails, and let your pipe out,
> And listen to the silence: on the ceiling
> There's one big, dizzy moth that bumps and flutters;
> And in the breathless air outside the house
> The garden waits for something that delays.

In this poem, and in another entitled "The death bed", Sassoon equates silence with safety and contrasts it favourably with the constant thudding of guns, whether it be the silence of a room or the silence of death itself.

Yet there are ways in which the dead themselves continue to speak to us, through memory and mood. Such a communicative presence is well illustrated, for example, in James Joyce's short story titled "The dead". And Madison Cawein (1865–1914) wrote in "Haunters of the Silence" how,

> There are haunters of the silence, ghosts that hold the brain and heart:
> In the mansion of my being they have placed a room apart:

Some of the ways in which the departed influence us are dependant on our own persistent regret or guilt about things that we did or did not do when people were alive. But there may also be a more positive silent legacy when the moral strength and thoughts of a person whom we respected influence our conscious or subconscious mind. One may regard such a legacy as a form of projection but can it be said to be entirely subjective? It is a lasting influence that may take the form of an imagined voice or dialogue and renders death a little less silent than it would otherwise be. In "To My Father's Violin", Thomas Hardy recalls seeing his father's old violin and visualizes his parent "in the Nether Glooms". He wonders if his father might "want you [the violin] down there"? For, "He might liven at the sound / Of your string, revealing you had not forgone him." Harrison believes that, "The violin does not 'speak his [father's] heart'; it speaks his absence and his silence" (p. 62), but it does also reveal the poet's heart. The violin is surely a metaphor for Hardy's continuing dialogue with his dead father's expectations of Thomas.

Silence itself can seem like death to people who are being silenced, and for some of these there is a dangerous choice to be made. Before his murder by extremists, in 1993, the Algerian novelist Tahar Djaout had declared his unwillingness to suppress his perspective on Islam. Using a phrase that would become the title of his biography by Sukys, he said, "Silence is death and if you say nothing you die, and if you speak you die. So speak and die" (Goytisolo, p. 22).

CHAPTER TWO

Busy silence

When we are busy at work, or trying to get something done at home, we may not notice silence. But it does not go away, and it seeps into our communications with one another in ways that can be significant. Our ability to misunderstand each other is frequently evident, even within personal and family relationships where the listener knows the speaker relatively well. How much greater, then, are the opportunities for getting it wrong when it comes to encountering work colleagues or strangers, especially those whose background or culture is quite different from ours? In this context, silence is one aspect of communications that may easily be overlooked or misconstrued. This can have unfortunate consequences for those engaged in business or other dealings, especially in cross-cultural or international contexts.

Pausing during speech may mean one thing to a European and another to an Asian. Remaining silent upon encountering strangers does not necessarily signify for the descendant of an American immigrant what it signifies for those descended from native American peoples. Waiting for some seconds before responding to what has just been said by another person can simply be a sign of good manners or courtesy in some places; it may be alienating in others. "Taking turns" within conversation is not a fixed or natural technique but is culturally and socially determined.

During the 1970s, I researched and presented a television documentary for Irish television about a controversy surrounding the publication of a book, published in the 1940s at the height of Irish censorship hysteria. The book contained the earthy fireside stories of an old tailor and his wife, named Ansty, who lived at Gougane Barra in a remote part of west Cork. Many of those whom I interviewed were very old (one aged 102 had attended the tailor's wedding), and they provided glimpses of a rapidly disappearing era. They also disconcerted me by conversing in a manner that often left me feeling that I had interrupted or spoken at the wrong moment, or that my speech was arid and staccato compared to their elegance and natural tempo. Without unduly romanticizing the oral fluency of west Cork and Kerry, which perhaps still owed something to ways of conversing in the days before general literacy and the speeding engine, it seemed to me that I had experienced a verbal culture that was quite distinct from that of the educational milieu in which children have been schooled more recently.

Rushing to speak and to fill gaps with "small talk" may be a feature of communications in our noisy electronic world, but it is by no means the only way of engaging in conversation.

Native America

In a seminal piece of research on silence and communications, conducted over 16 months between 1964 and 1969 in an Apache settlement in Arizona, Basso found that native Americans believe that "it is right to give up on words" in certain circumstances where other Americans find silence disconcerting. This is particularly so when it comes to meeting strangers, either Apache or non-Apache. Basso notes that, "In large gatherings the lack of verbal communication between 'strangers' is apt to go unnoticed, but in smaller goups it becomes quite conspicuous," and he repeats the following tale which was told to him by one member of a four-man group engaged in rounding up cattle:

> One time, I was with A, B and X down at Gleason Flat working cattle. That man, X, was from East Fork (a community nearly

40 miles from Cibecue) where B's wife was from. But he didn't
know A, never knew him before, I guess. First day, I worked
with X. At night, when we camped, we talked with B, but X and
A didn't say anything to each other. Same way, second day. Same
way, third. Then, at night on the fourth day, we were sitting by
the fire. Still, X and A didn't talk. Then A said: "Well, I know
there is a stranger to me here, but I've been watching him
and I know he is alright." After that, X and A talked a lot ....
Those two men didn't know each other, so they took it easy at
first (p. 72).

Where other Americans might rush to fill an empty gap, filling up
silence with nervous small talk, these descendants of native people preferred to "take it easy" at first. In this Apache society, formal "introduction" of one stranger to another by a third party was
regarded as presumptuous and unnecessary. Basso found that strangers who were quick to launch into conversation were "frequently
eyed with undisguised suspicion" by the Apaches and sometimes
assumed to be either in urgent need of assistance or else drunk.

    Related to this silence between strangers, is the phenomenon of
silence between Apaches in the early stages of courtship. Courtship
is discouraged between members of the same clan, so when girls
and boys meet it is often at public events that bring clans together,
such as rodeos or ceremonials. For up to an hour at a time, the couple may stand or sit, even holding hands, in complete silence. One
youth told Basso, "At first, it's better that way. Then, after a while,
when you know each other, you aren't shy anymore and can talk
good" (pp. 73–74). Much talking by a girl may even be interpreted
as a sign that she has been familiar with a number of men. Getting
to know people in silence is not a practice to which every culture
attaches high value. However, one may ask if filling spaces with
gabbled words or "chit-chat" is better.

    The Apaches of Arizona also maintained silence in the presence of
those who were recently bereaved, even weeks after a death, where
in other cultures one might seek to comfort or distract the bereaved
by engaging in conversation.

    Also, and somewhat sadly, related to the phenomenon of silence
between strangers is that between Apache parents and their children
when the latter return from boarding schools. According to Basso

(pp. 74–75), this appears to be because of past experiences that led parents to believe that exposure to such schools sometimes changed children and alienated them from their own culture and from their parents, upon whom they may come to look down. Instead of a flurry of verbal exchanges as children disembark from the bus, silences can last for as long as 15 minutes. It is deemed inappropriate for parents to interrogate their offspring and it may be some days before parents attempt to engage in sustained conversation. Were it not for the general phenomenon of silence in western Apache culture, one might fear that this silence between parents and children arose simply from a sense of powerlessness or shame on the part of the former, from concern about what might have been visited upon their children at boarding school besides the absorption of alien cultural values.

Basso's study was valuable not least because he studied silence in Apache culture as a phenomenon in itself and did not assume, as some others had, that silence among native Americans was predominantly a sign of their inability to cope with modern life. While social or other factors may well cow native peoples into sullen submission or mute defiance, Basso found that the Apaches had a particular cultural tradition that supported silence in certain circumstances.

One may not conclude generally that those who rush to talk are somehow superior at articulating the meaning of the situation in which they find themselves. One person's small talk is another person's silence. It is not a matter of judging that one style of communicating is intrinsically better than the other but of understanding the role and significance of each. To some people small talk may seem insincere rather than friendly. Constant talking can appear to be an effort to dominate an encounter, while silence may signify caution where one party to a meeting suspects that he or she is somehow weaker than the other.

Research among other native Americans, after that of Basso's with the Apaches, further echoes my experience with old people in west Cork over 30 years ago. In 1976, Philips found that Warm Spring Indians pause for longer in their speech than do Anglo-Saxons. They also take longer speaking turns and rarely interrupt each other. In 1990, the Scollons reported that Athabaskans are offended if, when they merely pause, an Anglo-Saxon takes the opportunity of their pause to start speaking again. Such an interruption means that the Athabaskans feel that they are not getting a chance to communicate freely. As the Scollons noted,

> The extreme of good Athabaskan conversation is, in fact, silence. People enjoy having a good quiet sit together with no topics being raised at all. While such an extreme is rare among the cultures of the world, of course, it does match our experience of the discourse of diplomats, for example, in which each word is carefully chosen (we hope) and new topics are broached with great care (2001, p. 98).

China and Japan

Gudykunst remarks that, "Our cultures influence the languages we speak, and how we use our languages influences our cultures" (p. 193). His is a statement of the obvious, but one that we may forget in our everyday encounters with different people. A vivid example of such influence may be discerned in the contrast between certain Asian and Western attitudes to silence. Europeans and Americans appear generally to regard talk as more important and enjoyable than do some Asians, with the former regarding speech as an instrument of social control, and the latter using silence as a strategy. Giving some advice on how Westerners can get along better with their Eastern counterparts, the Asian Studies Development Program (ASDP) recommended on its website that,

> It is especially important not to interrupt. This is considered very rude. While in the United States interrupting means to begin talking before someone else is through, in Asia you may be interrupting if you begin talking too soon after the individual is finished. There are often silences when talking with Asians, and these silences are uncomfortable for Americans. It may mean that the Asian is contemplating what you are saying and formulating an appropriate response. Don't try to fill in those silences! Sometimes silence is used to unnerve Americans and to get them to give in on negotiating points. During those times, lift your head a bit and stare into the space above your counterpart's head as though you are contemplating.

The ASDP is a joint national programme of the East-West Center and the University of Hawaii. Its personnel placed material online to guide the faculties at universities, colleges, and other institutions who wished to develop Asian studies units and curricula, although the above advice is unfortunately no longer online. However, it is partly echoed in this guidance given by the Commercial Service of the US Department of Commerce to small-to-medium sized companies seeking markets in China (at www.buyusa.gov/fresno/83.html):

> Don't be unnerved by long silences—these are an important part of Chinese communication. But note that silence can also be used to unnerve a negotiating opponent.

For their part, Glasser and Pastore note, in their assessment of Chinese business culture, that,

> The Western mode of teaching, which encourages students to question and challenge the instructor, is unknown to the Chinese. In China teachers lecture and students dutifully take notes—no exchange is heard. For a Western manager attempting to instruct IT [Information Technology] troops or train users, this silence can be unnerving.

One way of responding to such silence is to adapt one's strategies. Another is to try to change the Chinese. Glasser and Pastore report, "The Chinese must be urged to ask questions and interrupt, says Meimei Fox, a Meridian Resources consultant. Providing material in advance gives staff a chance to review a topic and think of questions." Quite why we "must" change the Chinese, rather than simply acknowledging their particular way of doing business, is not entirely clear.

In an analysis of Joy Kogawa's novel *Obasan*, which deals with the Canadian internment of Japanese citizens during World War II, Cheung notes that,

> In English, *silence* is often the opposite of *speech*, *language* or *expression*. The Chinese and Japanese character for *silence*, on the other hand, is antonymous to *noise*, *motion*, and *commotion*.

In the United States silence is generally looked upon as passive; in China and Japan, it traditionally signals pensiveness, alertness and sensitivity (1994, p. 113).

Billiet Lien, who studied cross-cultural differences in the use of silence by Irish and Chinese people, found that, "Where the Chinese respondents see silence as a higher form of communicating, the Irish experience it more as an embarrassing and uncomfortable situation" (p. 41). The Irish also believe that they would always speak their mind in situations of disagreement, where the Chinese respondents "mentioned disagreements spontaneously as situations in which they would remain silent"! Nevertheless, and somewhat paradoxically, Lien discovered that in situations where people in one's company are well known to oneself then the Irish seem to be more comfortable being silent than are the Chinese.

The rapid growth in the Chinese economy has greatly increased the number of opportunities for Westerners to do business there. Accordingly, there are very practical reasons why such cultural differences ought to be studied and understood. And China is by no means the only Asian country in which one may be disconcerted by silence. For example, Sabath cautions in the case of Indonesia,

> When establishing business relationships with Indonesians, be patient and diligent …. If the Indonesians with whom you are meeting make few comments, don't view their silence as a negative response. Frequently, part of the business practice in this country is to remain aloof until a group meeting can be held to gather a consensus. In addition, remember that these people are naturally soft-spoken, so be aware of your tone of voice and avoid being loud or harsh-sounding (pp. 63–76).

When it comes to Japan, Yasutaka Sai points out that few Japanese strike up a conversation with the person next to them on public transportation, and writes that,

> As a people, the Japanese are more reticent than Westerners. They make fewer statements, and explain considerably less, and generally speak less often. Japanese parents and school-teachers teach children to refrain from talking too much.

> If a child is talkative or too glib they are scolded as being gabby, shameless, vulgar and overall impolite. Adults who speak their minds freely also tend to be scorned; their vocalizing is taken as a manifestation of impudence and thus they become subject to negative social pressures to stop. Criticism tends to be especially harsh when directed against young people, women or new members of a group (p. 119).

In another discussion of silence in Japanese discourse, Takie Lebra reminds us that, "It is well recognized that silence is a communicative act rather than a mere void in communicational space." She adds that if cultures can be differentiated along the noise-silence continuum in a similar fashion to how Metz (1985) charts worshipping styles from the noisy Pentecostals to the quiet Quakers, then "there are many indications that Japanese culture tilts towards silence" (p. 343). One simple way of seeing this, she suggests, is to compare American and Japanese soap operas on TV. She believes that by just listening with closed eyes you will immediately notice the difference in the amount of vocalization. Indeed, Lebra has formed the impression that Japanese silence stands out even in comparison with that of Japan's Chinese and Korean neighbours. Silence is not only passively tolerated in Japan but is actively cultivated through a variety of cultural expectations or norms. Matsumoto has penned an engaging study of one particular phenomenon which mystifies foreigners, that of "*haragei*". This appears to be a particularly subtle use of silence to embrace those with whom one is dealing so that one achieves a mutually satisfactory outcome.

Paradoxically, silences in Japanese conversation give rise to a greater number of verbal prompts by the listener than is usual in English, and some other languages. These prompts ("*aizuchi*" in Japanese) are the equivalent of encouraging nods and utterances such as "uh huh" or "yes" in English. They support the speaker who has fallen silent and allow her or him to know that the listener is interested. Such encouraging vocalization by the listener qualifies the phenomenon of silence in conversation with which the Japanese are associated and is a vivid reminder of the relationship between silence and sound. Lebra writes that the absence of *aizuchi* indicates a listener's hostility or distrust and believes that "the amount of vocal backchannelling by the Japanese listener seems by far to exceed the

American counterpart". She adds, "I notice that the English speaker is annoyed by the Japanese listener uttering *aizuchi* too often, too untimely, and too loudly" (p. 344). It may be noted in this context that the Finns, also regarded as a quiet people who use fewer "verbal backchannel communications" than many other European people, still prompt the person who is currently silent and who is expected to start or to resume speaking. Lehtonen and Sajavarra write that the Finns do so by "head nods, mimics, on and off eye contact with the speaker (with the gaze typically directed towards the distance) and occasionally wordless murmurs" (pp. 195–196).

Lebra's treatment of Japan is measured and avoids the sort of exaggerated cultural exceptionalism that is misleading and that is sometimes implicit in cultural studies of particular nations. For can we not say of many peoples or even of individuals, for example, what Nishida writes of the Japanese?:

> … when a person who is requested to do something wishes to refuse that request, he or she will pause and not respond within an appropriate time period. This sends a negative message to the person who made the request, who will then be ready to receive the explicit message or refusal, when it eventually comes (p. 115).

The reasons why Japanese people value silence are somewhat contradictory in that silence may be, on the one hand, a sign of inner strength, while, on the other hand, it can also be a means of not revealing one's personal weaknesses or flaws, or of not getting into trouble or disturbing others even if what one might otherwise say is truthful and praiseworthy. Just as words may be used honestly or dishonestly, so too can silence signify either truthfulness or concealment. Politicians who are quiet or even clumsy in articulation are not necessarily at a disadvantage in Japan. The higher up you go in Japanese society, the more mute you may be. Where silence was sometimes your obligation as a humble inferior, it can become symbolical of your dignity as a superior.

Lebra remarks that Japanese respect for silence finds its way asymmetrically into public fora when one person speaks in turn while another listens politely, rather than engaging in the interruptive or competitive style of conversation so familiar to Westerners.

One style is not necessarily superior to the other, as that researcher also notes:

> I was struck with such asymmetry in conversation when I witnessed a group of Japanese tourists in Honolulu having dinner in a restaurant. About a dozen people, men and women, were talking with diners seated next to them. Soon, some voices became louder while the others settled into a listener's role, and eventually one man, obnoxiously loud, was yelling to the whole group as his audience (p. 352).

Clearly, silence is of great significance in Japanese society. That one ought not to romanticize its value relative to the spoken word, or see it in isolation from its social context, is indicated by Lebra's references to how silence may sometimes frustrate Japanese people and result in their engagement in compensatory activities such as the keeping of diaries or their subsequent communication with the silent person through a third party. However, the fact that cultures have differing attitudes towards silence is one of the reasons that Westerners and Japanese sometimes misunderstand one another. In a study of the various cultural factors that contribute to such misunderstanding, Haru Yamada illustrates varying perspectives by contrasting the style of two related films, one being John Sturges's *The Magnificent Seven* (1960) and the other Akira Kurosawa's *Seven Samurai* (1954)—on which Japanese original the former American film was based. She says, "The law of talk that regulates fair play in *The Magnificent Seven* is completely absent in the original movie …":

> The contrast between the use of talk by the American gunmen and the silence of the Japanese sword-fighters reflects a distinction between views of talk and silence that again finds its source in the religions and folklore woven into the respective histories of the United States and Japan (p. 15).

Yamada points to the way in which Buddhism, Taoism, and Confucianism often forefront the sacredness of silence and the ultimate emptiness of form, including the verbal form of words. She believes that this inclines the Japanese to attach less significance to speech than might otherwise be the case, and writes that,

According to this Japanese folklore of silence, only the belly
speaks the truth. The best communications is without words
in *haragei* (literally, belly art), silent communications. Such vis-
ceral communications is thought of as occurring between an
ideal couple in Japan through *a-un no kokyuu* (literally, ah-hm
breathing): if a husband says, "Ah", a wife would immediately
understand, "Hm". Ideal communication is communications
without talk (p. 17).

Such silence ought not to be confused with the silencing of a spouse,
which is an international phenomenon that will be considered later,
and it is in stark contrast to the verbalization that is considered ideal
and even essential in the West for couples who want their marriages
to last. Business people, as well as lovers, appreciate its value. Sai
writes that,

Being talkative is not only offensive to others' ears but can
be harmful if harmony is to be maintained. Above all, talking
too much can be equated with a lack of sincerity. Well-chosen
moments of silence in conversation with a Japanese are a more
powerful way of [exerting] influence and bonding than a long,
uninterrupted flow of cleverly chosen words. One would do
well to learn this rhythm of silence and indirect speech if one
wishes to convey a sense of personal integrity and encourage
trust. One may conclude that such an attitude of the Japanese is
a polar opposite of the American attitude expressed in sayings
such as "Dumb folks get no land", or "The squeaky wheel gets
the grease" (pp. 119–120).

The author adds that most Japanese businesspeople share the value
of "silence as eloquence". So, when it comes to business meetings,
it is crucial to understand the significance of silence. In an analysis of some such meetings, Haru Yamada discovered that Japanese
bank executives had more frequent and longer silences than did US
executives: "There was an average rate of 5.15 seconds of silence per
minute in the Japanese meeting as compared to 0.74 in the American,
and the longest pause in the Japanese meeting was 8.5 seconds,
almost twice as long as the longest pause of 4.6 seconds in the
American." She believes that the Japanese regard silence as a form

of bonding or an acknowledgement of interdependence, because it belongs to everyone, whereas words are closely associated with a particular speaker (p. 77).

In contrast to such Asian attitudes, Moran observes that "Americans associate silence in a negative context: anxiety, hostility or awkwardnesss ..." (p. 90). However, we shall see below how Deborah Tannen qualified such generalizations about the United States, and Bruneau has also recently argued that, "Contrary to stereotypical viewpoints about how Americans communicate, Americans do use silence, silences and silencing to help articulate," although they do so "in ways different from many sociological groupings elsewhere". He asserts that, "The din of noisy American social groups is not what it may appear to be on the surface" (2008, p. 83). Nakane (2007) also serves as a caution against stereotyping, and that author's study adds to our understanding of silence in intercultural communication in respect of the Japanese in particular.

Was silence more highly valued in earlier centuries in Western society? It is very difficult to assess historically the relative place of pauses in conversation, not least because of the absence of recording technologies in the past. Nevertheless, there are various folklore tapes that were, from the second half of the last century, recorded in rural areas and these might be examined closely with a view to seeing if silences or pauses were distinctive. Even in my own lifetime, it seems to me that Irish people did not interrupt one another as much as they do now, and being quiet or not being "pushy" was perhaps once more highly respected as a personal characteristic than it is today. An Irishman of my own generation who now lives in the USA but who has also worked in Asia, wrote to me in 2005 "from 39,000 feet above the Bering Sea on the way to Japan",

> Silence in communication may come from a number of sources and, as foreigners, we may be misreading the circumstances. It may be a language issue, where they struggle to communicate with us, or as a Zen society where perfection is always sought, they may not speak until they have internally reviewed their words. Or they may be polite in a way we are no longer, and while we rush to complete each other's sentences, they allow you to complete for yourself. I believe it is a mixture of the three but largely driven by respect and politesse. I believe you are

either open or closed to the possibility of other cultures and if
so, you may listen and absorb or be your Western self and step
on everybody's toes. The error is not to know which you are. But
without question, there is a different method of communication
in Japan based on culture, age, seniority, status and tradition.
And silence plays a role. While they understand the nuances,
we play the role of the bull in the china-shop to them.

Yet Haru Yamada points out a salient feature of Japanese silence that
suggests that those keeping silent are not necessarily as calm as they
may appear. There can be an inner ferment, as participants at a meeting think how best to achieve their objectives and to ensure that the
meeting is fruitful. She writes,

> ... an audience listening to an excerpt of conversation only hears
> empty silence [between words]. But for the actual Japanese
> communicators, silences demand the active listening work
> of *sasshi* (guesswork), and it is anything but hollow. In every
> silence, each section head is asking: "Is everyone getting this?",
> "Do we need/want to keep talking on this topic?" or "Should
> we move on to something else" (p. 77).

Yamada adds that the *kanji* (Chinese character used in writing
Japanese) "*ma*" (meaning "space" or "pause") is drawn to represent the sun shining through gates, illustrating how implied communication or meaning can shine through silence. She writes that
where Westerners tend to desire firm resolutions or outcomes at
the end of meetings, Japanese executives may prefer to let debate
about contentious issues just fizzle-out after a series of silences
rather than force a decision and reject a proposal. She recommends
that Westerners also learn to use such silences for reflections on
the process: "If nothing else, the silence will feel shorter" (p. 80).
However, it may also be noted that silence does not always work
to the advantage of Japanese business. According to Yasutaka Sai,
a tendency on the part of managers in Japanese companies not to be
expressive or explicit can give rise to a high level of ambiguity about
what was intended and, when dealing with non-Japanese, "vague
statements not only can invite misunderstanding but are also taken
as an indication that the speaker cannot be trusted" (p. 127).

Academics such as Yamada, as well as management consultants and others, offer advice to those engaged in cross-cultural negotiations. Brislin and Kim, for example, have drawn up a handy list of "ten concepts that summarise how culture affects intercultural interactions that are part of international business dealings". One of these is how people deal with long periods of silence. In summary, they advise,

- Try not to be intimidated by long periods of silence.
- People don't always have to fill gaps.
- Sometimes the period of silence symbolises the importance of an issue (p. 380).

Misa Fujio analysed a one-hour meeting between a US manager, a Japanese manager and a Japanese junior staff member of a US company operating in Japan. Fujio's study focused on miscommunication, especially relating to silence, the ambiguity of "yes", and different strategies of politeness between the US and Japanese managers. Misa makes some practical suggestions as to how both native and non-native speakers should make their approach "in order to understand each other and co-construct the conversation in intercultural communication in an age when English is becoming a global language and could be separated from the cultures of English-speaking countries". She advises that,

> ... as long as it is true that the Japanese have much more tolerance for silence, Japanese communicators should think about some devices to fill in silences, for example, some filling words such as: "Let me think about that", or just simple repetition, "So you're talking about xx" .... On the other hand ... it would be advisable that native speakers of English should be aware beforehand that the English spoken by non-native speakers, especially Japanese, is sometimes filled with pauses for their linguistic and cultural reasons (p. 337).

Corporate recruitment

Differences in the way that people from various cultural backgrounds use silence and other forms of non-verbal expression can be misleading for human resource managers who are engaged in recruiting the best-available talent. Without realizing it, they may be biased in favour of those whose modes of expression resemble their own. Jenkins and Parra examined the influence of non-verbal behaviour in the context of an oral proficiency interview test. The participants were four Spanish-speaking and four Chinese-speaking international teaching assistants. Had those administering the test rated only spoken words then they might have come to a conclusion quite different from that to which they did come, for as the authors of the study later wrote,

> Microanalysis of videotaped tests indicated that interviewees who employed nonverbal behavior considered appropriate by North American evaluators and who negotiated a degree of control over the interview process were able to compensate for perceived weaker linguistic proficiency. Active nonverbal behavior as listeners and turn-takers, together with appropriate paralinguistic features in their talk in interaction, created for the raters an impression of the test taker's interactional competence (pp. 90–107).

Participants who framed the interview as a discussion or conversation among peers were more successful than those who framed it as an examination. This suggests that, in situations of recruitment or personal assessment, both interviewers and those being interviewed have something to gain from an understanding of how oral communication may consist of more than the sum of the words spoken.

Overall, the danger of not respecting cultural differences when negotiating with other people is well summed up in the following advice by Mary Munter:

> Finally, resist applying your own culture's nonverbal meanings to other cultures. Vietnamese may look at the ground with their heads down to show respect, not to be "shifty". Russians may exhibit less facial expression, and Scandinavians fewer gestures, than Americans are accustomed to, but that does not mean they are not enthusiastic. People in Latin and Mediterranean cultures, on the other hand, may gesticulate and touch more often than Americans, but don't infer that they're "pushy". Southerners in the United States tend to speak slowly, but don't infer that they're dumb; northerners may speak more quickly, but don't

infer that they're arrogant. Compared to Americans, Brazilians may interrupt more, Asians may respect silence more, and Arabs may speak more loudly.

Silence in the workplace is not confined to cross-cultural encounters. It can also be, for example, a strategy for resistance by employees in the face of a company's own silence or pretence about its underlying values. Companies adopt fine mission statements and articulate elaborate corporate philosophies, but their effective organizational ethos may remain largely unspoken. Trainees are quick to pick up on the gap between aspiration and reality, sensing what to say and what not to say if they want to be regarded favourably by management. This is an example of that calculating silence that was considered in the previous chapter. A recent English study by Brown and Coupland found that graduate trainees at a large UK-based private sector retail chain (named "Beta" for the purposes of the study), illustrated this phenomenon. The authors paid attention to the ways in which trainees not only accommodated but also worked around what they interpreted as attempts to silence them. The employees' own expressive silence became part of a subtle strategy for the presentation of the self, underlining an earlier observation by Deborah Tannen that "silence alone is not a self-evident sign of powerlessness, nor volubility a self-evident sign of domination" (Wetherell et al., p. 158). Brown and Coupland note in particular how one graduate trainee answered a researcher's questions in a way that indicated how trainees used silence to protect themselves. Asked "Is it ok to say you don't know?", the trainee replied, "I sometimes think maybe I should do a little more research on this rather than asking someone. That's what Beta looks for when they are recruiting anyway, those people who are self-starters and, er, not relying on others too much." Another trainee remarked, " ... occasionally ... frustration leads me to speaking my mind to the wrong person. I need to be a bit careful," while another said, "I think ... you do have to be quite diplomatic sometimes and, you know, you have to think about how you are actually going to phrase things before you say things" (pp. 1057–1060). The authors concluded,

> Managerial identities are notoriously fragile, and conflicts between corporate rhetoric and people's first-hand experience of

work can result in a kind of "schizophrenia", which, in turn, leads to emotional dissonance and stress. "Silence" seemed, in part, to function as a resource for the graduate trainees that they drew on in elaborating the topic of themselves as newcomers, which was, importantly, enabling. For example, their depiction of the culture of Beta as officially inviting, but in practice actually highly discouraging of, new ideas from junior personnel, effectively relieved them from the responsibility to act .... This meant that they were able to secure and enhance their sense of self-identity without engaging in the "risky" business of speaking up too often or doing so when this might cause offence (pp. 1063–1064).

Managers may regard the cautious silence of employees as an appropriate form of humility, especially in the case of trainees who have much to learn. However, employers should also fear that their companies are not maximizing their full resources when their employees feel unable or unwilling to express themselves. Employees who give vent to ill-informed opinions or to emotional and inexperienced reactions may not necessarily benefit a company in the short-term, but the discouragement of such expression can have long-term negative effects on morale and performance.

In a book with an unambiguous title, Cooper and Theobald have recently made the business case for trying hard to understand what others think of you. Their work is simply entitled *Shut up and Listen!*

CHAPTER THREE

Theories of silence

When they are asked, "What is silence?", some people answer that it is "nothing", that it is merely the absence of sound. But in a quiet location, waking in the depth of a silent night, silence sometimes assumes the qualities of a presence, either pleasant or alarming. We may welcome relief from noise or we may project our fears and needs into the quiet void. There are those who prefer to whistle past the graveyard, not to dwell on how fleeting or insignificant are the sounds that we make during our lives. Others enjoy silence as a creative and nourishing space, or even a sign from God. The relationship between silence and sound is so subtle that observers differ on the question of which is most fundamental. In her "Cartographies of Silence", Adrienne Rich (b. 1929) has observed a fundamental tension between what is said and what cannot be or is not said:

> A conversation begins
> with a lie. And each
>
> speaker of the so-called common language feels
> the ice-floe split, the drift apart

as if powerless, as if up against
a force of nature

A poem can begin
with a lie. And be torn up.

A conversation has other laws
recharges itself with its own

false energy, Cannot be torn
up. Infiltrates our blood. Repeats itself.

Inscribes with its unreturning stylus
the isolation it denies (1978, p. 16).

Is silence more fundamental that sound? During the winter of 1838,
Thoreau wrote that,

> All sound is nearly akin to Silence; it is a bubble on her surface
> which straightaway bursts, an emblem of her strength and pro-
> lificness of the undercurrent. It is a faint utterance of Silence,
> and then only agreeable to our auditory nerves when it con-
> trasts itself with the former. In proportion as it does this, and
> is a heightener and intensifier of the Silence, it is harmony and
> purest melody (Torrey, vol. 1, p. 66).

On the other hand, more recently, the Lacanian psychoanalyst
Slavoj Žižek wrote admiringly of the Argentinian Pizarnik, whom
he believes is "arguably *the* poet of subtraction, of minimal difference: the difference between nothing and something, between
silence and a fragmented voice". Žižek conjured up the image of a
vase, and coined a metaphor that contrasts strikingly with Thoreau's
"bubble":

> The primordial fact is not Silence (waiting to be broken by the
> divine Word) but Noise, the confused murmur of the Real in
> which there is not yet any distinction between a figure and its
> background. The first creative act is therefore to *create silence*—it
> is not that silence is broken, but that silence itself breaks, inter-
> rupts the continuous murmur of the Real, thus opening up a
> space in which words can be spoken. There is no speech proper
> without this background of silence: as Heidegger knew, all

speech answers to the "sound of silence". Hard work is needed to create silence, to encircle its place in the same way as a vase creates its central void (p. 224).

Silence manifests in many forms, and theoretical approaches to the modes and functions of silence reflect that variety. Cultural, religious, and sociological insights, among others, have found their place in the growing body of research and writing on silence.

An early and enchanting work on silence is that by Max Picard (1888–1965), whose *Die Welt des Schweigens* appeared in 1948 (published in English in 1952 as *The World of Silence*). From his remarkable little book, it is clear that Picard regarded silence as much more than the absence of sound. He describes it as "an autonomous phenomenon", which is "not simply what happens when we stop talking". For him, silence appears to have some kind of essence, which is spiritual rather than material. It is, as he states, "an independent whole, subsisting in and through itself" (p. 15). He writes,

> Silence is the firstborn of the basic phenomena. It envelops the other basic phenomena—love, loyalty, and death; and there is more silence than speech in them, more of the invisible than the visible. There is also more silence in one person than can be used in a single human life. That is why every human utterance is surrounded by a mystery. The silence in a man stretches out beyond the single human life. In this silence man is connected with past and future generations (p. 21).

Thus, Picard portrays silence as a kind of web. For him, it connects past and future, God and the individual, and is the main support for everyday speech and meaning. Picard attributes to silence empowering characteristics that are related to language and the use of language. He sees silence as an important aspect of creation, through which the divine will is realized. His existentialist approach is poetic and imaginative, and is an example of how certain believers attach a theological value to silence. However, he does not exhaust the religious perspectives on silence. Buddhists, for example, regard phenomena as intrisically interdependent and would be unlikely to formulate their understanding of silence in quite the same philosophical manner that Picard does. They do, however, share his appreciation of its value in daily life.

Picard eloquently proclaims the value of silence, sometimes in a way that appeals to us intuitively while not necessarily bearing close logical scrutiny. For example, he writes that,

> When silence is present, it is as though nothing but silence had ever existed.
>
> Where silence is, man is observed by silence. Silence looks at man more than man looks at silence. Man does not put silence to the test; silence puts man to the test.
>
> One cannot imagine a world in which there is nothing but language and speech, but one can imagine a world where there is nothing but silence (p. 17).

However, can one really "imagine a world where there is nothing but silence", as Picard suggests in that last sentence? How can one possibily remove oneself, or *some* notional observer from such a vista of silence? This dilemma is a version of the well-known question, "If a tree falls in the forest and there is no one present to hear it fall, has it made a noise?" If there is no person present to experience or register silence then how can silence exist? What is the difference between such silence and sheer nothingness? One might as well attempt to imagine the space of our entire universe without anything in it and without any boundaries. It seems conceptually, and practically, impossible.

Picard notes that people, when they stop running and making noise, feel "observed by silence", and are indeed put to the test by it. Frequently, their response is not to contemplate it or not to meditate but simply to start running and making noise again. Yet he believes that,

> ... there is more help and healing in silence than in all the "useful things". Purposeless, unexploitable silence suddenly appears at the side of the all-too-purposeful, and frightens us by its very purposelessness. It interferes with the regular flow of the purposeful. It strenghtens the untouchable, it lessens the damage inflicted by exploitation. It makes things whole again, by taking them back from the world of dissipation into the world of wholeness. It gives things something of its own holy uselessness, for that is what silence itself is: holy uselessness (p. 19).

Picard is speaking here of silence that is embraced freely, and certainly not of that silence that is forced on the powerless by those who wish to suppress legitimate complaints. He is greatly interested in the vibrant relationship between silence and language. He sees language as liable to become unhinged from truth and beauty if there is not a place that is acknowledged within it and within us for silence. Picard's work greatly influenced the Trappist writer Thomas Merton, who believed that the recovery of silence is not an end in itself for the individual but "is necessary for the restoration of authentic communication" (Matthews, p. 62).

When communicating with one another at the everyday, unreflective level, we tend to regard language as merely a series of signs. In this regard, "cup" or "glass" are simple convenient verbal tags that distinguish objects in a descriptive or utilitarian way. However, even such simple words as cup or glass restrict our descriptive powers and we sometimes need to use a broader vocabulary to describe a particular drinking vessel that does not immediately fall into either simple category. How much more limited is language when it comes to expressing complex emotions and insights. Yet, we depend heavily on language to do so. So, our vocabulary determines or frustrates us to a significant degree. Through language's limitations we struggle to explain the world to ourselves and our understanding of it to others. We may sense that there is more to a particular set of circumstances than we can put into words—lacking as individuals the words and understanding to utilize a vocabulary that has been developed but that we have not yet learnt, or even lacking as a particular culture words that correspond sufficiently to our insights. From time to time, new words will be coined to meet that need. Sometimes, as translators know only too well, one language may have a word that a different language continues to lack.

At another level, language may somehow resonate with our very being, for example when we hit on "the right word" at a moment of heightened sensibility, and it is in this respect that Picard sees language as having an intrinsic connection with silence. It is not simply that words require silence around their sounds in order for them to be comprehensible. It is that their meanings somehow depend upon and reflect a potential that exists in silence. Remaining silent may indicate that there is simply nothing to say, but it may also signify a sort of quiet reconnection or recharging of one's psychic batteries. Picard writes,

Words that merely come from other words are hard and aggressive. Such words are also lonely, and a great part of the melancholy in the world today is due to the fact that man has made words lonely by separating them from silence. This repudiation of silence is a factor of human guilt, and the melancholy in the world is the outward expression of that guilt. Language is surrounded by the dark rim of melancholy, no longer by the rim of silence.

Language must remain in intimate relationship with silence. The transparent, hovering way of silence makes language itself transparent and hovering. It is like a bright cloud over silence, a bright cloud over the placid lake of silence. Silence provides a natural source of re-creation for language, a source of refreshment and purification from the wickedness to which language itself has given rise. In silence language holds its breath and fills its lungs with pure and original air (pp. 36–38).

That silence has had, unsurprisingly, a respected place in sacred liturgical and meditative contexts is a fact that will be considered in greater depth below. For his part, Picard recognized the sheer force of silence:

In silence there is present not only the power of healing and friendship but also the power of darkness and terror, that which can erupt from the underground of silence, the power of death and evil. *"Le silence éternal de ces espaces infinis m'effraie"* (The eternal silence of infinite space frightens me) (Pascal). The word that comes from silence is in danger of contact with the destructive and demonic power that is in silence. Every moment something subterranean and menacing can appear in the word and push out the friendliness and peace that also want to emerge from the silence into the world (p. 49).

In another passage, Picard suggests a way of understanding the proclamation of John the Evangelist that, "In the beginning was the Word and the Word was with God" (John 1:1). At some point, after that sacred beginning, people's way of seeing reality became self-consciously verbal and they were no longer "with God". Their will did not coincide with God's. This separation was a kind of sin, a falling away from perfection. Subsequent efforts to rebuild a linguistic Tower of Babel, back up to Heaven, continue to be confounded. One does not need to read a treatise on the place of "the word" or "*logos*" in classical culture to grasp the point expressed here by Picard:

> Silence calls forth sadness in man, for it reminds him of that state in which the fall caused by the word had not yet taken place. Silence makes man yearn for that state before the fall of man, and at the same time it makes him anxious, for in the silence it is as though any moment the word may suddenly appear and with the word the first fall into sin take place again (p. 46).

When singing the praises of silence, as he did for example in the passage below, Picard was evidently living in an age before estate agents and tourism promoters loudly claimed silence as a desirable feature of properties and vacation resorts. He wrote that,

> Silence is the only phenomenon today that is "useless". It does not fit into the world of profit and utility. It simply is. It seems to have no other purpose; it cannot be exploited ... it is "unproductive". Therefore it is regarded as valueless (p. 19).

Nearly 60 years later, silence is commodified in respect of locations that are prized and priced precisely because they offer respite from a very noisy world. Indeed, the aggressive nature of its exploitation in the case of luxury tourism is well captured by an adverb "fiercely" that has been used by the authors of a recent study of super-elite mobility when they asserted that "silence is being fiercely (re)incorporated into the bourgeois imagination" (Thurlow & Jaworski, p. 212). If Picard thought that the everyday life of citizens in 1948 was far from silent, what would he make of a planet today that is overrun by vehicles and bombarded by multichannel electronic stimuli?

Picard was by no means the only person interested in silence in the mid 20th century. Others included Sidney Baker, who developed a psychological theory based on the idea that the very aim of speech, conscious or unconscious, was silence. He distinguished (1955) between "negative silence" that results from a lack of identification between parties and "positive silence" that is pleasurable and that often occurs between intimates such as lovers or close working partners.

In 1959, Edward Hall's *The Silent Language* appeared. He paid close attention to the way in which culture influences behaviour, regarding culture itself as a form of communication that encompasses but transcends the merely verbal. We absorb our culture from the cradle and it forms our patterns of thought and speech. We and others may be unaware of how a particular culture works through us and moulds the ways in which we articulate thoughts and emotions or remain silent. Accordingly, we must bear in mind the possibilities for misunderstanding that are inherent in intercultural communication. Hall's work was influential, and later authors such as Jensen (1973), Bruneau (1973, 2008), and Johannesen (1974) took up the challenge of developing our understanding of those silences that constitute communication.

Meanwhile, during the late 1950s and into the mid 1960s, George Steiner wrote a series of brilliant essays that were subsequently collected and published as *Language and Silence*. These "essays on language, literature and the inhuman", as he called them, are written in a lucid and compelling style and are still a pleasure to read more than 40 years later. Indeed, their very style is a challenge to those academics who write in a technocratic manner full of jargon, and Steiner's clarity of expression is appropriate from an author who was very concerned about the erosion of literacy and the inhuman character of recent history. His essay entitled "The retreat from the word" (1961) was perhaps his most translated and influential. Yet, he appears to be seldom mentioned by sociologists and other academics writing about silence, notwithstanding the wide range of his concerns and observations. Divisions between "scientific", "literary", and "religious" perspectives on silence reflect divisions between disciplines within contemporary society but do not necessarily serve the individual reader who is attempting some integrated form of understanding in respect of silence and of the relationship between speech and silence. Indeed, Silvia Montiglio observed that, "… any study of silence risks being scattered and simply descriptive insofar as its object appears too variegated to be squeezed into a classificatory grid" (p. 7). Nevertheless, the complexity of the phenomenon of silence has not prevented her or others from finding recurrent features and patterns.

Steiner himself pays homage to the study of linguistics, which he regards as "close-bound" to literature. His collection is, as he writes in the first edition, "primarily ... a book about language", which he wishes to redeem before we fall into a dispirited silence:

> If silence were to come again to a ruined civilization, it would be a two-fold silence, loud and desperate with the remembrance of the Word (1967, preface).

He is fascinated, indeed horrified, by the failure of fine words to prevent ignoble actions even by those who are familiar with great literature and the arts. Recalling Nazi Germany, he writes that,

> We know now that a man can read Goethe or Rilke in the evening, that he can play Bach and Schubert, and go to his day's work at Auschwitz in the morning. To say that he has read them without understanding or that his ear is gross, is cant. In what way does this knowledge bear on literature and society, on the hope, grown almost axiomatic from the time of Plato to that of Matthew Arnold, that culture is a humanizing force, that the energies of spirit are transferable to those of conduct? Moreover, it is not only the case that the established media of civilization—the universities, the arts, the book world—failed to offer adequate resistance to political bestiality; they often rose to welcome it and to give it ceremony and apologia. Why? (1967, preface).

For Steiner, silence appears to be less a source of refreshment than a sign of shame and a form of punishment. He fears that language cannot stand the strain of murderous falsehoods that it has been asked to bear in the previous one hundred years. He is fascinated by the work of Ludwig Wittgenstein. Referring to the latter, he notes that, "The greatest of modern philosophers was also the one most profoundly intent on escaping from the spiral of language":

> That which we call fact may well be a veil spun by language to shroud the mind from reality. Wittgenstein compels us to wonder whether reality can be spoken of, when speech is merely a kind of infinite regression, words being spoken of other words. Wittgenstein pursued this dilemma with a passionate austerity (1985, p. 39).

During his whole lifetime, Wittgenstein was the author of just one published philosophical book, the *Tractatus Logico-Philosophicus*. It appeared first in Germany in 1921, being translated into English one year later. He himself wrote in the preface of this book that,

> Its whole meaning could be summed up somewhat as follows: What can be said at all can be said clearly; and whereof one cannot speak thereof one must be silent (p. 27).

Indeed, that philosophical tract by Wittgenstein ended with the following isolated proposition, which would come to be frequently quoted,

> *Wovon man nicht sprechen kann, darüber muss man schweigen.*
> (Whereof one cannot speak, thereof one must be silent)
> (p. 189, no. 7).

This was a proposition that reflected its author's own awareness of the limitations of language and philosophy. For some years after his book was published he abandoned his career as a philosopher to become a teacher of young children, a role that turned out to be unsuited to his personality.

Neither Wittgenstein nor Steiner let their perspectives on the limitation of language stand in the way of continuing verbal speculation. The former later became a professor at Cambridge, his further work there being published posthumously, while the latter's essays treat at some length of words and silence. Wittgenstein thought that certain silences have a religious significance that cannot be put into words, while Steiner has explored how certain aspects of reality appear to be capable of being accessed or expressed through mathematics and music but not through language.

The relationship of silence to forms of therapy is another aspect of the field that has been of growing interest, and will receive further attention in a later chapter. It is worth noting here that, as early as 1964, John Cook believed that he had a sound evidential basis for the theory that less successful therapy was associated with continuous speech. By this time, too, some researchers were already examining silence in the business environment, and the ways in which it is used by management for pragmatic purposes. James Farr, for example, observed how silence might function as a means of inviting someone to have their say, but it could also provoke anxiety or tension when it was unexpected and misunderstood. Other theorists such as Boomer have been interested especially in "hesitation pauses" within conversation and what these might signify.

As we have seen, during the 1970s, Keith Basso spent time among the Apache people of North America. His work then is often cited to illustrate how the meaning of silence varies depending on the cultural or social context. In an interesting comparative study, attempting to understand how an earlier generation in England used silence, Philip Bock refers to Basso's work when studying Shakespeare's plays. Silence presents particular problems for those looking back, because surviving historical and literary texts are clearly not audio recordings and do not include intonations or silences that were then used. The point has already been made above that it is quite possible that our direct ancestors spoke in a tempo or manner that is different from that of their descendents.

By the 1980s, B. P. Dauenhauer had built on the work of Max Picard, and of Martin Heidegger and Gabriel Marcel who had earlier influenced Picard. Dauenhauer developed his own theoretical framework, in which he asserted that silence is always connected with discourse. The question for him is never "Does silence make sense?" but always "What sense does silence make?". It is always in some sense "performative", even when deep, and requires to be understood in context.

One of the most influential works published in respect of silence was edited in the 1980s by Deborah Tannen and Muriel Saville-Troike. Their *Perspectives on Silence* was dedicated, "To those who suffer in silence and those who revel in it", and they prefaced it with this quotation from José Ortegay Gasset's *Man and People*:

> The stupendous reality that is language cannot be understood unless we begin by observing that speech consists above all in silences. A being who could not renounce saying many things would be incapable of speaking. Each language represents a different equation between manifestations and silences. Each people leaves some things unsaid in order to be able to say others.

Perspectives on Silence took shape over several years as the editors asked their students in anthropology and sociolinguistics at Georgetown University, in Washington, DC, to consider silence as part of the communicative code in their analyses of "speech" events. In introductory remarks, they describe silence as, "a relatively neglected component of human communications". They proceed to point out that, within linguistics, silence had traditionally been ignored except insofar as it marked the beginning and end of utterances:

> The tradition has been to define it negatively—as merely the absence of speech. Anthropologists and psychologists, however—less centrally concerned with language *per se*—have been somewhat less likely to ignore silence (p. xi).

If speech is a stone dropped into water, some types of silence may be compared to the ripples that flow from its impact. Indeed, silence is embedded even in speech itself. Tannen and Saville-Troike point out that, "The smallest unit of silence … is the normally unnoticed cessation of sound in the production of consonants, which creates the pattern of consonants and vowels that makes 'speech' of a vocal stream" (p. xvii). Also to be found within speech are pauses between words or sentences when a person is talking: these may be perceived as hesitation or may go unnoticed. They can provide clues to the attributes of a speaker's personality. Then there are further pauses that occur when one party in a conversation stops talking and another responds, and these may reflect cultural differences or social status. These authors note that,

> The next level of silence includes pauses that are perceived in interaction, such as those Goffman (1967) [Erving Goffmann, *Interaction Ritual*, New York: Doubleday] calls "lulls" in conversation. Longer than this is the complete silence of one party to a conversation, seen in Nwoye's example [see Nwoye, "Eloquent silence among the Igbo", p. 189] of a young Igbo woman who indicates her rejection of a marriage proposal by standing her ground yet not speaking. The broadest level of silence discussed is that which provides the structure and background against which talk is marked and meaningful merely by virtue of its occurrence. An example of this is the Igbo ritual … in which

a sacrifice is carried through the village. If this silent ritual is interrupted by talk, the entire sacrifice is profaned and, indeed, cancelled. (p. xvii).

This Igbo example indicates just how significant and socially specific silences may be. Saville-Troike further underlines this fact by reference to an exchange between a man and woman in another culture:

A: Please marry me.
B: [Silence; head and eyes lowered] (Acceptance).

The exchange occurred between Japanese speakers. For the girl (B) to say anything would have been considered very inappropriate in this very emotional situation (Williams, [unpublished manuscript] 1979). If it had occurred between Igbo speakers, silence would be interpreted as denial if she continued to stand there and as acceptance if she ran away (Nwoye, [unpublished manuscript] 1978), (pp. 8–9).

Examples such as these encourage us to reflect on the meaning of silence in our own speech and culture, and on how consciously or unconsciously we communicate messages to outsiders.

It is evident from the schema of Tannen and Saville-Troike that "the broadest level of silence discussed" by them does not extend far beyond social circumstances to encompass those existential concerns that preoccupy Max Picard (and in their book he appears to be mentioned only in its bibliography). They do not specifically ask how silence, in general, challenges humanity's understanding of itself or investigate if it is the key to some kind of transcendent experience or reality. However, one of the contributors to their book, Daniel Maltz, deals specifically with "Joyful noise and reverent silence: the significance of noise in Pentecostal worship" (pp. 113–138). Moreover, Saville-Troike herself refers to the importance of silence within the disciplines of religion and philosophy. Quoting the Chinese wisdom teacher known as Lao-Tse, who proclaimed that, "To talk little is natural," she acknowledges that,

Performances of silence are not merely passive acts, as can be seen in Catholic and Quaker worship, where silence creates

space within which God may work ... and in Eastern thought,
where silence is intimately related to action and desire (p. 3).

The contributors to Tannen and Saville-Troike's collection of essays
deal with, among other matters, psychological and ethnographic
views of pausing, non-verbal communication, meanings and uses
of silence and cross-cultural perspectives. For example, one essayist
addresses the effect of witness hesitancy on lawyers' impressions;
another an Italian case that illustrates how silence and noise may
be "emotion management styles"; one considers "The Silent Finn",
while another discusses some uses of gesture. In one influential contribution to *Perspectives on Silence*, Ron Scollon refers to "silence in
the metaphor of malfunction". He notes that our behaviour may be
governed by ways of seeing the world that project what we have
been told or learnt from our experiences in a particular time and
place. He believes, for example, that for modern Western man the
machine has so dominated life that we have come to interpret many
aspects of reality as types of machine. So, when there is no humming
and no noise, we think that there is something wrong and attribute
negative attributes to silences that we encounter. Scollon writes,

> Researchers still favour Descartes in taking the machine as the
> model of both human cognition and interpersonal interaction.
> This, in turn, has consequences both for the ways in which we
> do research and in our interpersonal interactions with people
> who do not build their understanding of communication in the
> metaphor of the machine (p. 21).

Reviewing the evidence of psychologists and psycholinguists that
"pausing is a factor of considerable significance in human communication", and considering important ways in which silences have
different meanings in different cultures, he notes that those who
speak more tend to dominate encounters with those who speak less.
Those who pause less frequently than others and who jump in to
speak when others pause during speech may leave other people
feeling that they could not get a word in edgeways. Compounding
their insensitive behaviour, they may mistakenly attribute sullenness, passivity, or even hostility to the silent other. He warns that
researchers have fallen into this very trap in their encounters with

alien cultures. Using such industrial terms as "productivity" to describe any reduction in "intra-turn" pauses during conversation, they tend to adopt the "generative metaphor ... of modern industrial society". He notes that,

> It is the metaphor of the machine. If one assumes the engine should be running, the silences will indicate failures. Smooth talk is taken as the natural state of the smoothly running cognitive and interactional machine (p. 26).

The metaphor of a "natural" humming conversational machine has surely been reinforced in our unconscious, since Scollon wrote, by the proliferation of electronic media, mobile phones, and background "music" in public spaces. In an aggressively consumerist world, people who are not "on the go" all the time may feel and appear out of tune. Indeed, Scollon believes that his own theoretical framework corroborates an earlier suggestion that even the tendency to classify people according to attributes (including, for example, "sober" or "detached") is culturally determined and, as he puts it, "is itself a significant aspect of modern industrial society" (p. 28).

However, within the volume itself in which this essay appears, there is an important qualification by Deborah Tannen of Scollon's research findings and theory. In an essay entitled, "Silence: anything but", she claims that, in fact, "slower-paced speech is more positively evaluated by 'mainstream' American [US] speakers than faster speech, and longer switching pauses preferred" (p. 119). She believes that negative evaluations are made in respect to communication encounters with others when the silence of the other is longer than expected by the standards of the culture from which the outsider comes. Thus, quick speech *per se* is not necessarily valued over silence by Westerners, and is even judged negatively in some circumstances. However, when people who value what they regard as slow speech in their own community meet members of other cultures with a different norm then their expectations of what is appropriate may give rise to misunderstandings if they hear what they consider to be (by their standards) abnormally long pauses or silences.

Saville-Troike places silence within an integrated theory of communication. She notes that, "Just as with speech, silence is not a simple unit of communication, but is composed of complex dimensions and structures" (p. 4). For one thing, some silence is a form of communication and some is not. In other words, not all silences mean something.

Moreover, not all silence that *is* a form of communication is non-verbal. It may simply be non-vocal. Thus, some forms of communication that do not require the use of one's voice may be silent but they depend on words or signs that correspond to words. The most obvious form of non-vocal communication is writing, but others include sign language for hearing-impaired people or for religious communities that live in relative silence. Forms of communicative silence that are both non-vocal and non-verbal include eye behaviour and body language. Two ambiguous areas are art and gesture, which may tend towards being verbal if deployed very literally but which may also and frequently do transcend what the artist or person gesturing could put into words if asked to do so. The gestures of a person giving directions to a motorist are much simpler than those of a mime performer such as Marcel Marceau. And a sketch of one's house for a property brochure says far more about some of its features and far less about others than the painting of it by an artist might. Saville-Troike points out (pp. 4–5) that even a verbal format such as writing can include non-verbal spaces, which are indicated by dots and which are used especially by Japanese writers to denote significant silences.

Saville-Troike concludes her own contribution to *Perspectives on Silence* with a bold and broad effort to classify silence into 20 categories that may be applied cross-culturally and that are intended to reflect the complexities and universal characteristics of the whole human communicative system, "within which silence serves variously as prime, substitute and surrogate, as well as frame, cue, and background" (pp. 16–17). Her perspectives on silence so impressed one young Polish student from Poznan that he arranged a research visit to Washington, DC. Adam Jaworski spent the academic year 1987–1988 at the American University in that city. Saville-Troike, who with Tannen had recently completed their volume at nearby Georgetown, lent him some assistance. In his book *The Power of Silence: Social and Pragmatic Perspectives*, published in 1993, Jaworski brought to bear on the topic his particular insights as a scholar of sociolinguistics. Since then, his continuing interest in the field has been reflected in a number of further studies.

He has attempted to achieve a broad theoretical framework within which silence may be discussed coherently. His approach draws on a variety of theories that are particularly relevant to his discipline, thus helping to highlight the many facets of silence as well as the complexity of comprehending its full significance in our lives. Some of the theoretical frameworks that he has specifically credited (1993, p. xii) are Brown and Levinson's theory of politeness, Leach's theory of taboo, Rosch's prototype theory, Sperber and Wilson's relevance theory and Goffman's frame analysis. He believes that by being open to numerous frameworks for analysing silence, he has "been able to suggest some unifying concepts and underlying theories that seem to warrant the formulation of hypotheses about what silence means and communicates" (ibid., p. 167). At the same time, he distinguishes between general underlying principles that may be universal in respect of silences and those important differences in the communication of various groups of people that demonstrate their uniqueness and their distinct world views.

Jaworski is careful to avoid treating silence as though it were some self-contained phenomenon that has its own intrinsic essence. He sees it always in relation to other aspects of reality, as part of some interrelated set of circumstances. He posits a range of linguistic items, with talk at one end and silence at the other end of his continuum. Within that framework, he approaches silence in three principal ways, suggesting that silences be divided into those that are states, those that are activities, and those that are formulaic ("lexicalized"). He says that, firstly, "Silence as a state has been argued to structure communication … when the non-verbal and/or visual aspect of interaction gains more importance in interpreting what is going on in a given situation" (1993, p. 168). In other words, there are instances when people's avoidance of words may reflect or signify a society's values and views. In this context, Jaworski refers to some work by Philips, who (as we have seen) had studied the lives of native Americans. By his second type of silence, silences as activities, Jaworski means to indicate non-verbal, conversational signals which comprise what he terms "propositional silences". When we "fail to mention something", or when we pause in speech for some psycholinguistic reason that involves rapid calculation or even evasion, our silences cannot be regarded simply as nothing, as the mere absence of sound. Words may be significant, but so too may be their absence. Thus, psychotherapists are well aware of the benefits of listening to their clients' or patients' silences, and later we shall consider some developing research in that field. The third leg of Jaworski's stool (his "three-way, prototype-oriented ... taxonomy of silences") refers to what he terms "formulaic silence", which is "related to formulaic speech in highly ambiguous, face-threatening situations" (ibid.). It may be, for example, that silences are sometimes an intrinsic part of politeness.

Jaworski's effort to characterize three principal types of silence is a useful exercise. His schema is by no means exhaustive of all possible kinds of silence, and may not even be clear-cut when it comes to the kinds of silence that he identifies. But it does serve to remind us that the meaning of silences varies with the circumstances in which they are observed. At times he seems determined to come at silence from as many sociological angles as possible, but there is no gainsaying the value of those insights that he uses his theories to support. For example, he writes that,

> I called on relevance theory to explain why certain forms of talk in the media can have the effect of silence understood as lack of any communication, and the oppressive silence[s] of dominated groups have been shown to follow the mechanisms of Leach's theory of taboo (ibid.).

In other words, he deploys relevance theory to argue that if media-babble says nothing significant then it may function as silence in respect of a story, especially where that story cries out for new perspectives to explain the significance of matters to which it refers. The items absent from a TV station's agenda may be at least as important as those about which it makes a great noise. Media-babble in general may displace reflective and inspirational programming. So, Jaworski uses the theory of taboo to indicate how the silencing of minorities, and the failure of society to hear them even when they speak, operate in effect.

Jaworski now works at Cardiff University, Wales, and has edited a special edition of *Multilingua* devoted to a consideration of silence in institutional and intercultural contexts. In the introduction to this, he remarks that, "It used to be customary to write about silence beginning with a bit of a lament that it was a 'neglected' or 'undervalued' area .... This is no longer necessary or possible." He also notes there that, since Tannen and Saville-Troike edited their volume, "a steady stream of monographs and anthologies on silence has continued to bring new titles":

> Final anointment to mainstream status, raising silence from the obscurity of one of the most esoteric researchable topics, is the inclusion of whole sections on "silence" in standard textbooks in sociolinguistics (e.g., Mesthrie et al., 2000), discourse analysis (e.g., Johnstone, 2002), and nonverbal communication (e.g., Guerrero et al., 1999) (2005, p. 1).

Among other essays in the special issue of *Multilingua* is Mary O'Malley's study of ante-natal care in Ireland that illustrates the importance of issues left unspoken as an indicator of status and of the quality or type of working relationship. In that instance alone, the value of understanding the significance of silence is demonstrated and the argument in favour of a theory of silence clearly vindicated.

The implications of acknowledging the "right to silence" in legal contexts has also been studied by authors such as Kurzon (1995) and Cotterill (2005), and has been considered above within the context of expressive silence. Sim argues forcefully that there is a more general right to be silent and to live in silence that citizens should be entitled to enjoy without constant instrusions by the state and by commercial forces. When U2 opened their latest tour in Barcelona in 2009, local residents complained that the band had rehearsed long past the permitted hour at night. Such intrusions are now commonplace in society. In his *Manifesto for Silence: Confronting the Politics and Culture of Noise*, published in 2007, Stuart Sim proclaimed himself to be a champion of silence in the face of the many forces that seek to invade its domain. Part theorist and part polemicist, he draws attention to the role of electronic amplification in particular. Formerly professor of critical theory at the University of Sunderland, Sim claims that "silence and quiet are generally anathema" for the business world, "being states of reflection and, in most cases, of non-consumption". He writes,

> In such an avowedly consumerist society as ours, the latter state will always be a target of attention, a test for the marketing temperament. Silence can therefore become a political statement, a refusal to accept the swamping of our culture by the imperatives

> of big business corporations and multinationals. Just as there is
> a politics of noise, so there can, and should, be an opposed poli-
> tics of silence (p. 2).

Sim prefers to use the terms "noise" and "silence" to "sound" and "quiet", partly because such usage is common but also "because they foreground the emotional content that is such a critical element in the debate" (p. 16). His book is well-written and succinct, and includes a chapter on the science and technology of silence. It deals with aspects of the arts, language, literature, philosophy, and religion in ways that highlight the relevance of his argument to each. The rationale for a politics of silence as espoused by Sim is further sup-ported by the findings of George Prochnik, who set out to discover if his sensitivity to sound and his longing for silence was ridiculous or not. Prochnik specifically identifies a distinguished precedent for those who would assert politically a right to silence when he recalls that the men whose labours in 1787 brought forth the Consti-tution of the United States had the street outside Independence Hall in Philadelphia covered with earth so that their deliberations would not be disturbed by the noise of traffic passing (p. 4).

Recently, the feminist writer Sara Maitland has also written an account of her personal odyssey towards silence. Hers is an engag-ing and thoughtful story, in which her eclectic theory is implicit rather than explicit. Maitland's work will be considered further in the chapter on sacred silences.

The ultimate value of involved participation in various kinds of silence is underlined also by the work of Swiss artist Salomé Voegelin, who writes that her philosophy of sound art is intended "to embrace the experience of its object rather than replace it with ideas". In following Theodor Adorno's advice, she attempts to pro-vide "insights which cause the question of their justness to judge itself" but insists that, "This does not make this philosophy irrational or arbitrary." She eschews "real conclusions" in favour of "strategies for engagement and efforts of interpretation" (pp. xii–xiii).

By thus relating theory to practice and experience in various domains our understanding of particular instances of silence is greatly enhanced.

CHAPTER FOUR

Silence and the arts

A rtists and other creative people have long made use of silence in their work, finding silence conducive to their Muse or incorporating it into the very fabric of their art. Artists may also, as we have seen, decide that it is appropriate to fall silent publicly in respect of their work or even of art in general. For James Joyce, who left Dublin and who for years lived in Trieste, silence was a means of avoiding close engagement with others who might have suffocated him creatively. He has the semi-autobiographical Stephen Dedalus say, in *A Portrait of the Artist as a Young Man* that was first published in serial form in 1914–1915,

> I will try to express myself in some mode of life or art as freely as I can and as wholly as I can, using for my defence the only arms I allow myself to use—silence, exile and cunning (p. 191).

Silence on the stage or during a film, in music or poetry or literature, is a powerful and moving force. Its presence, or references to it, can increase our enjoyment and understanding. Artists and architects can even evoke silence through the visual or spatial dimensions of their creations. Silence may be manifest in many different forms and techniques, enhancing the beauty and meaning of a creative work. It may be an object of contemplation or praise, or the theme of a narrative, or an intrinsic part of a work's structure. When considering types of silence in the first chapter above, various literary and poetic creations were mined for illustration. Literature and poetry are now revisited, along with drama, dance, film, television, and music, in order to underline the importance of silence in the arts.

Literature

The space between words can feature as a significant aspect of the construction of literary works and drama. Where space is at a premium, as in the case of the short story format, it may be particularly important to understand how words are used or arranged. They can say more than at first glance they seem to say. For example, a researcher who has looked at the Irish stories of John Montague, Bernard MacLaverty, Mary Beckett, Anne Devlin, and William Trevor has discerned a resonance between the short story form as they employ it and familiar features of writing about the Irish "Troubles" of the final decades of the 20th century. McDonald mentions, in particular, the emphasis on reticence and silence, the articulation of historical forces through narrative gaps, the use of symbolism, and attempts to express a social condition through non-mimetic modes. He argues that the short story form reflects problems of both articulation and representation, and yet with its characteristically wry, elliptical point of view it can become the mode of expression for a subversive strategy of understatement.

One American novelist who was fascinated by the barrier between the sayable and unsayable was Virginia Woolf. Laurence believes that Woolf was the first modern woman author to practise silence in her writing and that, in so doing, she created a new language of the mind and helped to change the metaphor of silence from one of absence or oppression to one of presence and strength. Woolf's struggle to find expression serves as a reminder of generations of people who, because of gender, class, race, or censorship, have not been heard in literature.

From medieval European romances to contemporary American novels, we find silence playing an important role within the novel. As Tille Olsen wrote, half a century ago,

Literary history and the present are dark with silences: some the silences for years by our acknowledged great; some silences hidden; some the ceasing to publish after one work appears; some the never coming to book form at all (p. 6).

Mireille Schnyder has studied what she regards as the significant if rather unexpected part that silence played in German courtly romance at the beginning of the 13th century. Focusing on the works of Hartmann von Aue, Wolfram von Eschenbach and Gottfried von Strassburg, Schnyder examined the language of silence, including its place in rhetoric, the silent act of reading, and the absence of speech and places of silence in the romances, "notably the night and the forest". In *Tristram Shandy*, Laurence Stern's curious 18th century English novel, even the text itself is silent sometimes, with blanks and asterisks taking the place of words. More recently, Hisaye Yamamoto and E. Annie Proulx have been among writers in the United States who, as we shall see, have explored the phenomena of silence and silencing.

The silence of an artist or writer himself may simply reflect a particular type of personality, or a disinclination to distract attention from the work of art itself. How else is one to understand J. D. Salinger (1919–2010), author of the highly successful novel *Catcher in the Rye* (1951), who published no original work from the mid 1960s and gave no interview in the decades before his death? Yet silence may be more than a mere personal preference. It may also be a judgement by a writer on the ultimate limitations of art forms and on their suitability for the expression or resolution of the contradictions of life. In a sense, as Sontag remarks, "art comes to be considered something to be overthrown":

> Rimbaud has gone to Abyssinia to make his fortune in the slave trade. Wittgenstein, after a period as a village school-teacher has chosen menial work as a hospital orderly. Duchamp has turned to chess. Accompanying these exemplary renunciations of a vocation, each man has declared that he regards his previous achievements in poetry, philosophy, or art as trifling, of no importance.
>
> But the choice of a permanent silence doesn't negate their work. On the contrary, it imparts retroactively an added power and authority to what was broken off—disavowal of

> the work becoming a new source of its validity, a certificate
> of unchallengeable seriousness. The seriousness consists
> in not regarding art (or philosophy practised as an art form:
> Wittgenstein) as something whose seriousness lasts forever, an
> "end", a permanent vehicle for spiritual ambition (pp. 5–6).

In fact, the self-imposed silence of intellectuals is not always "permanent". For example, as was noted above, Wittgenstein later returned to an active life as an academic philosopher after his unhappy experience as a village school-teacher. While he did not publish again in his lifetime, he kept copious notes that appeared posthumously. From 1946, for two decades, Duchamp worked secretly on a great assemblage known as *Étant donnés: 1. la chute d'eau, 2. le gaz d'éclairage* (Given: 1. The waterfall, 2. The illuminating gas). This is now in the United States (Philadelphia Museum of Art; Tomkins, p. 451). In a sense such artists are still in dialogue with their audience, albeit an audience that has no opportunity to respond to their later work until after their deaths.

For his part, Maurice Blanchot (1907–2003) was a writer renowned in France for keeping to himself. He lived in isolation and avoided publicity, yet he emerged occasionally to make political statements. He certainly did not think that artists were obliged to speak out and was committed to the idea that the author should stay silent and allow her or his words to speak for themselves. A work of literature has, in its own right, the power of contestation. As Johnson noted in his obituary of that Frenchman,

> Blanchot believed that it was in writing itself that the author
> found his purpose; there was the use of language, the reality of
> silence and the overwhelming reality of death.

Blanchot even eschewed storylines, concentrating on the quality of writing to communicate truths. Nevertheless, notwithstanding his reputation as a solitary, he did somewhat paradoxically also become in France a highly respected critic, writing columns each month for the *Nouvelle Revue Française* in which he refined his views on the role of the author. Thus, it was said by the anonymous author of another obituary that,

His review of Paulhan's *Les Fleurs de Tarbes*, entitled "Comment la littérature est-elle possible?" (1941), opened theoretical questions about the nature of literature and the status of the writer or narrator that were to be a constant theme of his writing. The predicament of the writer, Blanchot believed, was that of a solitary Orpheus who loses the object of his desire in the moment of turning towards it, losing his identity in what he called "L'espace littéraire", a locus of an anonymous, unmasterable, unspeakable experience.

In 1955, Blanchot had declared that,

> To write is to make oneself the echo of what cannot cease speaking—and since it cannot, in order to become its echo I have, in a way, to silence it. I bring to this incessant speech the decisiveness, the authority of my own silence. I make *perceptible* by my silent mediation, the uninterrupted affirmation, the giant murmuring upon which language becomes imaginary, opens and thus becomes image, becomes a speaking depth, an indistinct plenitude which is empty. This silence has its source in the effacement toward which the writer is drawn. Or else, it is the resource of his mastery, the right of intervention which the hand that doesn't write retains—the part of the writer which can always say no and, when necessary, appeal to time, restore the future.
>
> When we admire the tone of a work, when we respond to its tone as to its most authentic aspect, what are we referring to? Not to style, or to the interest and virtues of the language, but to this silence precisely, this vigorous force by which the writer, having been deprived of himself, having renounced himself, has in this effacement nevertheless maintained the authority of a certain power: the power decisively to be still, so that in this silence what speaks without beginning or end might take on form, coherence, and sense (p. 27).

What the lives of people such as Wittgenstein and Blanchot demonstrate is that silence is not an end in itself, an absolute, but is relative to some form of articulation or manifestation. Even the most solitary hermit is silent relative to creation in general or to a perceived Creator.

Not all French authors were as difficult for a general reader as Blanchot could be. For example, in his story entitled *Le Silence de la Mer* ("The Silence of the Sea"), which was published surreptitiously under the pseudonym "Vercors" in Nazi-occupied France in 1942, Jean Bruller, who was both a writer and (like Samuel Beckett) an active member of the French resistance, deals in an accessible way with a family that must interact with a German soldier stationed in their house but who are morally required to hold back from speaking with him.

The difficulty of pinning down silence as a coherently useful concept in studying literature has been raised eloquently by the author of a work on Pascal, Rousseau, and Beckett, who confesses to being unable to approach the subject entirely objectively. Loevlie writes,

> First of all, silence resists empirical observation and description. It cannot be analysed as a thing or an object, it cannot be pointed to or defined. Silence slips away from description; to talk of it is to lose it, or at least to defer it. As such, silence is always just ahead of our critical discourse, seducing us to follow it just one step further in the attempt to catch it, but never there to be caught. Critical discourse about silence lags behind its object of study. The seductive impact of silence is also linked to what might be called its flexibility. Silence, precisely because it is not a definable, graspable thing, is subject to numerous different understandings and can be used in a sufficiently vague manner to make it serve many purposes. It is available for various projections of meaning because no meaning or definition can "match" the notion of silence; it is always somewhere else (p. 9).

It is the silence of a snow-covered landscape that is central to the concluding force of one of James Joyce's most famous short stories, "The dead". And in the opening of his celebrated novel entitled *Snow*, Turkey's Orhan Pamuk (b. 1952) writes,

> The silence of snow, thought the man sitting just behind the bus driver. If this were the beginning of a poem, he would have called the thing he felt inside him the silence of snow.

In 1996, at the University of Athens, the Hellenic Association for the Study of English devoted its conference to the theme of "Autonomy in Logos: Anatomies of Silence". Among the writers whose relationship to silence were the subject of papers later edited by Cacoullos and Sifianou were Joseph Conrad, Celan, Charles Dickens, Seamus Heaney, Henry James and D. H. Lawrence. For his part, William Faulkner observed that, "I prefer silence to sound, and the image produced by words occurs in silence. That is, the thunder and the music of prose takes place in silence" (p. 248). That silence as a creative medium and silence as subject may be intertwined is suggested by David Jasper's contention that literature has a special value in terms of addressing silence, even in dreadful contexts such as that of the Nazi Holocaust. He argues that, "Literature continues to speak even in the midst of silence, and possibly because it has always been sensitive, in a way that theology paradoxically has often not been, to the inaudibility of the world, to the silence and darkness of God" (Hass, Jasper & Jay, p. 28). The Italian author Primo Levi, who himself experienced internment in a concentration camp, struggled throughout the remainder of his life to write appropriately about his experiences. Others who have had no such personal experiences need to be especially careful not to exploit for mere effect any misery that verges on the "unspeakable". Sometimes, falling silent is a better option.

Poetry

The richness of silence, its simultaneous delicacy and potency, has engaged many poets. In Africa, for example, the power of silence to move people was enunciated in detail in some Swahili verses of the 19th century entitled "Silence" (Harries, p. 257). They took as their starting point this old Swahili saying, "Deep silence makes a loud noise" (Madan, p. 154 at "Kimya"), and cautioned people to respect silence because it has a future! In Asia, Chong-Ju (1915–2000), perhaps the most important Korean poet of the 20th century, expresses silence's marvellous potency in a few simple untitled lines (translated at O'Rourke, p. 104),

> So hushed
> the sky
> an orchid

wondering
why
opened
its petals
wide

In a similar vein, the American poet Wallace Stevens (1879–1955) observed, in his "Thirteen Ways of Looking at a Blackbird",

I do not know which to prefer,
The beauty of inflections
Or the beauty of innuendoes.
The blackbirds whistling
Or just after.

The Russian poet, Fyodor Tyutchev (1803–1873), counselled reserve in his *"Silentium!"* (Latin for "Silence!"), believing that a thought once uttered becomes untrue. So valuable was silence to the authors of the old Jewish Midrash, as we shall see below, that they appear to have equated it to a precious stone. Indeed, George Eliot (1819–1880) suggests in her long dramatic poem entitled *The Spanish Gypsy* that precious stones may express more eloquently than words certain aspects of the unspoken:

FEDALMA (*taking out her ear-rings, and then
lifting up the other jewels, one by one*).

Pray, fasten in the rubies.

(DON SILVA *begins to put in the ear-ring.*)

I was right!
These gems have life in them: their colours speak,
Say what words fail of. So do many things –
The scent of jasmine, and the fountain's plash,
The moving shadows on the far-off hills,
The slanting moonlight, and our clasping hands.
O Silva, there's an ocean round our words
That overflows and drowns them. Do you know
Sometimes when we sit silent, and the air

Breathes gently on us from the orange trees,
It seems that with the whisper of a word
Our souls must shrink, get poorer, more apart.
Is it not true?

DON SILVA

Yes, dearest, it is true.
Speech is but broken light upon the depth
Of the unspoken: even your loved words
Float in the larger meaning of your voice
As something dimmer.

(*He is still trying in vain to fasten the second
ear-ring, while she has stooped again over
the casket*) (bk I, pp. 103–104).

One of a number of other poets who have dealt directly with the
ambiguities of silence is Adrienne Rich (b. 1929). In the ninth of her
"Twenty-one Love Poems", she seems both to fear and to respect the
silence of the loved other as she sings,

Your silence today is a pond where drowned things live
I want to see raised dripping and brought into the sun ....

I fear this silence,
this inarticulate life. I'm waiting
for a wind that will gently open this sheeted water
for once, and show me what I can do
for you, who have often made the unnameable
nameable for others, even for me (1978, p. 29).

Many poets have appreciated and jealously guarded the value of
relative silence as a creative milieu. So, for example, W. B. Yeats
(1865–1939), in the "Long-legged Fly", notably bid,

THAT civilisation may not sink,
Its great battle lost,
Quiet the dog, tether the pony

To a distant post;
Our master Caesar is in the tent
Where the maps are spread,
His eyes fixed upon nothing,
A hand under his head.
Like a long-legged fly upon the stream
His mind moves upon silence.

That the topless towers be burnt
And men recall that face,
Move most gently if move you must
In this lonely place.
She thinks, part woman, three parts a child,
That nobody looks; her feet
Practise a tinker shuffle
Picked up on a street.
Like a long-legged fly upon the stream
Her mind moves upon silence.

That girls at puberty may find
The first Adam in their thought,
Shut the door of the Pope's chapel,
Keep those children out.
There on that scaffolding reclines
Michael Angelo.
With no more sound than the mice make
His hand moves to and fro.
Like a long-legged fly upon the stream
His mind moves upon silence.

Another and less desirable kind of silence that we have considered earlier is paradoxically found embedded within a poem called "Silence" by Marianne Moore (1887–1972) of Missouri, USA. For in it Moore herself appears to silence a significant fact about her own life. The father whom she describes there as appreciating silence was not in fact her own father, whom she is said to have never met following his mental breakdown and committal to a hospital before she was born. Moore added a footnote to the poem, attributing the role of the daughter cited in it to another person, but the poem's 14 lines are frequently quoted without her gloss (Pollak, p. 109). They are,

My father used to say,
"Superior people never make long visits,
have to be shown Longfellow's grave
nor the glass flowers at Harvard.
Self reliant like the cat –
that takes its prey to privacy,
the mouse's limp tail hanging like a shoelace from its mouth –
they sometimes enjoy solitude,
and can be robbed of speech
by speech which has delighted them.
The deepest feeling always shows itself in silence;
not in silence, but restraint."
Nor was he insincere in saying, "Make my house your inn."
Inns are not residences (Moore, pp. 94–95, 168).

Annie Dillard is a US writer and poet who has won the Pulitzer Prize for her work. Poems included in her collection *Mornings Like This* were all original compositions but were constituted by sentences borrowed from other works. She dropped some words from those sentences but, so it is said, never added any. One of her poems, "Pastoral", was based on Max Picard's *The World of Silence*, which was discussed above in an earlier chapter.

The apparent silence of God, which will be considered later below, has engaged many poets, including not least the Welshman R. S. Thomas (1913–2000) for whom indeed it was "a dominant theme" (McGill, p. 23). And the Scottish poet Tom Leonard has written poetry for performance in a way that indicates explicitly the significance of what is absent in discourse itself. Manson has described Leonard's *Access to the Silence* as "incredibly moving".

Poetry occupies a suggestive space between articulation and muteness. In his study of Stéphane Mallarmé (1842–1898), Pearson contemplates its ability to express subtly what might otherwise be lost in silence or drowned out by words. He writes that,

Where everyday language, the "universal *reportage*" … may appear to mean everything, it actually means very little, is perhaps just another form of silence. "*Le Vers*" on the other hand, whether in prose or verse, may constitute a form of expression—and communication—at once purer and more dense than quotidian [everyday] verbiage. But by inhabiting this milieu the poet finds himself caught also between sense and nonsense, for in restoring the pristine imprint on his verbal coinage he discovers that language may mean more than he can ever control (p. 27).

Poetry is a kind of horizon of speech. It appears out of infinity, materializing at what in his poem entitled "It is born" the Chilean Pablo Neruda referred to as "the very edge where nothing at all needs saying" (p. 7).

Drama

Silences can constitute an especially important weapon in any dramatist's arsenal. The space around, between, or beyond words may be deployed to great effect, creating suspense or contrast, and highlighting the significance or insignificance of what is actually said. Audiences can be drawn into the stage by silences, or be fascinated by the ways in which playwrights evoke the inarticulate. However, silences are also feared.

In ancient Greece early dramatists affirmed the value of voice. Voice was to them what Silvia Montiglio describes as "an organizing principle". For such writers, reasoning and words ("*logos*") manifestly distinguished human beings from other forms of nature and allowed people to communicate directly with the gods and to organize political affairs. Voice celebrated creation, whereas silence boded annihilation. In Greek society, silence might threaten the fullness of sound. Montiglio notes that,

> As a troublesome, paralyzing interruption of the verbal flow within the speech code of the *Iliad*; as an impenetrable and concentrated attitude in tragedy; as a sudden suspension of the normal course of nature, silence heralds disruption and provokes anxiety. Ominous silences most often break out into cries; the horror of the void fills silence with its opposite, as if to reestablish a lost equilibrium through an overcompensation of sound (p. 289).

Silence in Greek drama is frequently associated with darkness, and is often an indicator of mood or character. Acts of silence are emphasized verbally. The Greek adage that "silence is a woman's ornament" had its counterpoint in the fact that silence in men was not generally regarded as desirable—and certainly not on the stage. As Montiglio points out, in practice even "the silence of real women in tragedy is never an ornament" but tends to indicate self-destructive behaviour or a subterranean plotting. Silence in men had once also been considered decorous in aristocratic Greek societies such as Sparta, but the subsequent development of the democratic city-state encouraged greater articulation within its relatively open fora and procedures. Men were expected to speak up, and this was so to such an extent that, according to Montiglio, in democratic Athens the spectators at dramatic productions did not regard themselves as silent observers: "As a vocal response, the uproar defines the audience as a group of potential speakers rather than of pure listeners. This may be the reason why Greek orators do not aim for silent admiration, as Roman orators do" (pp. 291–292).

In the contrast between noisy and participative audiences and those expected to remain passive or silent at all costs, Susan Sontag perceived a later shift in the nature of our idea of art. Referring to "audience in the modern sense, an assembly of voyeuristic spectators", she wrote that,

> At least since Nietzsche observed in *The Birth of Tragedy* that an audience of spectators as we know it, those present whom the actors ignore, was unknown to the Greeks, a good deal of contemporary art seems moved by the desire to eliminate the audience from art, an enterprise that often presents itself as an attempt to eliminate "art" altogether (p. 8).

Yet, notwithstanding their reputation as noisy audiences, Greeks appreciated the dramatic possibilities of silence itself. One recent study examines how Aeschylus, who is often regarded as the founder of Greek tragedy, uses the silence of Achilles to achieve effect. Working with fragments of Aeschylus's *Myrmidons*, the first part of a lost trilogy about Achilles, Pantelis Michelakis suggests that Achilles maintained his silence perhaps up to the middle of that play:

> In Greek literature silence is usually imposed on those who are in an inferior position, either individuals, or groups. In the *Myrmidons* it is not silence which is equivalent to impotency, but

language. Unlike, say, in the Homeric assemblies, where silence is an undesirable reaction ... manifesting somebody else's power, in Aeschylus it is a self-conscious decision, a weapon against those who attempt to impose their will on Achilles.

The provocative and disruptive silence of the Aeschylean Achilles is one of the focal points of Aristophanes's parody of Aeschylus in the *Frogs* .... Aeschylus features as an angry and silent Achilles. When he first enters the stage together with Euripides he remains mute for over 10 lines, a silence remarked upon by Dionysus and commented upon by Euripides: [Dionysus]: Why are you keeping so quiet, Aeschylus? You hear what he says. [Euripides]: He'll be all disdainful and aloof to begin with, the same hocus-pocus act he always used to put on in his tragedies (1999).

Michelakis adds that, in this way, "Aristophanes does not simply point to Aeschylus's provocative use of silence; he also seeks to reinstate the normative association of silence with powerlessness and inferiority."

Across the globe, in Japan from the 14th century, Noh plays became a classical form of theatre that artfully engaged with emptiness and silence. Noh plays are not so much the dramatic reenactment of an event as the expression of emotions associated with it. They utilize understatement and suggestion, dance and mime and music. However, the fact that they do so within a social context to which their elite audiences bring a certain understanding of what is intended is an indication of the fact that the absence of words in themselves does itself not necessarily indicate an absence of conceptual communication. Noh plays fascinated and influenced the Irish poet and playwright, W. B. Yeats who understood how the author of the plays "set before us all those things which we feel and imagine in silence" (Murray, p. 103). More recently, Japanese directors Munakata Ueda and Yoshihiro Kurita have each attempted to translate Shakespeare's English plays into Noh form. Discussing this challenge with Kensuke Yokouchi, the playwright and director, Kurita said that,

The movement that is allowed in Noh theatre is only a moment's movement. You need to stage the silence after that moment of movement so that it becomes movement that extends beyond that moment. It is a reversal of silence and movement (Yokouchi).

Shakespeare and other English dramatists of the Elizabethan period were themselves attuned to the possibilities and significance of silence. Ben Jonson, for example, wrote scenes in which the focus was not primarily on the person speaking. Thus, in one particular scene in Jonson's *The Alchemist*, Abel Drugger has scarcely any lines, yet this scene may be directed with him as the focal character (Woolland, passim).

In addition to its use for effect, silence also features as a theme or object of attention in Elizabethan drama, perhaps most famously at the end of Shakespeare's *Hamlet* (Act 5, sc. 2), when the mystery or annihilation that lies beyond death is acknowledged in a declaration that "the rest is silence". Shakespeare's vision of life as passing noise and ephemeral action before silent sleep is also expressed in other fine lines, including these from *The Tempest*:

> Our revels now are ended. These our actors,
> As I foretold you, were all spirits, and
> Are melted into air, into thin air:
> And, like the baseless fabric of this vision,
> The cloud-capp'd towers, the gorgeous palaces,
> The solemn temples, the great globe itself,
> Yea, all which it inherit, shall dissolve,
> And, like this insubstantial pageant faded,
> Leave not a rack behind. We are such stuff
> As dreams are made on; and our little life
> Is rounded with a sleep (Act 4, sc. 1).

Drama can also be a powerful medium for voicing objections to those silences that are undesirable. Thus, a group of Somali women in England were in 2005 encouraged to participate in a multi-media production at Birmingham Repertory Theatre that gave them a voice in relation to both Somali men and the foreign society in which they found themselves. *Breaking The Silence—Somali Women Speak Out*, by Evlynn Sharp, was created by "Exiled Writers Ink" with "The Horn of Africa Women's Association". Whenever Westerners provide such platforms to people from poorer countries, the former need to take care that the creative work produced expresses the perspectives of the latter and is not primarily about the points of view of facilitating agents, groups, and publishing companies, however benign their intentions.

Mime

One particular and ancient theatrical form that dispenses with words is mime. It features gestures and movements that spark an audience's imagination. The performance of Greek tragedies, for example, sometimes included an introduction in mime. In Roman times, mime or "pantomime" was an entertainment in its own right, detached from dance and from conventional speaking theatre. During the Middle Ages, a comedy theatre known as "Commedia dell' Arte" developed in Italy. By no means dependent on mime, it could be loud and colourful, a kind of slapstick. However, as the players from Italy travelled throughout Europe they came to compete with established local theatres and the latter eventually persuaded their respective authorities to oblige the Commedia dell' Arte to perform without words. Players survived by relying on mime and other techniques.

Mime may be simply a substitute for sound, a silence that is the absence of words while fully expressing human emotions through gestures. Sometimes, however, the silence of mime suggests a deeper truth that words obscure. It may hint at a transcendent reality.

In France, Italian characters of the Commedia dell' Arte took on new identities. Arlechinno became Harlequin, in his patchwork costume, and Pedrolino became Pierrot, with his white face that is believed to be the original of that worn today by circus clowns. The main home of French mime was the Théâtre des Funambules that opened in 1816. The Funambules remained a silent theatre until the revolution of 1830. Oisín Kenny writes (p. 22) that, "The Funambules used this restriction to its advantage and the silence of this theatre became a unique feature of a visit here." However, he adds that, when visiting the Funambules after 1830, Nerval expressed disappointment that, "[T]oday, all these small theatres babble and hum like the big ones" ("*aujord'hui tous ces petits théâtres babillent et fredonnent comme les grands*").

One famous mime artist at the Funambules was Jean-Baptiste Debureau, who drew all classes of Parisians to the theatre. The combination of simple plots with his complex and subtle performances earned him great acclaim. In the years following his debut at the Funambules in 1819, he developed the character of Pierrot in a new way. Debureau used the standard plots of the Commedia dell' Arte, involving Colombine being pursued by Harlequin and his wealthy rival, the gross Pantalon. Pierrot was the oppressed, ill-treated clown character:

> However, Debureau made these characters relevant and contemporary. Janin said, "Pierrot is the people", while Gautier compared him to, "the ancient slave, the modern proletarian" (Wechsler, p. 45). He transformed Pierrot into a crafty figure, often outwitting his master. Debureau played to his strengths. He accentuated the expressiveness of his long, composed face by applying white make-up. He exchanged Pierrot's traditional floppy hat for a black skullcap, got rid of his ruffled collar, and wore a baggy, white tunic (O. Kenny, p. 23).

Debureau's character helped to sustain the tradition of mime that came to find new forms in silent cinema when Charlie Chaplin and Buster Keaton played the roles of "little" men. But mime also survived on the stage, most notably in the work of Marcel Marceau (1923–2007). Marceau was a student of Etienne Decroux, who himself was regarded as the father of modern mime. Marceau developed a character called "Bip", whom he described as follows:

> Bip est une synthèse de la pantomime blanche qu'on a vu jouer par Jean-Louis dans Les Enfants du Paradis qui reproduit toute cette époque du Boulevard du Crime et des Funambules. Il y a d'une part le mélodrame où « Margot a pleuré », comme dit Victor Hugo, et de l'autre le Théâtre des Funambules.
>
> Bip est un petit-fils de Pierrot, le héros silencieux, et de Petrolino qui était un personnage qui a influencé Pierrot dans la pantomime française (Wagner).

The film that Marceau mentions, Les Enfants du Paradis (1945), which is highly regarded, was directed by Marcel Carné. The "paradise"

of the title is that of "the gods", as one says in English, being the
highest part of the theatre where one finds the least expensive seats.
A reviewer has noted how this film acknowledges the popular
appeal of mime in Paris of the mid 19th century:

> The dreamlike passions and fragile sensitivity of Baptiste the
> mime form a strong contrast to the loud and blustery Frederic,
> who booms, "I will die from silence like others die from hun-
> ger and thirst." Yet, while Frederic later achieves fame as an
> actor-star on the boulevard, the common folk are drawn to
> Baptiste and his delicate stories wrapped in the gauze of panto-
> mime. In one poignant piece, Baptiste plays Pierrot as he loses
> his beloved, a statue, to Harlequin, played by the flamboyant
> Frederic. (Shambu).

During 2000, Marceau visited Buffalo, New York, as a guest of the
Irish Classical Theatre Company and the local university in that city.
Lewandowski reports that he told his audience of 400 people that,
"With the breathing of the emotion, you create thought. Breathing
is ... poetry—how to sing inside, the stream of life, the feeling of
life .... When you speak words, you create an image, and when you
are silent, the attitude of the moment creates image." She continues
that,

> What began as a discussion about the history of mime—and
> Marceau's foray into the art—quickly evolved into a string of
> vignettes in which, among them, the 77-year-old was perched,
> arms crossed, over the rail of a cruise ship—swaying to and fro,
> a face reflective of both giddy pleasure and severe nausea; he
> tore a man's heart out of his chest in a fit of unabated rage, and
> struggled to walk against the wind—perhaps one of his most
> familiar "moves," which Marceau said was the inspiration for
> Michael Jackson's "moonwalk."
> ... though silence does not truly exist, he said, mime—a
> metaphor for, or "certain poetry about," reality—affords
> respite from present conditions, such as hate and war, that
> weigh heavy on him. "[It is] so wonderful to live in silence—
> there is such noise in the world!" he exclaimed, gesturing

with his hands—the tools of his livelihood that he said are "so important"—and filling his pause with a crescendo of sound emulating "noise."

This article reminds us that the gesture of mime renders its silence relative rather than absolute: "Emotional and animated, Marceau's speech circles back always to the 'sound' of silence—the gesture. 'The sound reveals the rhythm, the gesture [reveals] inside of man,' he said."

A modern playwright closely associated with the use of silence is Samuel Beckett (1906–1989), so closely indeed that Seán Ó Mórdha decided to entitle his special television documentary about the writer's life and work, "Samuel Beckett—Silence to Silence". Beckett wrote mime plays (*Act without Words I* and *Act without Words II*) and the influence of mime is evident throughout his works for the stage. To Beckett is attributed frequently the remark that, "Every word is like an unnecessary stain on silence and nothingness." However, the truth appears to be that, in his case certainly, he saw words in fact as a *necessary* stain on silence. This is the import of his views as reported by Deirde Bair and quoted above, "I could not have gone through the awful wretched mess of life without having left a stain upon the silence." Some of his best-known lines suggest that our lives are inevitably a stream of words, even if they will run their course and empty into silence: "I don't know, that's all words, never wake, all words, there's nothing else …."

> I'll go on, you must say words, as long as there are any, until they find me, until they say me, strange pain, strange sin, you must go on, perhaps they have carried me to the threshold of my story, before the door that opens on my story, that would surprise me, if it opens, it will be I, it will be the silence, where I am, I don't know, I'll never know, in the silence you don't know, you must go on, I can't go on, I'll go on (*Unnamable*, p. 132).

Not surprisingly, when they decided to direct six short plays by Samuel Beckett at the DePauw Theatre in Greencastle, Indiana, in April 2006, they referred to them collectively as "In the silence you don't know" and the theatre announced,

> Five short plays. 3 with no words. 1 with no actors. 1 with just
> heads sticking out of urns. Sample the existential world of the
> Nobel Prize-winning author of *Waiting for Godot*, Irish play-
> wright Samuel Beckett. When it's quiet, with the silence scream-
> ing in your ears, you see the bleakness, the pointless vacuum
> of nothingness before you, and you go on anyway .... *Parental
> discretion advised for children* ....

The English playwright Harold Pinter (1930–2008) was also
renowned for his dramatic deployment of what is not said. For this
reason, especially, his plays need to be acted and directed by those
who are mature enough to appreciate this dimension. Pinter cleverly
uses silence, understatement and cryptic small talk to create a mildly
menacing atmosphere in which a darker or greater reality seems to
lurk. He has sometimes been dubbed "Master of the Pause". In 1959,
The Caretaker was the first of many successful plays that accustomed
audiences to his style, a style that eventually gave rise to the adjective "Pinteresque". One of Pinter's short plays was even entitled
Silence. It and another one-act play by the author, *Landscape*, were
first produced on 2 July 1969 at the Aldwych Theatre, by the Royal
Shakespeare Company. An admiring reviewer wrote that,

> In either play the audience has to piece together into some
> sort of shifting coherence the fragmented details of the partly
> recollected past, and in each case what is important is not the
> past, but the continuing influence that this past exercises on the
> present which is before our eyes on the stage of the Aldwych
> Theatre (Hobson).

Eighteen years later, demonstrating the persistent force of Pinter's
silences, John Travolta starred in a film production of that dramatist's
Dumb Waiter (which had first been produced in 1960). It is the story
of two men hired to commit a murder, and its title is appropriately
ambiguous. Alan Bennett, the English writer, is said to have suggested jocularly that the most suitable way of celebrating Pinter's
birthday would be by a two-minute silence.

Among other European writers who have been interested in
the significance of silence was Nathalie Sarraute, the Russian-
born French novelist and critic. She was fascinated by the way in

which the subconscious may barely hint in speech at underlying intentions and wishes, and she studied our capacity to govern our lives by things that are not said. A theory of "tropisms" underlay her work, being the idea that existential principles are prelinguistic and incline us towards certain courses of action or speech. Her works are difficult for many readers. In 1963, she wrote for Radio Stuttgart a piece called *Silence*, the first of a number of theatrical explorations of voice and sound, and of what lies outside conversation (Rothenberg, p. 386).

In an acknowledgement of the central role of silence in drama, Athol Fugard of South Africa has written that, "Theatre—and I am a practitioner of the purest form of it, 'poor theatre'—is unique among the live arts in what it occupies: the three dimensions of space and then time and then silence" (Boyd).

Silence and dance

When dancers take to the stage, they too play with the possibilities of silence. The wordless grace of dance can be both a pleasure and an inspiration. The absence of words does not make dance silent, but silence may at times be an intrinsic element of dance productions. Silence may even be discerned in the space that such movements conjure up or suggest. The Puerto Rican choreographer Ana Sánchez-Colberg (b. 1962) took a phrase coined by Merleau-Ponty in his *Phenomenology of Perception* and wrote that silence can signal, "the entrance into a corporeal dimension which, rather than foreboding a retreat from the world, is in fact 'our general medium of having a world'" (p. 146).

Virpi Pahkinen of the Stockholm House of Dance draws inspiration for her work from the Tibetan *Book of the Dead*, among other sources. When Pahkinen's *Silence of the Trembling Hands* was produced by the Polish Dance Theatre, at Poznan in 2002, Izabela Przyluska commented that, "This barely few [17] minute-long dance etude ... enters the memory as a clean and deep illumination experienced through art, a drawing towards perfection and harmony, a touching of mystery ...." It is unsurprising to learn that Pahkinen earlier worked with Ingmar Bergman, the great Swedish director of silence in film, at the National Dramatic Theatre of Sweden.

A different kind of relationship between theatrical silence and dance is evident in *Hamlet, … the rest is silence*, a production of the Synetic Theater in Arlington, Virginia, USA. William Triplett of the *Washington Post* wrote of this award-winning but wordless interpretation of Shakespeare's classic that, "ultimately, this is not Hamlet as most of us have probably ever seen it—this is Hamlet as we know it in our bones". Again, one finds artists translating to another medium (in this case to dance from theatre) the underlying implicit truths of a work of art that are not fully articulated in its script.

Kalichi has eloquently addressed the question of a fundamental relationship between silence and dance. He is interested in both the physical and psychological healing powers of dance. Reminded by the editor of a recent book that he had asked people, "What kind of dance would emerge from your attention to silence?", Kalichi replied,

> I woke up from a dream several years ago and wrote the words, "God is a singing sound in the heart of silence." I've kept the piece of paper with these words written on it in a tin in my desk since 1988. The phrase "God is a singing sound in the heart of silence" won't go away. The words "heart", "silence", "singing sound" still resonate somewhere in me. Perhaps I shall be able to answer that question, *"What kind of dance would emerge from your attention to silence?"* from a deeper place somewhere in the not too distant future (Theodores, p. 166).

Between dance and drama lie certain experimental forms of stage production. One example is *Silence Silence Silence*, an imagistic, movement-based work in five visual "sequences" directed by Vito Taufer of the Theatre Mladinsko in Ljubljana, Slovenia. *Silence Silence Silence*, first performed in Ljubljana in 1996, is described as a work of dream images, anthropological fantasies and myths. When brought to New York City in 2001, its hosts at the La MaMa Experimental Theatre Club wrote that,

> The play is divided into five episodes of imagistic, slow-motion movement theater, each staged with a delicate soundscape that includes heartbeats, air sounds and soft instrumental music. With keenly skillful movement, six actors "break through"

silence, both real and metaphorical, in elaborately-designed scenes that nearly defy realistic description .... A mother earth or Lilith figure with bulging eyes, wrapped in Aluminum foil, shatters the silence with her piercing voice ....

One powerful influence on this piece was said by La MaMa to be a widespread feeling among Slovenes during the Yugoslavian conflict that, "we are condemned to be separated" and "whatever we do, there will be an infinite silence and distance between us":

> Taufer sensed that Sarajevo, after the bombings, dwelt some-where "in a hole, completely isolated, lonely" and that "inde-scribable, terrible things were happening there and there is nothing you can do or say about it." The situation recalled Hamlet's statement, "The rest is silence." From that notion, the title was born (La MaMa).

It is an interesting idea, even if at least one critic (Dunne) was not entirely persuaded by the actual performance of *Silence Silence Silence*.

Architecture

Certain places, natural and man-made, enhance our experiences of silence. This may simply be a matter of them being quiet places, with their quietness achieved in part by the avoidance of such errors in design and construction as give rise to wind-noise or harsh echoes, for example. But design itself is also capable of enhancing silence, with the proportions of a well-executed Zen garden being one instance of how this is achieved. There can be a sacred dimension to the construction of even secular spaces. Indeed, places may be expe-rienced as dumbly evocative even when they are intrinsically noisy. The sometime French minister for culture, André Malraux penned *Museum without Walls*, a well-regarded work that treats Paris itself as a sort of museum. He argued that the city speaks without using words, is a talking space, a voice of silence. Merleau-Ponty (1964) rejected that somewhat romantic view, seeing cities instead as con-structs or languages. As is the case with any ordinary museum, social and other forces determine their complex of meanings. Nevertheless, there are cracks in the footpath and silences in the street. Architects such as Louis Kahn (1901–1974) have recognized the important role of silent spaces, and have strived to ensure that their work acknowledges it in concrete ways (Lobell, pp. 20–22). Other architects have considered how a society's own cultural attitudes towards silence permeate the practice of architecture itself, specifically for example the Finnish attitudes towards silence to which reference was made earlier (Quantrill & Webb). In this context, generally, a planned book on silence and spaces by the president's professor of architecture at Arizona State University, Max Underwood, promises to be particularly interesting.

Visual art

The "retreat from composition" of certain visual artists such as Kasimir Malevich and Alexander Rodchenko in the Soviet Union, or Robert Rauschenberg, Robert Ryman, and Ad Reinhardt in the United States has been treated by Sim as a form of silence about the world (pp. 116–123). Yet, their blank canvases may also be interpreted as statements of a kind. The statements can be so vague or sparse as to promote anxiety rather than reflection, but the absence of visual reference points within a frame or boundary is principally silent in a metaphoric way. For just as solitude and silence are not necessarily the same thing, neither are open/blank space and silence identical. In its own way, a painting such as David Hockney's *American Collectors (Fred & Marcia Weisman)* can be more eloquent of silences than is any attempted retreat from composition. In that work of 1968, the subtle relationship between objects and people, light and shadow, says at least as much about what is not spoken or cannot be spoken as about what is diplayed.

In any event, it is quite evident that any suggestion by those involved in a retreat from composition that visual artists no longer have something to say to the world through the content of their work, and might therefore fall silent, is not a perspective shared in practice by many contemporary artists. This is not to say that some installations do not make use of space in a way that inspires silent reflection. For example, walking into the wonderful old telescopic building known as "Arsenale" at the 53rd Venice Biennale in 2009, the first piece encountered was Lygia Pape's dreamlike silvery fibres in a dark space, a sort of three-dimensional moonlit monochrome rainbow that generated a hushed sense of awe in its immediate observers. Even work like that of Tony Conrad, that seemed at first sight simply to be blank hangings, actually consisted of sensitive white paint applied at different dates to fragile paper. Thus his collection ostensibly made a point about the passage of time, as each piece had faded to deeper shades. Its title, *Yellow Movies* seemed to reinforce this point. There was very little on show in Venice that suggested a retreat from composition. Indeed, some work suffered from noise pollution as the sound from adjacent multimedia installations spilt over to make the silent contemplation of neighbouring works impossible.

Outside such exhibition areas the artist has more control over the environment in which he or she plays with absences. Thus, in 1960, in his celebrated photographic composition entitled *Le Saut dans le Vide* (The Leap into the Void), French artist Yves Klein played with the relationship between space and what fills it. In it, he shows himself hurtling off a high gate-post, arms outstretched above the pavement below. However, this work underlines the futility of attempting to embrace either silence or space as absolutes, even if notes for an exhibition of his work at the Pompidou Centre in Paris in 2006 declared that "… the leap was not faked. When he carried out his action, Klein was met on the ground by an outstretched tarpaulin. This was the only [!!] 'precaution' that has been removed from the final image, by replacing it with a shot of the street before the leap" (Morisset).

The relative nature of silence, and our recurrent tendency to "make sense" of silence by projecting our ideas into it, are illustrated by Tom Morton's description of the video installation that won the Turner Prize in 1997. Gillian Wearing's *Sixty-Minute Silence* shows 26 people in police uniforms, arranged in three rows as if for a group photograph. They remain silent for the duration, although, "As time wears on some of them wrinkle their noses or scratch their bums, lost in their own thoughts." Morton writes that, "You find yourself wondering what's on their minds, and it's not long before you're spinning stories around their fidgety fingers." At the end of the video one of the officers lets out a scream or yelp. Morton believes that the piece lets us "get a purchase on the slippery surface of the screen", but he also acknowledges that it is "something of an endurance test". We are reminded that silence demands a response.

Some of those who favour a direct emotional relationship between a work of art and its readers or viewers have interrogated the function of any critical interpretation of content. However, while Susan Sontag's arguments for an "aesthetics of silence" (1970) may be attractive in the face of torrents of complex critical verbiage, and while one understands the inclination of certain artists and writers to silence themselves, the calming of creative traffic is seldom absolute and the artist usually continues to whisper her or his meaning with or without the assistance of critics or the conscious interpretation of her or his works by the public. Nevertheless, as Sim points out, there is merit in Sontag's somewhat elitist analysis in that it serves to remind us of the relative value of—and need for—silence as "a necessary complement to discourse" within the relationship between artist and the public (p. 107).

CHAPTER FIVE

Film, TV, and music

Our first inclination may be to regard film and broadcasting and music as entirely noisy media, but beneath their surfaces and surrounding them are silences with which their creators can consciously play.

Silence and film

Film, by necessity, first emerged as a silent medium. The technology did not exist to create a soundtrack to accompany early moving images, and spectacle was more important than plot. A few words could be written on a card and cut into a movie but, more often than not, any narrative depended primarily upon the coherence of sequences of images. Exhibitors enhanced the medium by means of various strategies. Pianists and other musicians were frequently employed by cinema owners to provide a dramatic or romantic aural backdrop for audiences. Sometimes, narrators sat next to the screen and provided commentary or dialogue. However, until the production of "talkies" began to change film forever, directors depended largely on images to speak for themselves. This presented particular challenges for D. W. Griffith and his contemporaries when it came to framing adaptations of plays and literary works in a manner that audiences could follow without hearing words spoken by the actors (Gunning, pp. 92–95).

During the transition phase from silent cinema to talkies, one Russian who struggled to bring sound to film was Stephen Poliakoff's paternal grandfather. Stephen, who was born in London in 1952, later based one of his plays, *Breaking the Silence* (1984), on that grandfather. Paradoxically, Bresson has asserted that "the soundtrack invented silence" (Cardullo, p. 215). More specifically, the arrival of sound provided opportunities for the creative inclusion of silences within and around a narrative. The necessary silence of early film was overtaken by the threatening or communicative silence of later works.

One late and unusual silent movie was called simply *Film* (1965, 24 minutes). It was the sole work that Samuel Beckett wrote specifically for the cinema. Something of a curiosity that was significant as much for its author's mastery of dramatic silence as for its place in cinematic history, *Film* starred Buster Keaton. The latter had been a popular actor in earlier silent comedies and was proposed for the part by Beckett himself when Charlie Chaplin and Zero Mostel would not or could not play it (Bair, p. 570). Directed by Alan Schneider, and shot in New York in Beckett's presence, *Film* has no dialogue or music. Beckett used this work to illustrate a statement by George Berkeley, the 18th century Irish philosopher, that "to be is to be perceived". In it, Keaton tries to elude the eye of the camera, only to discover in the end that it is in effect his own gaze that he is attempting to escape. Even if others are not watching us, we are watching ourselves. Somewhat oddly, in Deleuze's brief analysis of what he calls "The Greatest Irish Film" (p. 23), the author makes no specific reference to the distinctive silence of the work. However, implicitly, any attempt to escape perception implies that a character in such circumstances would avoid drawing attention to himself by speaking.

The first meeting between Beckett and Keaton was itself not just awkward but marked by silences. They sat in the actor's hotel suite, where Keaton kept watching a baseball game on TV and sipping beer. Schneider later recalled that,

> Now and then, Sam—or I—would try to say something to
> show some interest in Keaton, or just to keep the non-existent

conversation going. It was no use. Keaton would answer in monosyllables and get right back to the Yankees—or was it the Mets? .... It was harrowing. And hopeless. The silence became an interminable seventh-inning stretch [an interlude in a base-ball game when the crowd stands and stretches] (Knowlson, p. 522).

Following the arrival of talkies, silences continued to play a role in many movies, being deployed for effect. This is evident, for exam-ple, in the highly acclaimed Japanese films of Akira Kurosawa, including *Rashomon* (1950), *High and Low* (1963), and *Rhapsody in August* (1991). It is also evident in many ordinary Japanese crime and horror films, where long silences are frequently a prelude to violence or shocks. However, mainstream producers tended to regard silence as redundant, and even as undesirably alienating for audiences, and it was left largely to the directors of less commercial films to exploit its potential in order to enhance ambience, charac-ters, and plot. When they did so, it became evident that silences in the cinema were as many faceted as the silences in life generally that are considered throughout this book. For silence is intrinsically part of a creative duality at the heart of nature and not merely some optional effect.

In Europe, the Swedish works of Ingmar Bergman have frequently acknowledged the significance of silence. His best-known film is *The Seventh Seal* (1957), in which the personification of death plays chess with a man whose cries for meaning and spiritual succour ulti-mately go unanswered. The silence of God will be considered later, but this film is one of the most striking artistic treatments of that question. It is set at a time when the Black Death strikes Sweden, just as Antonius Block returns from the Crusades. He had gone to the Holy Land as a faithful young warrior but comes home tortured by doubt and uncertainty. "Do you never stop questioning?", the figure of death asks him. "No, I never stop," he replies. Nor does the silence that he meets entirely defeat him. Another of Bergman's films is actually entitled *Tystnaden* (Silence) (1963). It too deals with the consequences of people coping with the apparent indifference of their Maker. Ten years on, Bergman produced *Cries and Whispers* (1972), which is a study of isolation, family dynamics, and unspo-ken feelings at the time of dying. It begins with a long silence that is eventually broken by the strokes of several clocks.

Bergman is certainly not the only Scandinavian director who has used silence to great effect. Gabriel Axel's *Babette's Feast* (1987) was shot in black-and-white and is set in the 1870s, in an isolated, rural settlement of Lutherans. Two sisters who might well have left their small Danish village stay to care for their father and their community. They take in an outsider, Babette, when she arrives in need. Dealing with unvoiced personal concerns and with Babette's secret past, the film becomes a celebration of the complex relationship between faith and the senses. As one critic remarks, "Throughout, there is little accompanying music, a feature of films most American filmgoers might find unusual. Everywhere one is aware of silence, punctuated only by the natural sounds of waves, wind, the opening and shutting of doors, the rustle of paper" (Wright). This atmosphere makes the feast of the film's title all the more delightful when it eventually occurs. The celebration is not merely Thoreau's "bubble" on silence but is a lotus blossoming on Adrienne Rich's "pond where drowned things live".

One might expect the long winter nights of Scandinavia to incline people to ponder on the nature of silence. In the case of the Soviet Union, both nature and politics have conspired to produce the dark works of a director such as Andrei Tarkovsky (1932–1986). His films, including *Solaris* (1972) and *The Sacrifice* (1986), are filled with bleak and significant silences. More surprisingly perhaps, the relevance and uses of silence have not been ignored further south, in sunnier climes. There is, for example, a celebrated moment in Frederico Fellini's famous *La Dolce Vita* ("The Sweet Life") when a film star, played by Anita Ekberg, enters the waters of Rome's Trevi Fountain. She is joined there by a journalist, played by Marcello Mastroianni. As the film star and her gossip columnist friend kiss, the fountain's waters are turned off. All is strangely silent and still. When Mastroianni died in 1996, the Trevi pumps were again switched off and the fountain draped in black crepe, in his honour. Moreover, the Trevi scene is not the only significant reference to silence in the film. There are, for example, existentialist musings by one "Steiner", who reflects on the silence of the night that weighs upon him, and a final quiet moment for Mastroianni on a beach. It is worth noting that Fellini's collaborator on this and other work was Otello Martelli, a master of black-and-white cinematography who started his career during the silent era.

A fellow countryman of theirs used both silence and music to create evocative spaces in a remarkable English-language film. Luchino Visconti's *Death in Venice* (1971) is based somewhat loosely on a novel of the same name by Thomas Mann and tells the story of an ageing composer, Gustave von Aschenbach, who is played by Dirk Bogarde. Aschenbach appears to regret his own failure to transcend convention and expectation, or to express adequately the aesthetic and other complexities of life that he intuitively glimpses. Certain possibilities that forever recede are symbolized for him by the figure of a beautiful youth, Tadzio, who is staying at the same resort hotel in Venice in the early 20th century. The composer's own carefully constructed way of dealing with art and life has been challenged, as we learn during flashbacks that reveal his heated discussion with Alfried, a younger man who is also a composer. The elder character appears to stand for Gustav Mahler (1860–1911) and the younger for Arnold Schoenberg (1874–1951), who later came to revolutionize the concept of composition. Mahler's own music is used extensively on the film's soundtrack. Aschenbach's admiration of Tadzio is infused with melancholy as he recalls his own past youth and waning potential, as well as his dead wife and loving daughter. Such poignancy is manifest in both the sound track and the silences of *Death in Venice*. The film is, at one level, a representation of both the decline of old European society and the disintegration of convention.

The tension between Aschenbach's established mores and the alternatives that he has glimpsed exhaust him. As he abandons caution and bites into a juicy strawberry, sold by a beach vendor, he contracts the cholera that is ravaging Venice and that will shortly lead to his collapse and death in the street. The film's theme of death, and its depiction of the old man's fascination with a beautiful boy who is also staying at the hotel, have made some audiences distinctly uneasy. Bogarde's account of how three different audiences responded to first showings of *Death in Venice* is not only amusing but distinguishes three quite separate kinds of silence in the face of art. First, there was the disconcerted silence of the "American Money" as Visconti unveiled to them in Los Angeles his final version. Reportedly, when a studio executive eventually spoke it was to ask nervously who wrote the score. Informed that it was composed by Gustav Mahler, the "suit" is purported to have suggested that they should "sign him"! Then there was the reserved and uncertain silence of well-connected people in London who, together with the queen of England, attended a screening that had been organized by a rich friend of the actor in aid of the city of Venice. Finally, there was the rapt and appreciative silence of those at the Cannes Film Festival who eventually erupted in delighted appreciation of what was unfolding before them (Bogarde, pp. 72–89).

As it happens, Mahler did not actually die at Venice but Wagner (1813–1883), that great romantic whose operas later served as an inspiration for the Nazis, had earlier expired there. Later, and not far along the Adriatic coast, James Joyce made his home in Trieste from 1904 to 1915. His *Dubliners* includes a memorable tale of haunting death and silence entitled "The dead". "The dead" became one of the most highly regarded short stories of the 20th century and was itself transformed into a respected film of the same name by John Huston (1987).

In *Padre Padrone* (1977) Paolo Taviani and Vittorio Taviani explore the process of silencing and suppression. They tell the story of a boy struggling to emerge from mute isolation, following his father's decision to force him to tend sheep rather than attend school. It is based on a true story. In a more recent and dark British film, *The War Zone* (1999), Tim Roth depicts not a boy's emergence from silence but a teenager's retreat into silence when he discovers an incestuous relationship between his father and his older sister. Roth has acknowledged the importance of aesthetic considerations when constructing narratives,

> ... but only in so far as they look back to the kind of cinema I used to see as a teenager, which I now miss terribly. Widescreen, never drawing attention to the camerawork, no fancy footwork.

[Interviewer asks] Which film-makers in particular?

> Tarkovsky, Visconti, Bergman—that great art-house tradition. I miss stillness, I miss silence. *Death in Venice* was an inspiration for its use of the camera and the silence—just people being people. Just watching the physical and verbal interaction of people is interesting, though film-makers today seem less and less willing to acknowledge that (Danielsen, pp. 8–10).

One acclaimed exploration of the silencing of women in recent years has been *The Piano* (1993), directed by New Zealander Jane Campion. The film, set in the 19th century, tells the story of Ada, a woman who has willed herself mute but who expresses herself by playing a piano that she has brought with her from Scotland to the southern hemisphere. When her insensitive husband, Alisdair, disposes of the instrument, he sets in train a series of events that lead to Ada seeking solace in the arms of another man. *The Piano*, ostensibly, is inspired in part by two novels, Emily Bronte's *Wuthering Heights* and Jane Mander's *The Story of a New Zealand River*. As Claudia Gorbman writes, "Not only is Ada, the main character, a musician; she is mute as well, so that music—in this story about people's ability to 'hear' one another—doubly serves as her voice. Ada occasionally uses music, or its sudden cessation, as a language" (p. 42). Like gesture, such use of music lies somewhere along a scale of relativity between sound and silence.

Although generally hailed as a success, it must be admitted that not everyone liked Campion's film. Stanley Kauffmann wrote,

> An overwrought, hollowly symbolic glob of glutinous nonsense .... I haven't seen a sillier film about a woman and a piano since John Huston's *The Unforgiven* (1960), a Western in which Lillian Gish had her piano carried out into the front yard so she could play Mozart to pacify attacking Indians.

His harsh words serve as a caution that the creative use of silences may come across to audiences as pretentious and ponderous rather than meaningful and sensitive.

There are silences that hide not just personal but communal secrets. One witty and wonderful German film relates what occurs when the adolescent Sonja determines to tell the story of her village during World War II. In Michael Verhoeven's *Das Schreckliche Mädchen* (*The Nasty Girl*, 1990), the past turns out to be a lot less benign than Sonja as a child had been led to believe. The Nazi past was a factor too in Sidney Lumet's film *The Pawnbroker* (1964), where at the end of the story a silent scream enacted by Rod Steiger expresses the extent of a horror than cannot be adequately expressed in words. Its misery is redolent of "The Scream", that iconic work of art by the Norwegian artist Edvard Munch (1863–1944).

In respect of silences against which the oppressed must struggle, Pat Murphy's *Anne Devlin* (1984) is an introspective and slow Irish film that deals with both colonialist and feminist themes (Gibbons). Eleanor Mannikka has described it as "a study in the neglected role of women in history". The film looks at how Devlin was imprisoned and tortured for helping Robert Emmet, a doomed Irish rebel of 1803. Her silence itself became a weapon of resistance, and this is reflected in the silences and voids of the film. Another kind of resistance is represented by the muteness of three women imprisoned for murder in *A Question of Silence* (1983). Strangers to each other, the three had beaten a male shop manager to death after he accused one of them of stealing, and had given prosecutors no explanation for their crime. It subsequently transpires that each, in the past, has been treated brutally by other men and that the manager just happened to be the focus of their rage. Hailed by some people as an insight into the oppression of women across class boundaries, this Dutch film by Marlene Gorris has been regarded by others as a thinly veiled justification of murder.

If the women of Murphy's and Gorris's films have decided to be silent, those of Moufida Tlatli's *The Silences of the Palace* (1997) have had silence thrust upon them. They are the servants of North African princes, in the 1950s, who exercise certain royal "rights of the bed chamber" over the women. The Tunisian film tells the story of their virtual imprisonment. As one of the women says, "… in the palace we are taught one rule: silence". It is a slow, and often quiet, film in which the director seeks to come to terms with the role of women in her country's past.

As we have seen earlier, even those who are free to express themselves may find that they are at a loss for words to describe a particular set of circumstances that they encounter. This is the point at which old explanations and formulations fail, and new meanings must be found. Films that explore such disjunctions between language and reality are Bertolucci's *Last Tango in Paris* (1972), Wenders' *Kings of the Road* (*Im Lauf der Zeit*, 1976) and Coppola's *Apocalypse Now* (1979), among others (Hedges, pp. 18–31). The principal character in a recent Korean film remains entirely and mystifyingly silent throughout. In *3-iron* (2004), directed by Kim Ki-duk, this silence allows audiences to come to alternative conclusions about the story. Is this character a figment of the leading woman's imagination, or is he simply what he seems—a shadowy man who likes to break into people's homes and live in them when they are away? Kim Ki-duk's earlier *Spring, Summer, Fall, Winter ... and Spring* (2003) also features silences significantly and is even more beguiling, being the beautifully filmed tale of a monk who lives in a floating house or temple in the centre of a lake.

In *Under The Sand* (2000), Ozon explores the inner life of a disintegrating personality. This film tells the story of a university professor of English whose husband disappears. It is not clear if he has drowned or left her but she determines that she will act as if he is still alive. Cardullo discusses Ozon's choice of an older actress, in this case Charlotte Rampling, to "communicate subtle psychological states without words". This she does, he tells us, "through gesture, look and phrasing (when she actually speaks)". He says that, "... some of the best directors in history, including Bresson, have fixed silence on film. For them, silence is both aural and visual—not merely the absence of talk but the presentation of persons who fill our imaginations with what they are NOT saying" (pp. 215 and 222). Cardullo believes that film is peculiarly suited to using silence. Framing and close-ups allow the actor to deploy the slightest gesture or facial movement to convey meanings that would be lost on stage, while at the same time the audience understands (and enjoys the prospect) that such silence will be broken eventually by sound in ways that a still photograph cannot be. For that reason, says Cardullo, "Only on film can we have it both ways" (p. 7).

As we see from these examples of the use of silences in film, it is possible to speak of diagetic silence and non-diagetic silence. The former encompasses the signifying silences of actors, including pauses and gestures, while the latter refers to the dramatic background impact of a director avoiding speech and mood music. However, as also suggested earlier in this book, any attempt to distinguish too rigidly between categories of silence runs the risk of reifying it and of failing to register the fact that it is part of the warp and weft of our daily round. Simple categorizations of silence, such as "interior" or "exterior", may be misleadingly simplistic.

One of the boldest efforts to respect silence even in the narrative methodology used to depict it is a remarkable German documentary by Philip Gröning. Produced in 2005, this German work has been described by its makers as "the first film ever about life inside the Grande Chartreuse, mother house of the legendary Carthusian Order, a community of monks who remain silent much of the time". *Die Grosse Stille* (entitled in English *Into Great Silence*) is, according to its producers,

> ... an austere, next to silent meditation on monastic life in a very pure form. No music except the chants in the monastery, no interviews, no commentaries, no extra material .... A film to become a monastery [sic], rather than depict one. A film about awareness, absolute presence, and the life of men who devoted their lifetimes to god in the purest form.

This is slightly misleading, as a few significant statements have been elicited from one monk in particular and are included, while a number of biblical quotations are also reproduced on the screen. But the film is austere, and some people simply find it boring. However, it was well received by the national newspaper *Die Welt*, where a reviewer wrote that,

> It is only in silence that one really begins to hear: the dripping of dewdrops, the creaking of floorboards, the beating of the heart. And only when words become silent does one really begin to see. There is no guide to take you through the monastery, no voice-over, no inserts. Our years spent learning the language of cinema are of no use to us here. This film demands a very different kind of looking and listening (Rodek).

Also in 2005, but more conventionally, one finds silences used in *Tsotsi* as a powerful tool in the telling of that tale about poverty and hardship in South Africa. Directed by Gavin Hood, the film is based on the only novel by playwright Athol Fugard. Whitty wrote,

> Hood's acting mantra of "it's all in the eyes" shows during the most emotionally intense scenes when the actors' faces fill the screen, and in the moments of silence between short, sharp blurts of dialogue. It's an extremely well-written script.
>   Said Hood: "I chose to use dialogue sparingly and only where most appropriate and poignant and then rely on the

camera to catch the character's private moments to convey his inner world."

The way in which Sergio Leone deployed silence so effectively in his westerns was considered earlier within the broad context of various silent "types". He and the directors of certain other westerns such as Sergio Corducci in *The Great Silence* (1968) have well understood that words and sounds are not the only means of creating dramatic tension. Their enigmatic silent characters are coiled springs. They are a distinctive part of a broader filmic landscape of the American West, within which a Christ-like rite-of-passage has been seen to be performed by seriously wounded soldiers (Brereton, p. 99). However, while the silence of Christ before his tormentors was a prelude to his own acceptance of death (see Chapter Nine below), that of the heroes in "Spaghetti Westerns" tends to presage the death of others.

No discussion of silence and the cinema, even one as short as this, should end without reference to a well-known American film where the very presence of the word in its evocative title serves as a chilling reminder of the finality and reality of death. This is Jonathan Demme's *The Silence of the Lambs* (1991), in which a serial killer who eats his victims' livers refers to the spring slaughter of lambs to impress on interrogators the true horror of his crimes. The sound of silence here signifies absence. It is a film that is not quickly forgotten.

Broadcasting

In a standard textbook for radio journalists, McLeish points out that, "Acute embarrassment on the part of the over talkative commentator and considerable annoyance on the part of the listener will result from [the commentator] being caught unawares" by the need for silence during the playing of a national anthem, the blessing at the end of a service, or important words spoken during a ceremonial (p. 207).

When it came to choosing between silence and commentary, one particular event that provided an opportunity for observers to compare the different styles of television networks was the papal funeral of John Paul II. A controversial pontiff, his funeral was a notable ritual event that impressed even some people who had disagreed with him about Church teaching and policy. McDaniel thought that,

> Those who arose early and surfed the television channels discovered there are two ways to cover the funeral of a pope: a quiet way and a less quiet way. Most of the TV news networks opted for solemnity, choosing to let Friday's service for Pope John Paul II speak for itself.
>
> "This Mass is about to begin," said CBS anchor Harry Smith as the service started at 3 a.m. Houston time. "We're going to try to stay as much out of it as possible ...." ABC, on the other hand, chose a busier presentation.

Bianco, on his part, was uncomplimentary about what he described as,

> ... the rituals of TV's cable and broadcast newscasters, who believe no momentous occasion is complete unless they talk over it. They're not merely witnesses to history; without them saying so, apparently, history doesn't happen ... reporters understand the value of a no-chatting rule collectively but can't imagine it applying to them individually. Your comment is intrusive, mine is indispensable, even at a funeral, which of all events on Earth is meant to be absorbed in silence.
>
> Grating at all times, the constant chatter was particularly unwelcome here because it was so markedly unnecessary.

If big television spectacles are a chance for TV commentators to be uncharacteristically quiet, much television today is undoubtedly a babble of noise. Any sudden silence may result, if extended for more than a moment, in automatic or hasty apologies for the loss of sound. As mentioned below, special provision was made by the BBC to avoid such a response when the station broadcast a performance of John Cage's quiet work entitled 4'33".

On occasion, a playwright or producer may explore the particular characteristics of television, or even radio, to dramatize a moment by being unexpectedly silent, or by using sound to simulate or signify silence. Samuel Beckett wrote some works especially for radio that are effective precisely because they treat of silences in a way that suits the medium. *All That Fall* and *Embers* were a creative challenge that Perloff has analysed approvingly. The final phrase spoken in *Embers*, "Not a sound", is itself a sound and this paradox serves to remind us that Beckett himself chose to continue writing even as his work indicated the limitations of language.

In the domain of factual programming, the director of a television documentary that was produced in 2005 by Harvest Films for RTE, about the Irish writer John McGahern who wrote *Amongst Women* and *That They May Face the Rising Sun* among other novels, underlined the exquisitely sparse nature of McGahern's later work by refraining from adding a busy soundtrack where, on the basis of usual production practice, one might have expected such added sounds. As McGahern walked slowly down through a field near his home, viewers of *A Private World* were allowed to share the peace while contemplating his quiet progress. Such a moment of sustained reserve is not unique in television, but it is quite uncommon.

Silence and music

You may currently buy silence. You can acquire it by mail-order on CD and DVD or by downloading dedicated tracks from internet services. Thus, for example, iTunes offers silent tracks among the hundreds of thousands of songs it sells at Apple Computer's online music store. Apple points out online that, "The silent tracks sell for the same 99 cents as other songs, feature free 30-second 'previews' and are all wrapped in Apple's usual digital-rights management software to prevent unauthorized copying"! Three tracks for sale, by hip-hop group Slum Village and each entitled "Silent", are labelled as "explicit", even though there is nothing but silence on them. Among the other silent tracks are "Silence", by Ciccone Youth (off *The Whitey Album*), "Silence" by Bill Schaeffer (from the album, *Grain of Sand*), and "One Minute of Silence" by Project Grudge, which is offered only as a single-song download. These tracks, presumably, owe much in respect of their conceptualization to what is probably the best-known composition associated with silence, namely John Cage's 4'33". Indeed, the genesis of that work itself may have been partly commercial, with Cage at one point having envisaged himself composing a piece called "Silent Prayer" and selling it to the

Muzak corporation for insertion in its "mood music" tapes that were purchased by corporations for playing in public spaces (D. Kahn, pp. 563 and 571; Cage, 1981, p. 43).

In 2002, a dispute arose over a noiseless track on an album by The Planets called *Classical Graffiti*. Its "writer" Mike Batt partly credited Cage. Batt's track, "A One Minute's Silence", consists of the absence of any digital signal, whereas Cage's 4'33" is a work that depends for its effect on what can or might be heard in a room when the musicians are present but not playing. An English newspaper reported pertly that, "this dispute has commercial implications. *Classical Graffiti* has been number one in the classical charts for three months. Peters Edition [publishers of Cage's work] would like a slice of the royalties. Well, wouldn't anyone?" (*Guardian*, 18 July 2002). The legal challenge succeeded, being reported to have been settled for about a six-figure sum. It is not known if Cage's estate was amused by Mike Batt's assertion that, "Mine is a much better silent piece. I have been able to say in one minute what Cage could only say in four minutes and 33 seconds" (CNN).

Silence is both a condition and a compositional feature of music. Silence in the acoustic environment must be regarded, as Voegelin remarks, "not as the absence of sound but as the beginning of listening as communication" (p. xv). For the composer and the audience it constitutes both context and content.

Silence actually features, subtly or otherwise, in the work of all composers. It is the necessary counterpoint to sound. Admittedly, certain rock bands seem to some ears to pump out non-stop sound by using electronics to sustain noise between notes. However, generally speaking, the deployment of silences of varying duration, sometimes lasting no more than a fraction of a second, is an intrinsic part of the construction of a musical work. Understanding a composer's use of silence may be a central part of appreciating what he or she is about.

One of the most influential and serious instances of silence being used artistically in the 20th century was by Schoenberg, in his great, unfinished opera, *Moses und Aron*. This is a complex work of art that, at one level, tells the story of two brothers, Moses and Aaron, who led the Jews out of captivity in Egypt. Moses is the greatest Jewish prophet, whom Schoenberg depicts as a man struggling to tell the truth but who finds that the boundaries of language fall far short of his experiences of divine reality. Aaron, his older brother, is depicted as a more practical man, an organizer and doer and peacemaker who makes compromises in order to retain his people's loyalty and maintain their sense of united purpose. The tension between them is searing, and reflects Schoenberg's own experiences of life both as a Jew in Nazi Germany and as an avant-garde composer. Schoenberg (1874–1951) does not simply tell their story as a verbal narrative, "putting the Bible to music" as it were. His interpretation of the biblical story is itself composed in a manner that structurally reflects the complex struggle between Moses and Aaron. He pushes out the boundaries of opera in radically new ways, and also creates a delicate relationship between language and music. Finding themselves at a point in the development of music where Mahler had, in a manner of speaking, "had the last word", 20th century composers such as Schoenberg broke the old mould and tried to move forward. In a similar way, during the early decades of the 20th century, James Joyce was experimenting with the form of the novel in both *Ulysses* and *Finnegan's Wake*. This is not to say that Schoenberg disrespected the great European classical tradition. On the contrary, he loved works by Bach, Mozart, and Schubert, among others, and was himself a protégé of Mahler.

Arnold Schönberg (later Schoenberg) was born in Vienna in 1874. He is remembered as one of the first composers to embrace atonality, and is renowned for his distinctive twelve-tone technique. Atonality does not make easy listening for people reared in the tonal harmonies that increasingly characterized composition in the years between 1500 and 1900, and which is associated with Western "classical" and "traditional" music as well as with many subsequent popular formats. The particular mode of atonal musical composition that Schoenberg devised is known as "twelve-tone", which he himself described as "a method of composing with 12 notes which are related only to one another". There is, ostensibly, a reference to the twelve-tone technique in the German title of Schoenberg's opera, *Moses und Aron*. Thus, "Aron" with a single "a" is a German variant of the man's name, making a total of 12 letters in the title where the English variant gives it 13.

In a brilliant and remarkable essay on this opera, George Steiner discusses the way in which Schoenberg deploys silences to express the experience and perspective of Moses, a man portrayed as being frustrated by his inability to find words for his experience of God and unwilling to attempt an imperfect form of articulation when others traduce the divinity that he has glimpsed. In the Jewish and some other traditions, images of God have been prohibited precisely because no image can ever truly describe a reality that lies outside the boundaries of our finite senses. Even the name of God may not be pronounced in certain forms, for much the same reason.

In Schoenberg's opera, Moses speaks in a highly cadenced, formal discourse. Steiner writes,

> The fact that the protagonist of a grand opera should not sing is a powerful theatrical stroke, even more "shocking" than the long silence of Aeschylus' Cassandra or the abrupt single intervention of the mute Pylades in *The Libation Bearers*. But it is also much more than that.
>
> Moses' incapacity to give expressive form (music) to his vision, to make revelation communicable and thus translate his individual communion with God into a community of belief in Israel, is the tragic subject of the opera. Aaron's contrasting eloquence, his instantaneous translation—hence traduction—of Moses' abstract, hidden meaning into sensuous form (the singing voice), dooms the two men to irreconcilable conflict. Moses cannot do without Aaron; Aaron is the tongue which God has placed into his own inarticulate mouth. But Aaron diminishes or betrays Moses' thought, that in him which is immediate revelation, in the very act of communicating it to other men. As in Wittgenstein's philosophy, there is in *Moses and Aaron* a radical consideration of silence, an inquiry into the ultimately tragic gap between what is apprehended and that which can be said. Words distort; eloquent words distort absolutely (1985, p. 157).

Central to any understanding of Moses as depicted in Schoenberg's opera is the fact that Moses regards God as that which ultimately cannot be imagined, conceived, or represented. Aaron, on the other hand, exults in imagining such a God, in finding words and symbols for him. Uekermann writes that, "Moses' spoken words become, in Aaron's sung interpretation, subtly modified and adapted to his hearer's expectations" (p. 16). Aaron's compromises leave Moses confounded, while the people move on towards the promised land. At the end of Act II, as Steiner observes,

> Moses is left alone. Is Aaron right? Must the inconceivable, unimaginable, unrepresentable reality of God diminish to mere symbol, to the tangible artifice of miracle? In that case all he has thought and said (the two are identical to Moses) has been madness. The very attempt to express his vision was a crime. The orchestra falls silent as the unison violins play a retrograde inversion of the basic twelve-tone set. Moses cries out, "O word, thou word that I lack!" and sinks to the ground broken.
>
> This is one of the most moving, dramatic moments in the history of opera and of the modern theatre. With its implicit allusion to the *Logos*, to the Word that is yet to come but which lies beyond speech, it gathers into one action both the claims of music to be the most complete idiom, the carrier of transcendent energies, and all that is felt in twentieth-century art and philosophy about the gap between meaning and communication (1985, p. 161).

The philosophical challenge of speaking about God, of defining reality in words, will be considered again below. But Steiner points out that the story of this opera also has a more specific, historical bearing, which may help to explain why Schoenberg did not complete it. He refers to Adorno's belief that the opera *Moses and Aaron* was "a preventive action against the looming of Nazism", as Schoenberg in his opera prominently deployed the German words *Volk* and *Führer* in an appropriate way to designate Israel and Moses, the former being a people at their most complex and the latter a leader at his most moral. But Schoenberg's efforts to save language from its decent into the barbarous mouths of a million voices bawling slogans at Nuremberg were doomed. As he laboured on this *magnum opus*, conceived by him during many years of experience in the opera houses of Germany and written at Barcelona, he surely knew that German culture and the lives of many German people were heading for ruin. Steiner believes that,

> It is this which gives the end of Act II its tremendous authority and logic. The events that were now to come to pass in Europe

were, quite literally, beyond words, too inhuman for that defining act of humane consciousness which is speech. Moses' despairing cry, his collapse into silence, is a recognition—such as we also find in Kafka, in Brock, in Adamov—that words have failed us, that art can neither stem barbarism nor convey experience when experience grows unspeakable. Thus *Moses and Aaron* is, despite its formal incompletion, a work of marvellous finality. There was no more to be said (1985, pp. 162–163).

Schoenberg began work on a final act for his opera but this remained unfinished. The final act was intended to see Moses emerge vindicated, as a man who stuck to what he saw as the truth. While dialogue (libretto) was written for the planned Act III, virtually no music was composed for it before the composer died. In 1933, faced with growing anti-Semitism, Schoenberg travelled to Paris and reconverted to Judaism, having become a Lutheran when younger. From Paris, he moved almost immediately to the United States and remained resident there until his death in Los Angeles on 13 July 1951. Some have asserted that it is appropriate to read aloud his third act at the end of a performance of the first two: but not Pierre Boulez, one of his greatest interpreters, who wrote, "If you were simply to speak the text, you'd see—as with Wagner—that it needs music to achieve its impact. If you were to stage this dialogue between Moses and Aaron, it would be a real anti-climax" (Schaufler, p. 14). In one way, it seems appropriate that Schoenberg never finished this opera, because the Bible tells us that both Moses and Aaron died in the desert shortly before their people entered the promised land (Numbers 20).

One of Schoenberg's early pupils in Los Angeles was the young John Cage (1912–1992). Cage, a highly respected innovator who was influenced by the Zen tradition, himself struggled with and celebrated both chance and silence in his works. In 1952 Cage composed his all but silent piece 4'33". On 16 January 2004, the BBC Symphony Orchestra gave 4'33" its first orchestral performance in the UK, in the opening concert of the annual "Composer Weekend" at the Barbican Centre in London. BBC Radio 3 broadcast the performance live and thus became the first broadcaster to risk airing nearly five minutes of ambient silence. Radio 3's emergency back-up systems, designed to cut in when a breakdown is signalled by prolonged silence on air, were switched off. BBC Four broadcast the performance on television an hour after its radio airing. According to a contemporary BBC press release (12 January 2004), 4'33" demonstrates Cage's view that all sound is music and that, "Wherever we are what we hear mostly is noise." The BBC release reported of its performance at the Barbican that,

> Despite having no notes to play, the musicians tuned up and then turned pages of the score after each of the three "movements" specified by the composer.

Not even in an anechoic chamber can we entirely escape some faint sound, for we must breathe, and Cage's ostensibly silent work is drawing attention to the absence of absolute silence. His 4'33" is a kind of canned silence that has been compared to Marcel Duchamp's bottled air, *Air de Paris* (D. Kahn, p. 571). Greatly admired by Cage and best known as a visual artist, Duchamp himself had also turned his hand to minimalist forms of musical composition, despite being untrained. The Frenchman ultimately silenced his own public persona, ostensibly retiring to play chess. However, on one occasion, Cage himself subverted Duchamp's retirement into self-imposed creative isolation. He lured him onto the stage of an arts festival in Toronto some months before Duchamp died in 1968. At Toronto, Cage and Duchamp, who had quite frequently met privately for chess, proceeded to play on a chess board that was wired in such a way that each move activated or cut off the sound coming live from several musicians. The performance, or piece, was called *Reunion*. Cage himself had written (1958, p. 191) that,

There is no

Such thing as silence. Something is

always happening that makes a sound.

No one can have an idea

once he starts really listening.

It is very simple but extra-urgent

The Lord knows whether or not

the next

(Bang fist)

Later, the composer asked,

> Is there such a thing as silence?
> Even if I get away from people, do I still have to listen to something?
> Say I'm off in the woods, do I have to listen to a stream babbling?
> Is there always something to hear, never any peace and quiet?
> If my head is full of harmony, melody and rhythm, what happens to
>   me when the telephone rings, to my piece [sic] and quiet, I mean?
> And if it was European harmony, melody, and rhythm in my head,
>   what has happened to the history of, say, Javanese music, with
>   respect, that is to say, to my head? (Cage, 1958, p. 42).

In 1959, Cage wrote in his "Lecture on nothing" (thus),

I am here   ,   and there is nothing to say   .

                                                             If among you are
those who wish to get   somewhere   ,   let them leave at
any moment   .   What we re-quire   is
silence   ;   but what silence requires
          is   that I go on talking   .

About that same year, he also penned a "Lecture on something":

This is a talk about   something   and naturally   also a talk about
nothing   About how something   and nothing are not   opposed to each other
but need each other to keep on going   .   It is difficult to
talk when you have something to say   precisely because of   the words   which
keep making us   say   in the way   which the words need to
stick to   and not in the Way which   we need for living.

If Cage's silences are revelatory of the actions of man and nature, John Tavener (b. 1944) uses silences in his music to express also "the longing for God", and has compared this kind of compositional silence to the transfixed or frozen gazes of angels in Orthodox religious icons (p. 157).

Noise pollution

The pollution of silent spaces by noise is a matter for growing concern in our crowded contemporary world. A Dutchman visiting the USA at the close of the 20th century may have somewhat exaggerated the problem in that country but he expressed a heartfelt anxiety when he wrote that,

> First of all the things I experienced while travelling through the United States, I found the complete lack of silence one of the most striking things. In all the cities, in all situations you encounter other people, there is a buzzing, a constant noise. One would get the impression that people are afraid of silence. At the same time the constant noise intensifies the superficiality. The French philosopher Roland Barthes observes that there exists a kind of acoustic pollution, whereby everybody notices that it forms an attack on the intelligence of the individual: the pollution disrupts true listening (Haan).

Haan, who was then the executive manager of the Blaise Pascal Institute, Vrije Universiteit Amsterdam, made an unfavourable comparison between his experience in the United States and his experience studying among several African peoples for whom traditional music is still part of their culture: "Within the traditional African music silence is as it were allotted an organic place. This should not surprise us knowing that the sounds of nature are incorporated into the music. Also silence is part of nature." He writes,

> Francis Bebey—some call him the guru of African music—describes in his book *African Music: A People's Art* the phenomenon that non-Africans find traditional African music at first hearing strange, difficult and unattractive. The conclusion then is that the music is uninteresting. Beby emphasises that the study of African music requires time and patience. True understanding of African cultures and music demands many hours of attention, of careful watching and listening, of doing away with prejudices and abandoning all too hasty judgement.
>
> The biggest problem may lie in the fact that the purpose of African music is so radically different from what we generally expect of music. African musicians set out to express life and all its aspects in sound. Their primary goal is not to combine sounds in such a way that they sound "pleasant", it's rather the

other way around: natural sounds are incorporated, absorbed
into the music (Haan).

Noise levels are even rising beneath the sea, and environmentalists
grow concerned about the measurable impact of the engines of very
large ships, as well as other sources of sound, on marine life. We have
already seen how Sim suggests strongly that silence deserves a place
on all political manifestos.

The recent phenomenon of "silent discos" is not, disappoint-
ingly for those concerned about noise pullution, a reaction again
cacophony. The term does not describe events where young people gather and move together in peaceful harmony. It is, instead,
used to refer to a place where people dance to music played through
personal headphones rather than speakers, selecting whatever track
they wish from their portable player. While this is less likely than
a normal disco to disturb the neighbours, it may be no less noisy
subjectively for those who are involved in it. As Ian Johnston writes,
"[C]lassical music fans waltzing to Schubert can, in theory, share the
same floor as ravers partying to hard-core techno music."

CHAPTER SIX

Constraints of silence

Francis Bacon (1561–1626), chancellor of England, observed that, "All kinds of constraints are unhappy—that of silence is the most miserable of all" (Spedding, Ellis & Heath, vol. 4, p. 485). The constraint of silence may be self-imposed, as a result of shyness or of a sense of personal inadequacy. However, directly or indirectly, it is frequently imposed by others. A most obvious form of silencing is the denial of freedom of speech through censorship or other legal mechanism, but it certainly does not require action by the state to deter citizens from articulating their views. Powerful personal, cultural, or social factors may act to silence people as effectively as any law. Those most affected include women, members of ethic minorities, students, and employees.

Personal relationships

Moments of silence between two people in a relationship may be a sign of that couple's deep understanding of one another, and of their wonder at the experience of love and of their shared perceptions of reality. Such "visible silence" finds expression in poetry. Thus, in his beautiful sonnet entitled "Silent Noon", which was later set to music

by the English composer Ralph Vaughan Williams (1872–1958),
Dante Gabriel Rossetti (1828–1882) recalled being with his lover on
one especially warm day:

> Your hands lie open in the long fresh grass –
> The finger-points look through like rosy blooms:
> Your eyes smile peace. The pasture gleams and glooms
> Neath billowing skies that scatter and amass.
> All round our nest, far as the eye can pass,
> Are golden kingcup-fields with silver edge
> Where the cow-parsley skirts the hawthorn-hedge.
> Tis visible silence, still as the hour-glass.
>
> Deep in the sun-search'd growths the dragon-fly
> Hangs like a blue thread loosen'd from the sky: –
> So this wing'd hour is dropt to us from above.
> Oh! clasp we to our hearts, for deathless dower,
> This close-companion'd inarticulate hour
> When twofold silence was the song of love.

Yet, even when two people have an intimate relationship, one party
may be unable to articulate her or his feelings and ideas in a satisfactory manner. He or she may be very shy or have been reared
in a repressive household, or may never have learnt from another
person or from books the language needed to express emotions.
Such failures to articulate can have long-term consequences. Thus,
Harper and Welsh write that self-silencing adolescents report poor
relationship satisfaction overall, with self-silencing or the inhibition
of self-expression appearing to play a role in shaping adolescent
romantic relationships. The results of the US study that they discuss
suggest that self-silencing impacts on multiple aspects of intimate
relationships, including communication patterns, sexual activity,
and ultimately the quality of relational and individual functioning.
Self-silencing individuals reported engaging in sexual intercourse
earlier than others, and had greater discomfort refusing sexual activity when their partners desired it. They conceded to their partner
at times of conflict, complaining of poor communication in their
relationships. Perhaps unsurprisingly, in the circumstances, they
also reported a greater experience of depression. The findings thus

suggest that ostensible shyness in expression may be manifest, simultaneously and paradoxically, when one is sexually more active than one's more articulate contemporaries.

Within the home, silence can be very frustrating for an individual who feels that a partner is freezing her or him out. This may be so notwithstanding the fact that the silent partner appears to wish to continue the relationship and even denies that there is a problem. Such silences arise in various circumstances. For example, a man may simply feel inadequate and self-conscious when it comes to expressing his emotions, or even be fearful of them or of being perceived as "wimpish" if he refers to them. Particularly at times of economic or other external pressure he may think that he can best protect his sense of self and appear strong by being distant, perhaps while playing in his head some male role model from a film or play. This can leave his partner feeling spurned and neglected, and even angry or frustrated if her man still expects to have sex with her. Women also may not articulate, perhaps because they feel inadequate or self-conscious or wish to appear "modern" rather than emotional or dependent.

Marriage therapists frequently hear complaints about self-silencing within relationships. Some men who are eloquent when wooing and winning a partner, making what is evidently an effort, thereafter become quieter or even taciturn. Perhaps they believe that words are a frivolous waste of time. Whether harmful or not to the future course of a relationship, such silence may be well intended and expressive of a person's idea of what is appropriate.

One sympathizes with those for whom silence becomes a hallmark of their apparent failure as lovers or partners. What a sorry sight it is to see two people in a restaurant who are quiet because they have nothing to say to one another or could not be bothered to try to sustain a conversation. Yet, if both parties find depth and peace in silence then it may mark a maturing of their relationship. In 1913, Irish poet George William Russell ("A. E.") wrote in "The Silence of Love":

> I could praise you once with beautiful words ere you came
> And entered my life with love in a wind of flame.
> I could lure with a song from afar my bird to its nest,
> But with pinions drooping together silence is best.

In the land of beautiful silence the winds are laid,
And life grows quietly one in the cloudy shade.
I will not waken the passion that sleeps in the heart,
For the winds that blew us together may blow us apart.

Fear not the stillness; for doubt and despair shall cease
With the gentle voices guiding us into peace.
Our dreams will change as they pass through the gates of
    gold,
And Quiet, the tender shepherd, shall keep the fold.

However, there is always a danger that, for one party or for both, taciturnity will turn into isolation in the long term.

There are of course occasions when one or both parties in a relationship should keep silent, at least in the short term. On the "Christianity Today International" (CTI) website, for example, Les and Leslie Parrott counsel that, "… there are times when conversation isn't necessary, and is even hurtful." They add, "There can be power and wisdom in not talking—in biding your time, walking away, or simply shutting up and getting on with things." The authors suggest that occasions when a partner should try not talking include those when one of the couple is preoccupied with something else and is not ready to talk, or when a spouse has already said the same thing "a million times" without effect or when what is really needed is time to think. On other occasions what is actually needed is action but couples put it off by discussing "issues", with talking about sex being an example of this in certain circumstances. The Parrotts also note astutely that exchanges between irritated partners in marriage may reach a point where two participants forget what they had been disputing, a fact which suggests that "biting one's lip" instead of indulging in recrimination is wise.

The Parrotts' advice is not sexist and many couples in a reasonably balanced relationship will recognize its relevance. However, there will also be those who are suspicious of advice emanating from a Christian group like CTI, not least because of their reading of St Paul's opinion on the role of women (discussed below). They may note that CTI was founded in the United States by the famous evangelist Billy Graham and wonder if this is part of an effort by "the Christian Right" to roll back feminism and to silence women. Moreover, there will be times when talking about a problem such as sexual tensions may be precisely the best course, rather than bungling into bed and later leaving one or both of the partners feeling exploited and unhappy.

Silence in response to anger or abuse is not always a sign that the silent person is weaker than the abusive individual. Sometimes, as Shakespeare writes, "discretion is the better part of valour" (*1 Henry IV*, Act 5, sc. 4), and one avoids responding to or answering an angry person for the very reason that one believes the person more likely to calm down quicker and return to a normal and even contrite state of mind when not opposed. Angry people frequently displace their anger onto the nearest object, slamming a door or kicking the cat or launching into a tirade against some hapless family member. Adopting "wise silence" of the type considered earlier, one makes the assessment that it will simply make matters worse to respond. Of course if such a strategy becomes habitual within a relationship then it may be a sign that one person is in fact being silenced or intimidated, but in other instances the silent response is simply due to one partner recognizing the ways in which people behave when emotional and not descending to the level of the abuser. This kind of silence is found around the world and is by no means unique to the Western Apache of Arizona whom Basso studied. One of the people whom Basso met put it well when he said of being "cussed-out", "People like that don't know what they are saying, so you can't tell about them. When you see someone like that, just walk away. If he yells at you, let him say whatever he wants to. Let him say anything" (p. 77).

Self-silencing, the situation in which a spouse decides to fall silent entirely for reasons of her or his own, must be distinguished from the silencing of one spouse by another. Silencing of the other involves some form of oppression. The complex nature of interpersonal and social silences within the context of sexual relations has been explored by John and Nair, in their case in the sophisticated society of India. The fact that India is known as the home of the *Kamasutra*, which is perhaps the world's most famous sex manual, is a reminder that the availability of explicit depictions or discussions of sex is no guarantee that communication between couples will be free of difficulties.

Silencing in one sphere does not necessarily mean that the silenced party is generally quiet in others. Paradoxically, the fact that someone cannot articulate or voice her or his heartfelt needs because of a lack of understanding or a fear of retribution may result in that person compensating by talking at length about other matters. There can be something superficial about such chatter. One notes in this context how humorists raise many laughs by assuming that women are more inclined to talk than men. To what extent some of their jokes are, in effect, a misogynistic diversion from the phenomenon of silencing is a matter of opinion. Such quips include these on an aptly-named "Misogyny Unlimited" website: "When a woman suffers in silence, the phone is probably out of order", or, "An optimist thinks the woman in the phone booth will be right out because he heard her say goodbye", or, "I haven't spoken to my wife for 18 months—I don't like to interrupt her". Such jokes may serve to relieve tensions between men and women but they can also condition men to be indifferent towards, or misconstrue, the words of women. The jokes are consistent with many proverbs in international folklore which, as Thiselton-Dyer demonstrates in a chapter on "Woman's tongue", "has generally held that whatever a woman says must be received with caution"; and, according to an African adage, "If a woman speaks two words take one and leave the other," with which may be compared an Eastern saying, "A woman's talk [is] heat from grass [worthless]." We saw earlier that a long line of notable European writers also thought that a silent woman was the best type.

Women may sometimes overwhelm and silence men but the available studies concentrate on the evidently more common phenomenon of silenced women. This phenomenon is closely related to social circumstances, with women in some societies and certain classes of society more easily silenced than in others. The extent of silencing may also vary from one individual to the next, but its consequences can be destructive and extreme. Suzanne Vega has poignantly sung of it, in a song called "Luka" that tells of a woman who would rather not be asked by neighbours about violent noises that come from her apartment late at night.

Even in non-violent situations, a partner who demands or desires sustained silences between partners within a relationship, regardless of the needs and wishes of the other person, runs the risk of alienating that partner and driving him or her into another's arms. Dalma Heyn has written a collection of stories entitled, *The Erotic Silence of the American Wife*. These remind us of the importance of women's needs in respect to pleasure and eroticism. Heyn urges women not to sell out their sexuality in order to fit the socially prescribed criteria for "good girls" and "perfect wives". However, her prescribed remedy in the face of silencing appears to be the pursuit of surreptitious affairs rather than communication. This looks like a counsel of despair, and perhaps a dangerous one at that.

A more constructive, not to say moral, approach to the problem of silencing is taken by Orly Benjamin of the Department of Sociology and Anthropology at Bar-Ilan University, Israel. She seeks to weave several feminist and sociological perspectives into her discussion of the subtleties of silencing, turning her attention to the situation in which the need for unsilencing may not be consciously understood by either party in a relationship, even when "one of them is actually undergoing an inner struggle ..." (Benjamin, p. 1). In response to which situation some people might be inclined to advise an outsider "to leave well enough alone", to advise that it is not the role of any third party to stir up dissension by encouraging the struggling spouse to express his or her doubts. However, Benjamin's objective clearly is to understand the process and help to improve the quality of relationships. She instances (pp. 1–2) the case of a social worker whom she met who "felt outraged" about an arrangement in which her husband managed the couple's finances when they travelled abroad and gave his wife an allowance, so that when she wished to spend the money, it had to be mediated by his agreement: "Once, upon finding herself without money away from him, she planned to confront him, but this plan somehow evaporated and the arrangement persisted." By contrast, the social worker had raised for discussion with her spouse the topic of how it came about that she always ironed her husband's shirts at home, notwithstanding the fact that he was "a generally egalitarian man who certainly contributed his fair share at home". Benjamin explores the subtle process that is at work between these points of mild "silencing" and negotiation, regarding the concept of "self" as central to any understanding of the issue, and asserts that,

> The notion of unsilencing challenges the classical Marxist distinction between consciousness and action that has been adopted by some feminist sociologists (e.g., Gerson & Peiss, 1985). This distinction assumes a notion of self or agency that can resist false consciousness through a liberating realization of

the truth of oppression. Unsilencing, in contrast, is based on a
more complex understanding of the self that encompasses inner
struggle and ambivalence. It is based on a feminist notion of
the self as fragmented and continually changing, where frag-
mentation reflects not only the various power hierarchies that
shape us (such as race, ethnicity, sexuality, class), but also our
ideological positions, including our changing understanding of
ourselves as either accepting or rejecting our position in a given
social interaction (p. 2).

Such a "feminist notion of the self" is by no means unique in its
subtlety or complexity, but this statement by Benjamin is a useful
reminder of how the processes of silencing may be internalized and
may be difficult for the individual to recognize and even, at times,
to explain to her or himself. Moreover, the processes are further confused by emotional expectations and responses that are intertwined
with domestic relationships of power and status. This can make it
very tiresome to break established patterns of relationship and may
create an environment in which nagging dissatisfaction alternates
with periods of resignation and acceptance. Benjamin observes that,
at certain moments,

> ... the tendency for a legitimacy crisis starts to increase,
> possibly with the help of parallel crisis tendencies occurring in
> public discourses [e.g. a radio discussion involving "real" peo-
> ple]. This may weaken the position of the hegemonic meaning
> structure and support the possibility of unsilencing. At such
> moments, the feminist alternative gains power so that a reflex-
> ive process of power struggle between the different positions
> occurs and unsilencing may emerge. However, shortly after-
> wards, unsilencing may seem to exact too high a price in terms
> of the woman's resources. At that stage, the pendulum of power
> relations swings back, and silencing is reinstated ... the woman
> returns to the position where the hierarchical meaning structure
> is experienced as safe and authentic (pp. 10–11).

Her description of the way in which attempts by a spouse to unsilence herself may run out of steam is useful, even if Benjamin
appears to deny agency to those people who believe that hierarchical

relationships within marriage are indeed "natural" and "freely chosen". One does not have to regard such men and women as dupes to find value in the author's general analysis. It can be frustrating for caring men as well as for women when relationships revert to a type in which the woman is ultimately dependant.

Women and society

It is not Jesus but Paul and his companions who are found in the Bible silencing women. The Old Testament has little to say on the subject, although the author of the apocryphal and conservative Book of Sirach (Ecclesiasticus) observes that, "A silent wife is a gift from the Lord, and nothing is so precious as her self-discipline" (Sirach 26:14). Jesus is not recorded as having made any such observation. Errico and Lamsa point out (pp. 73–74) that he was surrounded by supportive women and appears to have transgressed social custom in order to have conversations with a woman at the well and other women. King discusses (passim) an early second century papyrus of fewer than eight pages that suggests Jesus gave advanced teachings to Mary and that indicates there was resistance to her conveying these teachings to others. However, when Paul begins to lay down what is appropriate for men and women he says that women should be silent in church, for they are "subordinate" and "it is shameful for a woman to speak in church". This is notwithstanding his earlier reference to some women prophesizing (1 Corinthians 11:5 and 14:34). Paul opts for the second of the two creation myths found in Genesis, when he claims also that woman was made from man, and uses it to preach again the subordination of women (Genesis 2:21–22; 1 Corinthians 11:8). Before he became Pope Benedict XVI, Joseph Ratzinger wrote a series of Lenten homilies on the Creation story but did not consider this aspect relating to the status of women.

Paul's ideas on the matter are advanced once more in the New Testament by the unidentified author of a letter to Timothy (1 Timothy 2:11). Paul seems to rely on Jewish law or regulations to support his arguments. Indeed, he wishes to curtail dissent in general, believing that "every mouth may be silenced" by that law (Romans 3:19). Attempts have been made to contextualize or explain away his comments. However, Collins rejects on textual grounds any suggestion that someone other than Paul himself later inserted these remarks about women, while also noting that Paul cites no particular scripture or "law" to support his statements (pp. 513–517 and 521). Even more striking, in the context of silencing people, is the declaration by Paul's companion Titus that there are at Crete "many rebellious people, idle talkers and deceivers, especially those of the circumcision" who "must be silenced, since they are upsetting whole families by teaching for sordid gain what it is not right to teach" (Titus 1:10–16). While Titus appears to recommend only a sharp rebuke for such people—the nature of whose "sordid gain" is not clear—therein may lie a seed of the future persecution and suppression of non-Christians and of Christians who have disagreed with their Church's leadership.

Women have, individually and collectively, fought back against silencing by Church and secular authorities. As Armstrong indicates, some are still struggling for an equal role in many Christian Churches.

While folklore in general may have encouraged women to be silent, there has always been an undercurrent of folk wisdom that acknowledged the power of feminine articulation:

> ... the Chinese have a favourite saying to the effect that "a woman's tongue is her sword, and she does not let it rust;" with which may be compared the Hindustani proverb, "For talk I'm best, for work my elder brother-in-law's wife;" which has its counterpart in this country, where it is said, "A woman's strength is in her tongue," and in Wales the adage runs thus: "Be she old, or be she young, a woman's strength is in her tongue" (Thiselton-Dyer, ch. 5).

When earlier considering silent types, we saw how the classical world recognized that some women resisted attempts to silence them. It was seldom easy for them to do so effectively. Later, the protestant Reformation appeared to encourage education for English women, and this might be thought to have been a way of empowering them to speak out. However, as Hannay indicates, the education they received was intended to equip them to read, translate, and meditate on the Bible and on approved commentaries, and was not meant to encourage them to articulate any original thoughts of their own. In a sense, the royal court replaced the convent as a place of scholarship for aristocratic women.

One of many women who have felt silenced by society in more recent times is the Afro-American poet, Audre Lorde (1934–1992). In her case, speaking up also meant "coming out" as a lesbian. She had been married and had two children before breast cancer led her to the realization that, "I was going to die, if not sooner then later, whether or not I had ever spoken myself." She decided that, "... it is not difference which immobilizes us, but silence." Proclaiming "your silence will not protect you", she asked,

> Of what had I ever been afraid? To question or to speak as I believed could have meant pain, or death. But we all hurt in so many different ways, all the time, and pain will either change or end. Death, on the other hand, is the final silence. And that might be coming quickly, now, without regard for whether I had ever spoken what needed to be said, or had only betrayed myself into small silences, while I planned someday to speak, or waited for someone else's words.
>
> And of course I am afraid, because the transformation of silence into language and action is an act of self-revelation, and that always seems fraught with danger .... In the cause of silence, each of us draws the face of her own fear, fear of contempt, of censure, or some judgment, or recognition, of challenge, of annihilation. But most of all, I think, we fear the visibility without which we cannot truly live .... And that visibility which makes us most vulnerable is that which also is the source of our greatest strength (p. 42).

In 1990, Judith Plaskow observed that, "When a silence is sufficiently vast, it fades into the order of things" (p. 520). She writes that it took her a long time to notice that as she went through three years of graduate school she was not reading a single word written by a woman. Her consideration of the process of first hearing silence, then making a space to name silence and then further creating structures for the silenced to speak with authority are germane not only to feminism but to many walks of life.

In *The Shipping News* and elsewhere, according to Seiffert, the US novelist and short-story writer E. Annie Proulx "interrogates the right to silence as well as the wrongs that provoke speechlessness". According to this viewpoint, Proulx's writings about silenced people,

... make the reader listen more closely to the careful quietness that can be misread—misheard—as awkward silence. The dumb show of Proulx's characters, whether tongue-tied through trauma or tactical manoeuvre, can inhibit and estrange, but it can also engender a muted musicality, eloquent and empowering (Seiffert, Abstract).

Proulx's work reached a wider audience when one of her short stories became the basis for a successful film, *Brokeback Mountain* (2005). This story deals with the fearful silences surrounding a homosexual relationship between two farmhands. When in 2006 *Brokeback Mountain* failed to win the annual Oscar for best picture, although its directors and others involved in making it did win Oscars, Proulx dashed off for *The Guardian* newspaper in Britain a sour account of the awards ceremony. It was an occasion when silence might have been the better option.

Finding new words to describe our experiences is a process that enriches our lives. It may help us to overcome pain or injustice. Yet, articulation can threaten others near us. For this reason, Gill proclaims of her own recent research with Asian women that,

By speaking out, by naming violence, the women in this study have broken a significant silence .... To tell is to voice and release the emotional victimisation; this is a violation of the social hierarchy, and entails putting self above the family. To do that in Asian cultural traditions, ancient or modern, is more immoral and shameful than rage itself. Telling would dishonour the family by making public something that it is felt ought to remain private (p. 474).

Li points out that women and other silenced groups may be complicit in their silence. To say so, adds Li (p. 162), does not justify acts of public silencing but acknowledges human agency. At what point may third parties determine that such complicity is unacceptable? On 22 June 2009, President Nicolas Sarkozy made clear his opposition to Muslim women wearing the burqa, a garment regarded by many feminists as a form of silencing. He said that it was "not welcome" in France because "it is a sign of subservience". Some women objected in reply that they wished to be free to dress as they choose. In their enthusiasm to unsilence women everywhere, reformers enjoying the individualistic ethos of Western, capitalist societies may inadvertently offend and alienate those whom they wish to help, and make more difficult the possibility of even gradual improvements in the lot of women elsewhere. Before embarking on their crusades, they need to interrogate their own social contexts and to examine their own assumptions, interests, and "discourse systems" in order to avoid the danger of appearing to others as the latest version of that well-intended missionary or modernizing imperialist who believes that he or she knows what is best for the natives. Western liberals must be alert to the various ways in which their own societies oppress others, being sensitive to unjust economic and social realities from which they benefit materially. Thus, for example, the Scollons write that,

> At the Earth Summit in Brazil in 1992, it was reported that Third World feminists had engaged in extended discussions with North American feminists on the question of cultural and gender identity. As it was reported, the problem was that Third World women felt that American feminists were asking the women of the world to take on aspects of identity which were not, in fact, those of the discourse system of women, but rather the discourse system of North Americans. They argued that American women could not set their American identity aside and claim to be simply world feminists as a means of escaping responsibility for the worldwide ecological problems which they had gone to the Earth Summit to discuss (2001, p. 259).

Moreover, we ought not to jump to the conclusion that women have come to be progressively less silenced by a process of modernization. Thus, for example, Mitchell and Franklin, who have researched the history of First Nation women in British Columbia, Canada, found that, "There was a time, before European conquest of North America, when the voices of Native women were strong and clear." However, one must also avoid romanticizing the past. While the idea that women had a higher status in pre-Christian Ireland than they had later in a christened society is sometimes aired, scholarly evidence suggests that it ought to be treated sceptically (Folsom, p. xi; Kelly, pp. 68–98).

Being sensitive when dealing with people from other cultures need not blind us to the shortcomings of those cultures in respect of their treatment of the individual. Just as Pope John Paul II wanted people not even to discuss the possibility of women priests in the Roman Catholic Church, so some Muslim authorities do not like it when their Western friends raise the issue of the status of women in their societies. Indeed, Muslim women may point out that they are treated with great respect in such societies, even if they have fewer civil rights than their male partners. However, reasonable concerns persist about the way in which Muslim women appear to be silenced by their men. For example, in one extended journalistic study, Jan Goodwin interviewed women in ten different Muslim countries, reporting on how they are submitting to or fighting against such practices as polygamy, arranged child marriages, and the wearing of the *chador*.

On 29 November 2004, reporting from Rawalpindi for the BBC, Nadia Asjad told the story of a Pakistani girl called Najma who was being stalked by a man who had written her name in blood on his flesh, and who groped her and uttered obscenities at her. The girl had contacted a lawyer but subsequently refused to act on the latter's suggestions because Najma feared the reaction of the stalker and feared that her family would confine her to the house:

> "Right from the moment a girl is born, she's taught to keep silent no matter what happens to her," says Shahnaz Bokhari, a psychologist and chief co-ordinator of a non-governmental organization, the Progressive Women's Association in Islamabad.
>
> "Girls are taught that it's a sin to speak up for yourself and contradict your father, brothers or husband. We have snatched away all the courage and confidence of our girls but when something happens to them, we say 'Why didn't she protest, why didn't she raise her voice?'"

Georgina Ashworth, as director of CHANGE in London, has argued that even the human rights agenda itself can be gender orientated while seemingly neutral. CHANGE is said to have been the first contemporary organization with the objective of raising awareness of the "human rights and human dignity of women" as distinct from "women's rights". Ashworth asserts that,

In fact, the belief in neutrality disguised trenchant masculine bias in the selective promotion and protection of human rights. This in turn contributed to the hierarchy between men and women, their legal capacities, and their approved behaviours (p. 259).

Given the fact that some feminists blame the Bible, and more specifically St Paul, for lending strong support to the silencing of women in Western countries, it is quite ironic that Smart complains of the silencing of the Bible itself within Christian Churches. Religious critics throughout history have suspected that Church authorities favour their own interpretations and teachings over the voice of Jesus Christ as encountered directly by a receptive reader of the Bible.

Ethnic minorities

Audre Lorde's struggle to express herself was, as we saw above, that of an individual who happened to be black and lesbian in a predominantly white and heterosexual society. However, the difficulties of expressing ourselves can be exacerbated by our being members of ethnic minorities, either in relationship to the wider society or within the culture of the ethnic minority itself. Thus, a woman struggling to articulate her concerns may encounter prejudice against all members of the ethnic minority to which she belongs, and she may further encounter within her own minority community a specific type of prejudice against women.

Of women in ethnic minorities, Patel has written that, "Our experiences show us that when Asian women who are victims of domestic violence make demands of the [United Kingdom] state for protection, they are likely to confront the racism of the state in the form of indifference and even hostility" (P. Patel, p. 163).

Members of ethnic minorities, generally, may find that their point of view is unwelcome in the wider community in which they live. This is especially so if they are critical. It is as if they ought to be grateful and know their place in the society to which they or their families have migrated. Hisaye Yamamoto has penned an interesting fictional treatment of this phenomenon. In "Wilshire bus", a renowned short story first published in *Pacific Citizen* on 20 December 1950, one migrant speaks out and thus indirectly challenges another nearby to break her usual silence. We join a quiet Japanese woman who frequently takes a particular bus ride in Los Angeles. An elderly Chinese couple come on board. The Chinese woman objects to the boorish behaviour of a white American passenger. This creates a dilemma for the Japanese woman who had been enjoying her bus rides in silence until that moment. Should she remain silent or support the Chinese?

Yamamoto's various uses and treatments of silence have led to her being one of three second-generation Asian-North American women writers whose work is considered by King-Kok Cheung in her *Articulate Silences*. The others are Maxine Hong Kingston and Joy Kogawa. Cheung believes that these writers demonstrate clearly how silences, including voiceless gestures and textual ellipses and authorial hesitations, can themselves be articulate or expressive.

European immigrants to the United States also had difficulties finding their voice. The Italian-American poet Maria Mazziotti Gillan has explained how she found a way to express herself through poetry, writing that, "... my work springs from shame and silence, the shame I felt growing up as an Italian American, a shame so strong, so overwhelming that I spent the first twenty-five years of my life unable to speak." She says that her poem "Arturo" "explains most clearly how we learned shame and silence" (Gillan, 2003a, p. 1).

Immigrants around the world have faced similar problems. For example, Pepe Choong writes of the poor 19th century Chinese immigrants to New Zealand and of their "contentment to be allowed to live in someone's land—borrowed space by trying to be as invisible and quiet as possible for fear of drawing attention that might lead to further discrimination". One of those interviewed by Choong was "Christine", a Chinese-New Zealander born in Wellington in 1944. The interviewee was not surprised by such silence:

> Besides, as Christine nonchalantly added: "What would we write about?"... the underlying question and issue was not just "What to write?" but also "Who would read it?" Would there be a target audience at all? A receptive target audience? In all fairness, I would hardly think so, taking into account the political and social climate of that era. Hence, to this generation of

women it would seem their silence is an indication that they instinctively knew their place (pp. 45–46).

This New Zealand example is a reminder of the fact that silencing and prejudice can function passively when we make no effort to hear certain voices in our community, perhaps because we unconsciously rate them as insignificant, troubled, or disturbing.

Over and beyond general experiences of prejudice in the wider world, an additional impediment to speaking out may arise within the immigrant's own migrant community. Gill instances the case of some South Asian women living in London, with particular reference to their culture's concepts of honour (*izzat*) and shame (*sharam*). She writes,

> Fear of bringing shame on the family routinely acts to silence women about their experiences of violence and discourages them from resisting such coercive control. The social significance of female shame is also reflected in the prevalence of victim blaming, consistently identified in women's experiences (p. 476).

As Gill also notes, "… silencing is complicated by a range of issues relating to the requirement to not disturb or challenge long-standing community silences about violence against women" (p. 476). The situation for such women is rendered even more complicated by the fact that a vocabulary may not have developed in their own tongue to name or articulate their experiences. Even a concept such as "domestic violence", that many Westerners today take for granted, may be assimilated, understood, articulated, and validated more slowly in the daily language of people from more conservative and non-Western cultures than it has been in liberal democratic societies.

One must be careful also not to forget the extent to which social restraints have played an important role in many parts of Western societies themselves, even until recently. Urbane academics and polemicists, living in anonymous modern cities, may be unaware of the continuing importance to many people of what one's relatives and neighbours think or say. Exposing the family to gossip or shame in such a community may have socially unpleasant consequences for all its members, and one may come to repent of "washing one's dirty linen in public".

Employees

If one of the ways in which the silencing of women is achieved is by means of bullying, women are by no means the only ones who experience bullying. An awareness of the problems associated with bullying in the workplace is evident in a number of societies. One aspect of bullying is the suppression or silencing of points of view within organizations, and this is particularly easy to achieve in the case of younger employees. They feel vulnerable and may have much to lose if they do not toe the boss's line. Laughing or sneering at their point of view is just one of the ways in which their superiors may silence them.

Another form of silencing is simply implicit in the ethos of many big organizations, where managers employ those who not only seem to be self-starters but who also appear unlikely to rock the boat by challenging practices that express the institutional ethos. In that recent English study by Brown and Coupland which was mentioned earlier at p.64, graduate trainees at a large UK-based private sector retail chain (named "Beta" for the purposes of the study), talked about being silenced. They learnt to shut up, put up, and get on with their work. Although "Beta" insisted that trainees were part of a team that was to take initiatives and to be creative, many employees felt that it was safer to project a positive image and not to contradict institutional practices. Might the global banking crisis of 2009 have been avoided had employees felt encouraged to articulate their personal reservations about certain financial practices and lax regulation?

The extent to which one is willing to silence oneself for the sake of staying employed is a subjective matter, and may depend on the level and type of one's personal commitments elsewhere. The silence that one maintains at work is also relative, in that one may compensate for it by loudly complaining to a spouse or friend about one's job. It is the case, too, that speaking up at work is not always personally counterproductive, especially if it is done in a constructive or helpful way. The degree to which one is genuinely free to say what is on one's mind varies from one employment context to another. At the end of the day, one either opts out or remains inside and adapts to organizational realities in a manner that is, hopefully, compatible with one's personal dignity. The silencing of an individual usually occurs within a social context that requires a price to be paid for publicly breaking the silence. One must weigh up a number of variables before deciding to pay that price.

Students and scholars

Silencing is not confined to the home or workplace. Children may also experience it in the classroom, and students at college. Gillan has written of her sense of humiliation at being the child of immigrants in an American school. She reminds us forcefully that,

> Before I went to school, I spoke a southern Italian dialect inside my home, but as soon as I stepped outside the old brown doors, I was in America, and I soon learned that I had to speak English in school and on the streets. In school I was always terrified that the Italian word would come flying out of my mouth before I could prevent it from happening. I was intimidated by the teachers and I learned from them how to be silent, how to sit with my hands folded neatly on my desk, how to be a good girl. In truth, I was afraid to be anything else (2003a, p. 1).

She explores here feelings in her poem, "Public School No. 18: Paterson, New Jersey". This describes her search for words to express her sense of being an outsider and invisible, as well as the courage and empowerment that came when she was able to find words to express her anger:

> Miss Wilson's eyes, opaque
> as blue glass, fix on me:
> "We must speak English.
> We're in America now."
> I want to say, "I am American,"
> but the evidence is stacked against me.
>
> My mother scrubs my scalp raw, wraps
> my shining hair in white rags
> to make it curl. Miss Wilson
> drags me to the window, checks my hair
> for lice. My face wants to hide.

At home, my words smooth in my mouth,
I chatter and am proud. In school,
I am silent, grope for the right English
words, fear the Italian word
will sprout from my mouth like a rose,
fear the progression of teachers
in their sprigged dresses,
their Anglo-Saxon faces.

Without words, they tell me
to be ashamed.
I am.
I deny that booted country
even from myself,
want to be still
and untouchable
as these women
who teach me to hate myself.

Years later, in a white
Kansas City house,
the Psychology professor tells me
I remind him of the Mafia leader
on the cover of *Time* magazine.

My anger spits
venomous from my mouth:

I am proud of my mother,
dressed all in black,
proud of my father
with his broken tongue,
proud of the laughter
and noise of our house.

Remember me, Ladies,
the silent one?
I have found my voice
and my rage will blow
your house down (2003b, pp. 15–16).

Pupils and teachers may have different understandings of the value of silence. Some pupils, particularly those who are shy or who come from families where their parents' or guardians' first language is not English, may regard listening, thinking, and reflecting as a "facilitative device" that allows them to gain access, organize, and absorb new material. Teachers, on the other hand, may judge such silence negatively (Jaworski & Sachdev, pp. 286–287).

Recently, a study of some Chinese-born children in a New York school suggested more than one reason why immigrant children fall silent in class, and some of the reasons are also those why some non-immigrant children are quieter than others. Hu and Fell-Eisenkraft identified four types of silence in the Chinese students' perceptions of their own behaviour. These were silence as a result of being shy; silence as a result of fear of not having the correct answers; silence as a result of unfamiliarity with talking to learn; and silence as a result of a lack of confidence in speaking the English language. Hu discusses the cultural significance of these students' perceptions from her own perspective as a cultural insider, while Hu's co-author, herself a teacher in New York City's Chinatown, describes from her standpoint as a classroom insider ways to facilitate effectively the learning of these students. Hu reminds readers not to take the epithet "shy" for granted. It may not be a simple character attribute. She writes,

> I often hear the word "shy" being used as a general label to characterize those who display a tendency to remain silent in class discussions. However, according to McCroskey (1991), shyness is a behavior that could be the result of any one or a combination of the following seven factors: skill deficiencies, social introversion, social alienation, ethnic/cultural divergence, unfamiliarity with academic discourse, lacking confidence in subject matter, and/or communication apprehension (p. 56).

Teachers must be careful not to transfer any negative judgement of a child's shyness onto that child personally, but to understand its origins. They must also bear in mind that there may be additional cultural reasons why children remain silent and are, indeed, regarded positively within their own culture for being reserved rather than being eagerly expressive. Such "ethnic/cultural divergence", as Hu has categorized it (above), may spring from that respect for silence and hierarchy that is, as we discussed elsewhere, a feature of various societies. So, even if a school has excellent and sensitive teachers and does not "silence" immigrants, those migrants themselves may stay silent when they indeed could benefit educationally from being more involved in classroom activities and discussions. Their various cultures become another aspect of that complexity with which every teacher must struggle if attempting to deliver the best possible quality of schooling.

Helping children to understand that they are not required to speak perfect English before they may contribute, or that "the right answer" is not always at issue, or that they need not be "pushy" to be articulate, are means through which their involvement in class discussions may be increased.

Cultural attitudes have implications that of course are not confined to schooling young children or adolescents but that are relevant too at a higher level. In a recent study of some Turkish graduate students in the United States, the researcher has related their behaviour to the fact that,

> Placed in the lower end of the individualist-collectivist continuum, Turkish society traditionally socializes children not to talk much because "[i]t is widely accepted that being quiet is a well-behaved attitude for a child" (Bichelmeyer & Cagiltay, 2000, p. 12). Similarly, in the classroom, the student is expected to listen, respond only when asked a question, and not ask questions, an act that might be perceived as a threat to the teacher's authority (Tater, p. 286).

While there are ways in which it is possible to address creatively the anxiety surrounding such silence (Poulos), it is always necessary to bear in mind that the relationship between teacher or professor and student is one of power. Some discussions of this problem do not acknowledge that students may be afraid of teachers for a number of reasons that reflect poorly on those teachers either personally or pedagogically. There are professional and moral obligations on teachers to examine their own conduct as well as that of the students.

However, Petress may have gone too far in claiming in respect of student "reticence" that there is an "obligation" on the individual student, teacher, classmate, and educational administrator to reduce or "eliminate" such "reticence". This assumption begs a number of questions. For example, should "silence" and "reticence" be equated? Are they really the same thing? Secondly, are all of us—professors and students and even college administrators—ethically obliged to "reduce or [even to] eliminate" such student reticence or silence, as Petress appears to believe? Might it not in fact be an unethical imposition to put peer pressure on a student to speak? Should students, like the criminally accused, not enjoy a "right to silence"? It is easier to agree with his more general observation that,

> If one engages in communication with another, one implicitly agrees to respect and pay attention to the other and we can expect others to pay attention to us when communicating. These lessons need to be taught to children in school in addition to how to communicate (Petress, p. 105).

Research

It is not only in the classroom that scholars may inadvertently, or otherwise, find themselves silencing those whom they encounter. Researchers in the field must also tread lightly if they are not to be reproached because of their methods. Thus, using insights from a comparative qualitative study undertaken in Zimbabwe and Senegal, Randall and Koppenhaver have discussed some problems inherent in qualitative data collection and analysis in this context. They have proposed ways in which such data should and should not be used. Focusing in particular on semi-structured in-depth interviews, they consider issues of representativity, respondents' silence on specific topics, and the role of interviewer characteristics in influencing the interview subject matter. Respondents' silence on a subject may give rise to a major problem of interpretation and understanding. They write that,

> If a topic is brought up frequently, in a variety of contexts, and with a range of different emphases, (e.g., the deteriorating economy or AIDS in Zimbabwe, or good upbringing

in urban Senegal), then one can assume that not only is it a pre-occupation, it is also perceived as a fairly safe topic to talk about. The benefit of qualitative research is the increased respondent control over subject matter, but we must beware of the flawed assumption that everything can be talked about. There may well be certain subjects which people are not only prohibited from *discussing* but which they are discouraged from *thinking*. Thus, silence on a subject should make an analyst pause. Does it necessarily mean that the subject is unimportant, or might it mean that the subject is potentially extremely important but not to be discussed with just anyone? (pp. 74–75).

The problem became clear from the Senegalese data in particular when the researchers tried to establish whether the Wolof people reasoned in the same way as the demographer reasoned in respect of mortality risks. Islam is very important for the Wolof, and, "… the general interpretation of Islam in the study communities is that a believer must not challenge God's will. There are substantial demographic ramifications of this …" (pp. 74–75 and 81). Thus, silence did not mean that people had not considered and taken a view on the issue.

So silence on a specific subject must not lead a researcher to conclude necessarily that the topic is unimportant or irrelevant. Indeed, the extent to which a researcher asks specific questions, and how often the researcher probes a particular aspect of the matter under investigation, may alter the response of the person interviewed, thus influencing perhaps the incidence of silence, the amount and nature of "noise" or speech, as well as the findings of the research. Randall and Koppenhaver persuasively argue that, "… it is essential to have an idea of interviewers' interests, prejudices, and socio-demographic characteristics in order to interpret silences; a basic knowledge of their preoccupations can also help interpret noise" (p. 81). Thus, through bias or ignorance, researchers may effectively silence a true expression of the group that is the subject of their demographic research.

Understanding the relationship between interviewer bias and research outcomes is similarly important when assessing the accuracy of public opinion polls in any society, a subject to be given greater attention when "the spiral of silence" in public discourse is considered below.

The politics of unsilencing

A majority of people in any given society simply may not acknowledge that there is a particular silence to be broken about some oppressed group within its sphere of influence at home or abroad. And those oppressed individuals or groups who do speak out may not be heard clearly or in a way that leads to an amelioration of their circumstances. The struggle to reverse marginalization and to break such silences is a political struggle. It takes many forms. Sometimes, powerful forces of the state must be tackled. Sometimes, popular prejudice and assumption are the insidious barriers to be dismantled. The very noise of daily politics, in which big groups and vested interests play on popular support to get their way, can drown out weaker voices. Citizens do not especially enjoy hearing about problems that make them uncomfortable, or that might require change or sacrifice in their lives. Mass media organizations are sensitive to the tastes and interests of their audiences or readers and do not readily run the risk of alienating them by running stories that interpret facts in ways that continually irritate such audiences and readers. Even when a reporter writes about some silenced problem or point of view, and even when an editor approves such an account for publication, the report itself may fall on deaf ears. The breaking of silence requires not only a speaker but also a listener.

In a significant address against the US war in Vietnam, the civil rights leader Martin Luther King identified circumstances in which we may come to summon up the courage to speak or hear the unpalatable truth, to take a public stand on issues when our silence may otherwise be regarded as concurrence with an undesirable course of action. On 4 April 1967, at Riverside Church in New York City, he said (1967),

> The recent statements of your executive committee are the sentiments of my own heart, and I found myself in full accord when I read its opening lines: "A time comes when silence is betrayal." And that time has come for us in relation to Vietnam.
>
> The truth of these words is beyond doubt, but the mission to which they call us is a most difficult one. Even when pressed by the demands of inner truth, men do not easily assume the task of opposing their government's policy, especially in time of war. Nor does the human spirit move without great difficulty

against all the apathy of conformist thought within one's own bosom and in the surrounding world. Moreover, when the issues at hand seem as perplexed as they often do in the case of this dreadful conflict, we are always on the verge of being mesmerized by uncertainty; but we must move on.

And some of us who have already begun to break the silence of the night have found that the calling to speak is often a vocation of agony, but we must speak. We must speak with all the humility that is appropriate to our limited vision, but we must speak ....

Over the past two years, as I have moved to break the betrayal of my own silences and to speak from the burnings of my own heart, as I have called for radical departures from the destruction of Vietnam, many persons have questioned me about the wisdom of my path. At the heart of their concerns this query has often loomed large and loud: "Why are you speaking about the war, Dr King?", "Why are you joining the voices of dissent?", "Peace and civil rights don't mix", they say. "Aren't you hurting the cause of your people?", they ask.

To King also is frequently attributed a declaration that, "Our lives begin to end the day we become silent about things that matter"; although it is not certain that he ever said it.

If it is sometimes difficult to summon up the courage to speak out against the dominant forces in a democracy, it is all the harder to do so in a dictatorship. Dictators frequently and violently suppress dissidents and minorities. For example, many people outside the Soviet Union long remained unaware of the extent of the system of prison camps within that state. Then, Alexander Solzhenitsyn, a former inmate of the "gulag" or camps, began to write about them, forcing both Russians and foreigners to face reality. He put himself at risk of re-imprisonment or worse, but his bravery in exposing what had been happening hastened the demise of the Soviet Union itself. His was an example of what an individual can do in the face of mighty forces, and it comes as no surprise to find that, in his lecture on the occasion of his being presented with the Nobel prize for literature, he quoted an old Russian proverb that proclaims boldly, "One word of truth shall outweigh the whole world." In that speech, Solzhenitsyn spoke of the Soviet experience,

Silent generations grow old and die without ever having talked about themselves, either to each other or to their descendants. When writers such as [Anna] Achmatova and [Evgenij] Zamjatin—interred alive throughout their lives—are condemned to create in silence until they die, never hearing the echo of their written words, then that is not only their personal tragedy, but a sorrow to the whole nation, a danger to the whole nation. In some cases moreover—when as a result of such a silence the whole of history ceases to be understood in its entirety—it is a danger to the whole of mankind.

Yet even in a small state such as Guatemala, which has experienced long periods of repression, writers and poets continue to emerge to break the silence and give voice to the experiences and suffering of their people (Zimmerman et al.).

Sometimes the effective silencing of writers is a function of economic poverty more than of deliberate political repression. Nadine Fettweis has called such unpublished authors *"écrivains du silence"* ("writers of silence") because of the absence of publishing outlets in states with scarce material resources (Gikandi, p. 214). Even states that are mighty and free do not guarantee liberty of expression to all, for the temptation for governments to silence their critics or those who are deemed to be "undesirable" is a recurrent one. When the government of the United States launched its so-called "War on Terror" following the destruction of the Twin Towers in New York, it soon found various ways of justifying to itself the silencing of prisoners. Some were interned by the United States in foreign countries where there was little respect for the rule of law or human rights and where the very existence of such prisoners might be kept concealed while they were being interrogated or even tortured. Others were sent to the US prison camp at Guantanamo Bay, Cuba, where they were denied rights of expression and confidential access to visitors. Such rights had formerly been established as due to prisoners of war and to civilian prisoners within the United States.

After its Vietnam War, the US government and that of other democracies had also sought ways of silencing the truth about war itself. Manipulation and restriction of media in the Falklands and in Iraq, among other places, have fettered the freedom of journalists to go where they wish and to report openly what they see, even assuming that the corporations that own the media allow them to do so.

Direct censorship is a way to silence the voice of minorities, although it may be argued that such silencing is sometimes necessary to protect democracy from violent subversives who use freedom of speech in an attempt to destabilize society. Such was the rationale for that Irish law known as "Section 31", and its UK equivalent, which for years partly barred representatives of Sinn Féin, the IRA, and other paramilitary organizations from the airwaves. Political parties affiliated with those organizations spoke for some members of marginalized minorities in Northern Ireland, who were free to vote for other parties if they wished. Some political and media analysts believe that the exclusion of their representatives from media debates ultimately exacerbated problems within Northern Ireland and delayed the day when politicians on both sides of the Irish Sea realistically addressed the causes of alienation and conflict in Northern Ireland (Corcoran & O'Brien, passim).

Spiral of silence

As already noted above, it does not always take direct censorship or government pressure to silence certain voices in society. Public prejudice or fear or ignorance alone can work effectively to stifle the articulation of points of view that are different from those of the mass of people. Members of the general public who are in a minority may be reluctant to express their opinions even to individual researchers if they think that those opinions are out of date or unfashionable. In one influential work, first published in 1980, Elisabeth Noelle-Neumann coined the phrase "spiral of silence" to explain this latter phenomenon. She represents public opinion as a form of social control and argues that individuals, almost instinctively, sense the opinions of those around them and then shape their behaviour to prevailing attitudes about what is acceptable. In other words, people in a minority may not say what they think because they fear being ridiculed or hounded. They do not need to read opinion polls to sense what the prevailing opinion is, and they have no wish to isolate themselves by expressing a minority opinion.

The fear of what one's neighbours might think or say has always been a powerful one, especially in small communities. People are guarded when it comes to doing or saying something that appears to constitute a rejection of the consensus of the majority. What Noelle-Neumann has done is to study this tendency and demonstrate that it may even influence what people say privately to researchers. She came to this conclusion on the basis of her experience as the founder and director of a leading German polling organization, the Public Opinion Research Centre in Allensbach, and as a professor of communications research at the University of Mainz. She herself did not allow her own political past to silence her. A former member of the Nazi student organization, who had travelled to the United States and elsewhere on a German state stipend, she had applied as a post-graduate in 1939 to join the Reich Chamber of Writers but was rebuffed on the ground that she had not published a sufficient number of articles. One article that she did write, published in *Das Reich* on 8 June 1941, attacked alleged Jewish influences in the US media, including in the *New York Times* and the *Chicago Daily News*. Forty-three years later, as it happened, it was the University of Chicago Press that published the English edition of her *Spiral of Silence*. Christopher Simpson of the School of Communication at the American University in Washington DC has written of her personal background and has published on the internet what are said to be original documents relating to her Nazi past. He claims to have been threatened with legal action as a result.

Not long after the war ended, Noelle-Neumann's researches revealed to her some of the strange ways in which democracies work. She later recalled that,

> It was in Munich in 1951/52, and I had ended up at this party of intellectuals by chance ... the last time we had seen each other ... was in 1943 or 1944 on the Limonenstrasse in Berlin-Dahlem, by the botanical gardens ... on the approach path for the bombers ... (1993, pp. 174–175).

Their conversation turned to the question of public support for Konrad Adenauer, a politician. Noelle-Neumann had been pre-testing questionnaires for her Allensbach institute:

> In fact, I had frequently interviewed the young wife of a railroad signalman with questions that repeated themselves, and I knew

her answers. I had already heard at least eight times that she did
not agree with Adenauer. But acting conscientiously and strictly
according to the rules ... I once again asked her: "Do you agree
with Adenauer ... or do you disagree ...?" "Agree," she said.
I tried to hide my surprise, since interviewers are not supposed
to show surprise (ibid.).

When results of the survey proper came in they showed that this
woman was just one of many who appeared suddenly to change
their minds at the time. This drove Noelle-Neumann to wonder,
"By what means had the wave of pressure in the Federal Republic reached this railroad signalman's wife? And what was such an
opinion worth?". Her study of that question led to the publication
of *Spiral of Silence*, which she does not claim represents an original
insight but which teases out some of the complex ways in which
public opinion may wax or wane in particular directions. One of
those whom she acknowledges as having long ago recognized the
reluctance of individuals to defend unpopular ideas was Sir William
Temple, sometime employer of the author of *Gulliver's Travels*, Dean
Jonathan Swift. In 1672, Temple wrote that a man "will hardly hope,
or venture to introduce opinions wherein he knows none, or few of
his mind, and thinks all others will defend those already received"
(cited at Noelle-Neumann, p. 238).

It is evident that assumptions, prejudices, group dynamics, and
fear of isolation are among the factors that shape our opinions. One
graphic demonstration of this was the series of experiments conducted in the early 1950s in the United States by Solomon Asch,
a psychologist. He asked people to judge which of three straight
lines best matched a fourth line in length. One of the three lines
was always exactly the same as that fourth line, and people spot-
ted this quickly. However, he then rigged the environment so that
initial respondents in tests would deliberately identify a particular
line wrongly as the matching one. Faced with this rigged consensus,
most subsequent participants in the tests frequently agreed with the
wrong answer. If people are so easily swayed in respect of such a
non-contentious and simple matter, then it will probably be difficult
for them to swim against the tide of public opinion in respect of
more complex or contentious issues.

The publication of Noelle-Neumann's *Spiral of Silence* also
sparked debate about the extent to which public opinion research

must take into account the possibility that the opinions of those being polled are shaped by respondents' pre-existing ideas of what public opinion already is and by their relationship to it, as well as factors such as media that present versions of public opinion while at the same time shaping it. She writes in that book,

> It was to be expected that the spiral of silence theory was not hailed as progress toward a theory of public opinion when it was first presented at the 1972 International Congress of Psychology in Tokyo or in 1980 or 1984 when my book appeared in English and German respectively. There was no room here for the informed, responsible citizen, the ideal upon which democratic theory is based. Fear of public opinion—fear on the part of the government and of the individual—is not provided for by classical democratic theory (p. 199).

The author asserts that, "Democratic theory does not deal with topics such as the social nature of man, social psychology, or what creates cohesion in society." If some see her book as implicitly providing an apologia for her earlier failure to resist fascism, it is also quite a lively and stimulating read. One of the more curious aspects of it is her periodic reliance upon and agreement with Walter Lippmann, a journalist and intellectual, whose widely read book *Public Opinion* was published in 1922. For, during World War II, when writing for one Nazi publication about alleged Jewish influence in the US media, she had described Lippmann as "a Jew of German origin .... He is the most clever user of this neutral camouflage, who shrewdly brings his readers to the conclusion that America is surrounded on all sides. He is the spokesman for huge finance who was once an opponent of Roosevelt, [but] who now supports intervention without reservation ...." (cited at Simpson, p. 149).

In general, it may be said that the extent to which one remains silent or, alternatively, is outspoken depends on variables such as one's psychological predisposition, fear of isolation or ridicule, and even nervousness about articulation. One does not have to believe that public opinion is entirely determined by social factors to see some value in the spiral of silence theory, and it is still being tested today. It may be that in a mature democracy, particularly one in which the market economy encourages certain kinds of individual initiative, people feel relatively free to say what they think and to disagree with the consensus. However, that fact does not exclude the possibility that they are influenced consciously or unconsciously by social forces that mould their thinking or inhibit them from forming views that would make them feel uncomfortable. Moreover, it is important to remember also that outspokenness may be culturally relative, with certain statements being considered outspoken in style and content in one context that may seem quite subdued or conservative in another.

The spiral of silence theory has received a great deal of attention, being described by Glynn as, "one of the most researched and controversial approaches to understanding public opinion" (p. 203). One test has involved a representative telephone poll of 668 adults conducted in Singapore in September 2000. Respondents were asked to indicate how likely they would be to discuss publicly two controversial issues: interracial marriage and equal rights for homosexuals. In Singapore, prior to the study, the topics of interracial marriages and equal rights for homosexuals were sensitive but had been written about widely in the newspapers and discussed by officials. The findings were said to provide partial support for the spiral of silence hypothesis:

> That is, the respondents' perception of the future opinion climate in Singapore interacts with their assessment of how important the issue is in influencing their level of outspokenness. The findings also indicate that outspokenness is associated with respondents' self-concept of interdependence, their fear of becoming socially isolated, their communication apprehension, and their perceived importance of the issue (Willnat, Waipeng & Detenber, p. 391).

Singapore is a society where people believe that disagreeing openly with the government may have serious consequences. According to one study by Leong (Willnat, Waipeng & Detenber, p. 396), 93% of respondents there said that they preferred to remain silent when they disagreed with official policies. In the study by Willnat and his colleagues, people were phoned and asked on a four point scale how likely they would be to join a conversation at a wedding banquet if people were discussing each topic and espousing views contrary to their own, where most of the those people were unknown to the respondents. The respondents' personal fear of isolation and fear of authority, their communication apprehension, and their self-concept in respect of independence or interdependence were ascertained in order to relate these to their responses to the main question on outspokenness. So too was the level of their interest in public affairs and their assessment of the salience of the issues, both factors that the researchers regarded as important variables. Finally, in addition to normal control measures, their individual exposure to the media was measured (based on their own assessment), because "people's perceptions of the public opinion climate are thought to be significantly influenced by the media" (p. 401, referring to Noelle-Neumann). The conclusions of the study were in line with earlier assessments of the spiral of silence:

> Similar to previous findings, perceptions of the dominant opinion climate alone were weak predictors of public outspokenness. However, when analyzed in combination with other predictors such as issue salience, significant interaction effects emerged (Willnat, Waipeng & Detenber, p. 406).

Most respondents in the Singapore study reported that they would be reluctant to talk about interracial marriages or equal rights for homosexuals in the hypothetical public setting. The researchers were somewhat surprised at their reluctance in respect of the former issue, given the fact that the government approves interracial marriages. In respect of the latter, they point out that sex between homosexuals had not been decriminalized in Singapore. It was found that the willingness or unwillingness of people to speak up was significantly related to their personal level of fear of social isolation and other anxieties. When such people remain silent, it does not mean that they have no opinions or feelings about a matter and it would be wrong to assume that they are politically indifferent or ignorant.

In another test of the spiral of silence theory, researchers in the United States (Jaffres, Neuendorf & Atkin) studied reactions to the trial of O. J. Simpson in 1995. Many people in the USA and beyond held very strong opinions about the former football player, regardless of their level of knowledge of the actual details of the case.

The arrest and subsequent acquittal of one of America's foremost athletes, on a charge of murdering his wife, polarized public opinion between blacks and whites. While the researchers' findings in this instance did not generally confirm the spiral of silence theory, they did discover evidence of racial differences in respondents' concerns regarding the impact of their expressed opinions. As they noted,

> One's willingness to be quoted varied significantly in an unexpected fashion: majority group members (Whites) interviewed by minority group members (Blacks) were significantly more willing to be quoted than were minority members interviewed by majority members (p. 115).

The authors of these recent studies refer to much previous work in the field and their findings reflect the nuances that have emerged through researchers qualifying and refining the methods employed by Elisabeth Noelle-Neumann. The spiral of silence theory is significantly circumscribed by many variables but it is still a useful starting point for addressing the process whereby, undoubtedly, many individuals and groups fail to express their opinions forthrightly in certain circumstances. Those circumstances may be encapsulated in the word "fear" (Neuwirth), but the spiral of silence that surrounds such fear continues to be worth exploring carefully.

"The silent majority"?

If there are "silent minorities", is there also at times a "silent majority"? Certainly, "the silent majority" is a political concept to which elected representatives like to have recourse when they find that their own ideas and those of the most vocal groups in society do not coincide. A politician may purport to speak for a supposed mass of people that the politician believes is subdued by government or by the mass media. Such people, real or imaginary, do not express opinions loudly and feel that their views are underrepresented in the media. In one notable speech, during the Vietnan War, President Richard Nixon invoked "the silent majority". Speaking on 3 November 1969, he recalled the noble reasons that his US predecessors such as John F. Kennedy and Lyndon Johnson had given for committing forces to Vietnam and he said,

Let historians not record that when America was the most powerful nation in the world we passed on the other side of the road and allowed the last hopes for peace and freedom of millions of people to be suffocated by the forces of totalitarianism. And so tonight—to you, the great silent majority of my fellow Americans—I ask for your support.

Silent myths

The complexities of silencing are illustrated by considering the situation of some people who find that even a minority to which they belong and which, historically, has itself been silenced can still be a powerful force for repressing their individuality and distorting the truth. Cultural and social self-conceptions of identity may become straight-jackets that leaders of a minority are reluctant to throw off lest political advances be reversed, or out of a sense of loyalty to pioneers or even out of their fear of losing the rationale for their being the current leaders of their minority group.

John McWhorter, associate professor of linguistics at the University of California at Berkeley, has argued that true racial equality requires new perspectives. He believes that, "… a tacit sense reigns among a great many black Americans today that the 'authentic' black person stresses personal initiative and strength in private, but dutifully takes on the mantle of victimhood as a public face" (p. 2). While acknowledging the rational basis for certain criticisms, including criticisms of the police, McWhorter notes that a *New York Times* poll, which was conducted in 2000, found that "a mere 7 per cent of blacks thought that racism was the most important problem for the next generation of Americans to solve" (p. 4). He suggests that the truths of advancement and improvement are silenced by some in the black community on the grounds that, "We can't let whites off the hook," adding that,

> Black Americans roughly sixty and younger have spent their mature lives where this phrase is as much a part of the scenery as the "one in three young black men are in jail or involved with the criminal justice system" mantra that I will discuss in the next chapter. Many ideological tendencies in the black community are based neatly on this "whites on the hook" idea, virtually unquestioned and spiritually resonant (p. 5).

The tendency that McWhorter identifies will be familiar in other contexts, such as that of Northern Ireland, where some of those who have succeeded in emerging from a period of systematic repression and are now relatively prosperous still struggle to adjust psychologically to their improved circumstances. Critics allege that a culture of complaint persists.

McWhorter's arguments, and those of others like him in other contexts, can seem like a betrayal of "the cause" or may be criticised as premature. However, in the same way that McWhorter thinks that his fellow Afro-Americans ought to "up their game", so some women feel that feminism has achieved much of what it sought and are impatient with those who adhere too readily to its litany of wrongs while doing very nicely from various reforms that have allowed them to get jobs and to lead lifestyles that their mothers never had available to them. Other women are convinced that the battle for equality and rights is far from over, even in Western countries. Whatever one's perspective on such matters, McWhorter's book is a healthy reminder that silencing can operate in many complex ways.

Minorities may find it particularly difficult to voice a different perspective at times of national crisis, when they are expected to show their loyalty by "coming on board". This point was well made in a review of McWhorter's book, when in 2003 Gary Dauphin wrote caustically that,

> During troubled times such as these—last-and-first days of conservative ascendancy, economic recession, biological anxiety and increasingly apocalyptic rumblings of war—the street value of black public intellectuals decreases precipitously .... The black spin on, say, Iraq or Al Qaeda may exist. But practically speaking—and I stress the word "practically"—those opinions tend to be almost invisible since they don't suit the disposition of wartime punditry. As the contretemps over Amiri Baraka's poem "Somebody Blew up America" would indicate, when America is under attack it's time to get with the program. Black punditry—an op-ed for example, or an appearance on CNN, or depending on the crowd you like to run with, a lecture or reading—with the words "as an African American, my reaction to 9/11 is" is seen as indicative of a damning lack of team spirit.

Black neo-con perspectives on Iraq are also hard to find on the tube and in the editorial pages, but for the very different reason that black neo-conservative opinions on foreign affairs are a kind of self-negating redundancy. The opinion in question is generally indistinguishable from general conservative cant by virtue of the neo-con's identification with "America" to the exclusion of all other ethnic and racial heritage. Unless the topic of the day is, say, "Islamic fundamentalism in Africa," there's just no reason to trot out the black talking androids to say just what Vice President Dick Cheney or Defense Secretary Donald Rumsfeld would. What would they have to offer, and who would care? (p. 53).

See no evil, speak of no evil

On the global stage, critics argue that the problems of poor countries are often ignored. A hurricane that hits the United States will be far more widely and more graphically reported that a hurricane (perhaps even the same one) that hits other states around the Caribbean, or an air crash in some Western country may receive greater media coverage internationally than a worse catastrophe elsewhere. This is partly because the advanced communications technology of richer countries means that there is a quick and ready supply of graphic media images; but it may also reflect an unwillingness or "inability" of people who are privileged to hear those who are not when the latter have unpalatable messages to convey. Only when a truly epic catastrophe such as the Haitian earthquake of 2010 occurs does it make headlines around the world.

On the other hand, even where one overcomes Western prejudice to hear certain news from far away, there may well be factors within non-Western countries that further distort the truth by fostering other silences. When the president of Pakistan suggested in 2005 that Westerners were quicker to send aid to the victims of the Indian Ocean tsunami than to the victims of an earthquake in Kashmir because, as he said, Western visitors had been caught up in the former, he was partly deflecting attention away from the failure of wealthy Asian and Muslim countries to do more. Similarly, some Africans who accuse Western governments and drug companies of not doing enough to help AIDS victims on that continent are silent about underlying cultural factors that contribute to the devastating spread of the disease there. Such factors include attitudes towards the sexual behaviour of men and their treatment of women.

In 2005, AIDS claimed even a son of Nelson Mandela. Just four years earlier, his successor as president of South Africa, Thabo Mbeki, had delivered a speech playing down the scientifically established link between HIV and AIDS, because he wished to avoid "over-medicalizing" AIDS. He wanted people to focus instead on extreme poverty as the principal cause of ill health in the world. It was a misguided way of addressing the AIDS issue, and officials at South Africa's Ministry for Health were said to be appalled. Mbeki ignored local circumstances that were exacerbating the AIDS crisis. This was ironic, indeed, for he delivered that speech at an AIDS conference in Durban in the very year of 2000 when the international slogan for AIDS awareness campaigners was "Breaking the silence". In an "Aids bulletin" later that same year, Suzanne Leclerc-Madlala of the School of Anthropology and Psychology at the University of Natal addressed what she described as "a mystery at the heart of the AIDS epidemic in Africa that scholars have explored but have been unable to explain". She, too, sought not to "over-medicalize" the issues. However, looking elsewhere for answers, she wrote that,

> The mystery ... has to do with that stubborn and multi-layered AIDS silence, or what the professionals call "the denial" that has consistently characterised the AIDS pandemic in Africa .... The silence has to do with ... that much used and abused, dearly beloved sacred cow ... called "culture". In the two weeks fol- lowing the AIDS 2000 Conference, incidences have impressed upon me, once again, the hopeless situation of women in the face of AIDS ....
>
> Admittedly, this epidemic is not only affecting women, but their stories have a special poignancy that is embedded in a kind of silence and helplessness that does not affect men. Millions of women are being squashed under the weight of the com- pounded multiple silences of AIDS. Has the AIDS 2000 "Break the Silence" Conference really helped them ...?

> Firm measures on the part of government to foster the transformation of the sexual attitudes and practices of young and middle-aged men will run the risk of inciting the hostility of, politically, the most dangerous section of the population. Perhaps this explains why the issue is so carefully avoided (Leclerc-Madlala, pp. 20–21).

Yet, in the opinion of some, she herself had still not said enough. When her article was published by the Women's International Network in 2001, the *WIN News* editor appended a commentary in which she identified some issues about which the author herself had been subdued or remained silent, including rape and polygamy: "Rape, which is rampant throughout Africa, is hardly mentioned in the article; but there are stories about rape in every newspaper all over Africa though it is almost never prosecuted" (ibid., pp. 21–22).

What the various perspectives on AIDS in Africa demonstrate, apart from anything else, is the political importance of paying attention to silence and to what it signifies in respect of the eventual resolution of any conflict or problem. The *Wall Street Journal* recognized this when, during the US presidential election campaign in 1998, it ran a series of articles addressing "absent agenda", including issues such as the US budgetary deficit that the editor believed to be important but that the two leading candidates apparently considered too awkward or uninteresting to address substantially.

CHAPTER SEVEN

Silence in therapy

Those who encounter silence during therapy have much to teach us about its power in our daily lives. Psychiatrists, psychotherapists, social workers, and other health service professionals meet clients who fall silent in ways that can be frustrating and even threatening to those around them. Silence on the part of the client or patient may be associated with feelings of pleasure or joy or even peace, but it may also be for them a means of expressing anger, apathy, resentment, and other emotions (see, for example, Zeligs and Liegner), or else be a sign of denial. Sometimes, silence stems from a disability. Whatever its base, it is a phenomenon that merits attention. As Sigmund Freud observed in 1905, in the case of Dora,

> He that has eyes to see and ears to hear may convince himself that no mortal can keep a secret. If his lips are silent, he chatters with his finger-tips; betrayal oozes out of him at every pore (pp. 77–78).

Silencing the self

A number of authors have studied ways in which we fall silent in order to defend ourselves against instinctual urges that threaten us, urges with which we have not come to terms developmentally. In 1961, for example, Zeligs discussed the function of silence in some cases as a type of displacement from the original erotogenic zones to the organs and functions of speech. And according to Sabbadini, a silence that displays such anal connotations is characterized by an ambivalent if not openly aggressive attitude. Fliess further differentiated all silences into oral, anal, or urethral, while Sabbadini postulates the existence of a "phallic silence". The latter writes that,

> Words can be experienced as an extension of the body, as well as of the psyche, with the capacity to penetrate the ears and minds of the listener; language itself is often eroticised and used for seductive (active or passive) purposes. In this sense, silence is unconsciously associated with phallic impotence and can become a defence against castration and possession anxieties pertaining to this stage of development. Keeping quiet is a way of protecting the parents, the analyst and oneself, from exposure to the dangers of sexuality, aggression and retaliation that characterise the Oedipus complex. Silence becomes a sort of self-censorship for one to reassure oneself not to say anything wrong (p. 237).

Like the statue that one may claim already exists inside the block of marble before the sculptor has touched it with her or his chisel, words are already "there" as potentials, before being uttered. This is so in any interpersonal situation, including the psychoanalytic one. Silence can protect words from exposure to hostile treatment—misunderstanding, sarcasm, attacks—or conversely become an impediment to their expression: the safely contained becomes a constraint, a prison, a dictatorial regime forbidding free speech. The statue might remain forever buried inside the block of marble (Sabbadini, p. 232). There are occasions when the pain of past events is simply too searing to acknowledge and so people deny even to themselves the reality of their own experiences. This can happen, for example, in the case of sexual abuse. Referring to what one survivor of incest, Kathryn Harrison, has described in her memoir as a process of "selective self-anaesthesia" that left her "awake to certain things and dead to others", the sociologist Eviatar Zerubavel explains that the process of denial may be not only psychological but also sociological, being a subtle interaction between the individual and the group (pp. 3–4).

Professionals themselves fall silent at times and must understand why they do so. At a very basic level, it is desirable that doctors and therapists hear clearly what their patients or clients are saying. They should listen attentively. It can be very frustrating for a patient to attend for a doctor's appointment only to find that it is necessary to struggle to be heard while a busy, possibly overworked, medical practitioner rushes to diagnose and prescribe.

Another problem occurs if therapists are tempted to believe that they are not doing their job unless they or their clients are speaking. It is the case that psychoanalysis developed as a "talking cure", whereby speaking was a means of relieving the psychological pressures that were thought to be causing clients to suffer. Failure to talk was seen as an evasion and regression, a form of conscious or unconscious resistance to the truth, a truth that might at least help one to cope if it did not actually set one free. In this context, silence was not highly valued. Thus, Freud could write, in the 1890s,

> The longer the pause … the more suspicious I become and the more it is to be feared that the patient is rearranging what has occurred to him and is mutilating it in his reproduction of it (Freud & Breuer, p. 26).

Thirty years later, in 1926, Freud remarked of the analyst and client that, "Nothing takes place between them except that they talk to each other …. The analyst agrees upon a fixed regular hour with the patient, gets him to talk, listens to him, talks to him in his turn and gets him to listen." Freud clearly suspected that his technique's dependance on words might be treated with contempt by sceptics, for he conjured up in his imagination what he calls an "Impartial Person" who thought: "Nothing more than that? Words, words, words, as Prince Hamlet says." And then, in a sentence that seems uncanny given its authorship just a few years before the ascent of Adolf Hitler, that supreme demagogic orator, Freud wrote of this imaginary sceptic,

No doubt he is thinking too of Mephistopheles' mocking speech
on how comfortably one can get along with words [*Faust*, Part 1,
Sc. 4]—lines that no German will forget (p. 187).

"So it is a kind of magic," Freud imagines his sceptic commenting,
"... you talk, and blow away his ailments." "Quite true," responds
Freud. "It *would* be magic if it worked rather quicker." However,
even as Freud himself thus stressed the importance of words, he also
came to appreciate the significance of silence as we have already
noted. And others explored the place of silence within this psychoanalytic process. That very same year of 1926, Reik noted that in psy-
cholanalysis, "... what is spoken is not the most important thing. It
appears to us more important to recognise what speech conceals and
what silence reveals" (p. 126). During the following half-century a
trickle of important articles on the subject of silence and psychoanalysis appeared.

More recently, Andrea Sabbadini has spoken eloquently of the
need to listen to silence. In 1989, at the 36th International Psycho-
analytical Association Congress in Rome, he commented in a paper
subsequently published in the *British Journal of Psychotherapy* that,

> If psychoanalysis is primarily concerned with the attribution
> of meaning to our patients' communications, and if we believe
> silences to be meaningful, it follows that one of our functions as
> psychoanalysts is to understand the meanings of our patients'
> silences ....
>
> Such listening is not a simple operation, as silence often
> makes others, and psycholanalysts are no exception, feel anx-
> ious. As soon as this happens—and until we become aware
> that it has and of why—our analytic faculties are impaired: our
> efforts are diverted away from our normal capacity to listen in
> a state of free-floating attention and, before we realize it, we
> might have become bored and sleepy, or provided inappropri-
> ate responses, such as a "retaliatory" silence or a rushed inter-
> pretation (p. 230).

Sabbadini also pointed out that, "Silence is an element of human
language, not its opposite." Indeed, he asked, "... is it not conceiv-
able that words [as much as silence] could be a form of resistance

to getting in touch with something in ourselves which language cannot reach?" (p. 231). People may speak many words simply to cover up their own confusion. We may write at length to conceal our muddled thinking. One is reminded of a verse by Alexander Pope who, in "An essay on criticism" in 1709, noted that, "Words are like leaves; and where they most abound, Much fruit of sense beneath is rarely found." The subtleties of silence in a therapeutic context are explored by Sabbadini who instances a patient who suddenly stops talking:

> Is your patient's silence related to the content of what he was talking about: his mother, elder brother or whatever? Is it the result of a sudden intrusion of a disturbing thought, or fantasy, or memory in his train of association? Is it a response to something he imagined you were doing, or thinking, or feeling while he was talking?
>
> Different silences can have different meanings, and they are all richly overdetermined. Silence is not, or not just, an absence (of words) but an active presence.
>
> A silence lasting a few seconds, for instance, is intrinsically different from one lasting several minutes; a silence at the beginning of a session is not like one in the middle of it; a silence after an interpretation is different from one following the report of a dream; a silence in a patient who is usually talkative is unlike one in someone who is often quiet; a silence in the first session is different from one after years of analysis ....
>
> Silence, then, can be a barrier. It can be a shield. It can be a bridge. It can be a way of avoiding saying something and it can be a way of saying what no words would ever tell. It can express anger, excitement, despair, gratitude, emptiness, joy, shame, helplessness or indeed any other emotion (pp. 232–234).

Sabbadini is of the opinion that behind all silence there is an unconscious fantasy which the silence—like the dream or the symptom—both conceals and expresses at the same time. In a phrase that those working in media might also take to heart, he concludes that, "As psychoanalysts we have the responsibility of helping our patients to understand not just *what* they do say, but also *why* they cannot say what they are quiet about."

Productive silence

If early psychological literature described silence as "a homogenous event", it has been recently noted that "psychotherapeutic silence now tends to be seen as a heterogeneous, multidetermined phenomenon stemming from various underlying processes" (Frankel et al., p. 627). Some patients (or "clients") may benefit from falling silent. Gita Martyres, the author of one Australian study, has written of such silence being "a language for emotional experience". She notes that, "... silence is an important aspect of human interaction, but is often experienced with discomfort and quickly filled with words" (pp. 118–123). Martyres believes that, while the quantitative parameters of silence such as timing and duration are easily recognized, qualitative experiential aspects are much more difficult to identify and describe. She asserts that, "... words used to describe emotions are generally inadequate and simplistic," and finds that silence is a useful experiential medium in which to identify and work with emotions. Like Sabbadini, Martyres believes strongly that, "It is necessary to recognise what is being communicated by silence in each silence." Her paper explores various types of silence encountered in clinical work, and how to deal with them.

Dr Heidi Levitt of the University of Massachusetts has conducted research interviews with psychotherapy clients who have experienced different therapeutic approaches. These clients identified for her silent moments that they found beneficial in various ways. Their silences may be divided into three principal productive categories, being emotional, expressive, and reflective. Levitt's lucid article of 2002 is a useful illustration of how the structuring of introspective pauses may, for both client and therapist, greatly enhance the quality of their encounters. Such narrative psychotherapy brings to mind the process whereby ethically responsible journalists or producers may also help individuals to articulate their concerns within a public forum, and it would be interesting to explore at some time the similarities and differences between therapeutic and journalistic processes. To what extent might the therapist learn from media practitioners something about the effective and honest shaping of stories that interviewees find hard to tell, while the producer or journalist might become more aware of the impact on the interviewee of participation in the media? Malcolm has accused the journalist of being a kind of confidence trickster, "preying on people's vanity, ignorance, or loneliness, gaining their trust and betraying them without remorse" (p. 3). Even assuming that in fact a particular journalist is well intentioned, that journalist may yet unconsciously betray an interviewee's ultimate wish to articulate her or his own experience accurately.

In considering the three main categories of what she terms "productive silence", Levitt turns first to those emotional pauses when clients feel overwhelmed by a realization or intimation that lies beyond what they are actually saying, that is to say to those moments when silence beckons as a relief from inadequate articulation. She quotes one client as stating that,

> I knew there was something deeper in those things that I was saying, I can tell by the tone of my voice as I'm saying it. I'm kind of trying them out, tried and true, things one might be afraid of, or I might be afraid of, but I knew that wasn't it, that there was something deeper (p. 339).

Levitt describes this experience as an example of what she calls a "sense of the unrealized depth" that appears to function as a guiding force for clients and that helps them to understand their experiences (p. 339). From the perspective of media studies, it is worth asking how this same "sense of the unrealized depth" may be exploited commercially when people are communicating not with a therapist but with their television set or Playstation or iPod. How intuitive or sophisticated are producers at anticipating people's emotional experiences the better to shape their meaning and orient or manipulate their choices at a subconscious level?

In considering her second category of productive silence, the expressive, Levitt notes that words may both arise out of and, at the same time, distance oneself from an emotional realization. She recounts this exchange between herself ("I") and a client ("C"):

> C: It's interesting, you know, as I'm talking to you about this, I'm really aware of the conflict between the two.
>
> I: Between?
>
> C: Feeling the feelings and trying to find the words to communicate the feelings, 'cause they're not the same thing at all, at all.

I: So you're becoming aware of the struggle in moving between those two?

C: Well, no, uh—it's not so much the struggle, but I'm very aware of how they are two very different states in a way that I've never been before.

I: Right.

C: Interesting, that uh, that being in the feeling, trying to find the words to communicate the feeling means trying to pull yourself out of the feeling (pp. 341–342).

Turning to her third and final category of productive silence, reflective pauses, Levitt sees these as moments of increased awareness in which clients appear to recognize the significance of experiences and then shift their narrative exploration accordingly. They are, in a manner of speaking, stepping back to get their bearings. She writes that one client put it this way:

Again that's … a silence of being with the awareness …. And as I recall the awareness of kind of coming back to myself, and I was going to say, a certain poignancy, I love that word. There's a certain poignancy of coming back to that place of refueling (p. 343).

She notes how another client recalled that,

In that moment I was literally doing an "A-ha! Oh my god!" Like maybe for me this might be a pattern. I might be depressed and not aware of it at all …. It was very much an "a-ha moment." Like Oh my god. Maybe that whole period. So it was identifying something (p. 343).

Clients speak of experiencing joy at such moments, and of a desire to take the time to allow things to "click" before verbally describing the idea to the therapist. For this reason, among others, Levitt suggests that therapists may wish to direct clients to lengthen their silences in order "to give them the time to check to see if their initial response fits". How different this is from the world of much of the media, where participants in broadcast programmes are not expected to pause for any noticeable period. Broadcasters fear having "dead time" on air. Levitt's research strongly indicates that such time is by no means "dead", even if it may be disturbing for others.

In a more recent study (2010), Stringer, Levitt and others have suggested in reference to various understandings of silence in therapy that "process research that distinguishes among various kinds of silences can exact more precision for understanding the role of silence in psychotherapy" than can purely empirical studies (Stringer et al., p. 497).

The silence of a client or a patient may be productive or unproductive, and in either case it challenges the therapist to observe her or his own reaction to it and then to respond skilfully. Consider, for example, the case of two analysts (Fuller & Crowther) who have worked with patients whose silences stretched over years. The two believe that persistently silent patients are projecting onto their therapists a need for containment, "which they [patients] can then disavow, leaving the analyst carrying the need, and feeling helpless, baffled and undermined". In the experience of these analysts, such patients taxed to the very limit their professional selves and their therapeutic repertoire of responses and techniques. The therapists found destructive fantasies developing in themselves in response to the lack of verbal interaction with their patients. They were able to counteract this destructive effect on the analyst-patient relationship by discussing between themselves what chronic analytic silence may mean.

Silent callers

The question of silence takes on a particularly trying aspect in the case of callers to crisis centres. According to Scott and Lester, for example, when suicide prevention services first began using the telephone as a primary mode for counselling it became necessary to develop techniques for responding effectively to the "silent caller". A person may be suicidal but cannot get past just telephoning and saying nothing. Scott herself, as chairman of the Samaritans, and Lester, as a former president of the International Association for Suicide Prevention, had each had extensive experience of suicide cases. Given the worrying incidence of suicide, including among young people, it is worth noting their advice that, "There is a need for individuals, for society, to listen to silence" (pp. 106–107). Brockopp and

Lester advise that no silent caller should be perceived as being a "problem caller" but rather a caller with problems, and no call should be regarded as a nuisance. Just being there and listening can help (p. 199). Scott and Lester cite the example of 16-year-old Susan, trying to complete important examinations while coping with a mother who was drunk each day by lunchtime. Her doctor recommended that she call a local "Befrienders Center". She did so many times, but always remained silent. Later, she explained that her experience of the centre had helped her through a crisis:

> To dial the number (…) and hear a voice was all that I needed. I was locked into my mind, my thoughts, my whole body. Words would not come—I felt strangled, voiceless (….) For weeks I phoned the Center, and always someone answered—the comfort of listening to a person! (….) I was sorry to be a nuisance but I needed someone to care for me, to worry about me, to listen to me (….) I knew it stopped me hurting myself; well, I mean killing myself. I made these calls late at night. Always after my parents had finished fighting and screaming and killing each other. The noise was tremendous, yet they loved each other. I don't think they loved me—I was never noticed (….) Twenty years ago this happened; all I can say is that each year I send a card to that center to say "thank you" (pp. 106–107).

These authors also relate the sad story of one of the first patients of a recently qualified psychiatrist. A young woman in her early twenties had been referred to the psychiatrist by her family doctor for eight sessions of psychotherapy. Each week, for five weeks, she did not talk but sat in silence. At the end of the fifth session, perturbed by her behaviour, the psychiatrist suggested to his patient that she was wasting both her time and his by sitting in complete silence, and that she should only make the next appointment with his secretary when she was ready to talk. On the following day, she committed suicide. Fifteen years later, the psychiatrist still felt bad about his failure to listen more attentively. The authors write that,

> (….) Listening to the silence is an essential role for counselors who are helping clients in crisis. Much of the pain, the suicidal feelings, and the turmoil are often shrouded in silence both for

the individual and for society as a whole. Communication is the focus of crisis intervention and befriending, and counselors are sometimes very uncomfortable at sharing the silence of their callers. But silence is an important aspect of human interaction; for, after all, verbal communication consists only of words strung together on a background of silence. Silence can have different meanings. It is not simply an absence of words; it can be an *active presence* (p. 108).

Silent therapists

So far, we have been mainly considering silences on the client's or patient's side. Silence on the part of a therapist may serve many purposes, not all of which are pleasing to a patient even if they are ultimately beneficial. Knowing that the silence of an analyst may frustrate a patient who him or herself falls silent and "backs away from even the shadow of demand", Lacan explained that analysts can use their own silence "in order to allow the signifiers with which the [patient's] frustration is bound up to reappear" (1958, p. 516). However, Sabbadini cautions that "Silence is part of communication and as such it can take place only within a relationship: it is an interpersonal phenomenon." He writes of a case where the therapist found that,

> Miss C's silences often created for me a serious technical problem. I knew that she was likely to experience my letting her stay quiet as evidence of my lack of understanding and caring; at the same time, I also knew that she would have experienced my breaking her silence as a painful and persecutory intrusion into her space. Pointing out my dilemma to Miss C was at times the only way to break through this impasse (pp. 235–236).

Sabbadini adds that the analyst can "feel acutely the need, almost an urge, to fill the vacuum; to say *something* without knowing *what* to say". That he regards this as a potentially catastrophic intrusion is implict in his remark that the danger of flooding a quiet patient with words reminds him of how some US soldiers who entered Nazi extermination camps in 1945 inadvertently caused the death of starving survivors by overfeeding them.

The therapist can use silence to communicate safety, understanding and containment but, as Lane, Koetting, and Bishop point out, "... if this intervention is not skilfully and sensitively employed by the practitioner, the client may feel the therapist's quietness as distance, disinterest and disengagement, leading to breaches in the trust and safety of the therapeutic alliance" (p. 1091). One might add that the client may also feel short-changed as a customer, that they are not getting therapeutic bang for their buck.

In a recent survey of 81 licensed therapists, who were experienced members of the American Psychological Association, respondents reported that they use silence primarily to facilitate reflection, encourage responsibility, facilitate expression of feelings, not interrupt session flow, and convey empathy. They said that, during silences, they observe the client, think about the therapy and convey their interest. According to Hill, Thompson, and Ladany's account of that survey, "Most indicated that they would use silence with clients who were actively problem solving, but they were more hesitant about using silence with all other types of clients" (p. 514). They did not use it where clients might misunderstand their motivation, had a history of silence being used as punishment, or were psychotic, paranoid, or potentially dangerous to themselves or to others. This survey found that basic helping-skills texts for therapists barely mention when and how to use silence, "raising questions about how therapists use silence in therapy and about how they learn about using silence" (ibid.). The authors note that both the theoretical and empirical literatures, some of which they briefly review, are contradictory about the advisability and effects of using silence in therapy.

Hill, Thompson, and Ladany's survey also found that the length that a therapist had been in practice did not significantly correlate with his or her attitude towards silence. However, male therapists more often than female ones used silence as a shield or boundary with all clients, and all therapists used silence as a shield or boundary more often with male clients as opposed to female clients. The authors conclude that, "... silence appeared to be more defensively used by and with men, which poses interesting questions for future naturalistic studies" (p. 522). They found also that a therapist's theoretical orientation was related to how he or she thought about using silence. Psychodynamic therapists more often used it to facilitate reflection, which fits with their emphasis on insight, while humanistic therapists more often used it to convey empathy, respect, and support. This is a useful reminder of how our own disposition or particular experience influences our choice of methods.

The spiritual in therapy

One very particular theoretical orientation is that of Piotr Rajski. He is a psychologist based in Edmonton, Alberta, who practises silence on his own, and sometimes with his patients, in the form of "Contemplative Prayer". He describes this technique as a mode of self-purification and self-balancing on the part of the therapist, and stipulates that "silence is a royal way to discovering God" (pp. 181–190). He believes that, upon finding this "divine particle" within oneself, the therapist is no longer alone with the client, "but God becomes an active participant in the therapeutic process through His love for both therapist and client". Clearly, such a technique will not be to the taste of some therapists and/or their clients, and may be quite inappropriate in some circumstances. But Rajski is convinced of its value. He writes,

> Around 1982 I had a patient in mania, which manifested itself mainly through his constant talking. The patient would fill every session with fast, uninterrupted, intensive talk, making sure that I wouldn't be able to say anything. I was a young and inexperienced therapist at that time and the dynamics of the situation were quite frustrating for me. Out of sheer despair I asked the patient to close his eyes. I don't remember how I persuaded him to do so, but he eventually complied.
>
> What happened next was amazing for me. He continued his fast talk for a while, but after about five minutes began to slow down. He also started to be more thoughtful about what he was saying. In another few minutes he was completely still. He started to breathe more deeply and to be aware of his body. He was silent for the rest of the session and I was silent with him (pp. 181–182).
>
> When he finally opened his eyes he was a transformed person. He noticed me and began to interact with me. We were no

longer a therapist and a patient—we were two human beings
who had finally met.

Rajski's story is impressive, albeit marred perhaps by his subsequent
admission that the patient never returned. But Rajski writes that he
had information from the patient's employer that his employee's
functioning, thereafter, dramatically improved.

The place of religious considerations in family guidance or therapy can be controversial. Internationally, many counsellors of couples are themselves associated with organizations that have their
origins in, or affiliations with, religious bodies. Secular therapists
may sniff at such counsellors broaching spiritual matters with their
clients, but secular therapists can themselves be accused of not having had the sort of religious experience that many clients regard as
a real and valuable part of everyday life, and of being ill-equipped
to help those who have had such experiences. The place of silence
in religion and meditation, as discussed in the next chapter, and its
place in therapy need to be understood as each has a potential value
in its own right.

In 1990, Bergin and Jensen compared the religiosity of several psychotherapy disciplines (psychiatrists, psychologists, social workers,
and marriage and family therapists) with those of the lay public.
They discovered that marriage and family therapists were the most
religious and that their way of life in this regard most resembled that
of lay people. Nevertheless, notwithstanding this ostensible fact, the
authors of one recent US study of family therapists' beliefs about
the appropriateness of addressing religious and spiritual issues in
therapy write that, "For many years the literature in the field of
family therapy was silent as to the religious and spiritual aspects
of clients' lives" (Carlson et al., p. 157). This seems to have been a
remarkable omission, given the role of religion in the world and its
special place in the lives of so many people. However, these authors
also note that the situation has significantly changed for the better in
recent times. They surveyed a large number of marriage and family
therapists and found that no less than 95% believed themselves to be
spiritual persons, with 82% stating that they "regularly spent time
getting in touch with their spirituality" and 71% praying regularly.
Most regarded their careers as part of their spiritual development.
The authors also found that "a surprising 95% of the respondents

believed in the relationship between spiritual and mental health", although just 62% believed that a spiritual dimension should be considered in clinical practice, 68% that it was appropriate for therapists to ask clients about their spirituality, and just 42% that it was appropriate to help clients to develop their own spirituality. This survey notably found too that when the word "religion" was used instead of "spirituality", there was a drop in the percentages of respondents who considered it a relevant factor. One may speculate that this drop signifies a fear on the part of therapists that if they are seen to be "religious" rather than simply "spiritual" then they may be thought more likely to proselytize or to be narrowly sectarian. Incidentally, more than three quarters of the respondent therapists had received no training in spirituality. The overall response rate was only 38% (153 out of 400 randomly selected members of the American Association for Marriage and Family Therapy) and the authors acknowledge that, "... it is quite possible that ... those who were not interested in these topics chose not to participate" (ibid., p. 169). It may also be noted that the survey did not measure behaviour but attitudes.

The survey by Carlson and others raises questions about the silence of some therapists in respect to spiritual or religious matters. One participant is quoted as arguing,

> While I have heard therapists say that religion and spirituality should only be talked about if the client opens the door by raising the issue, I am concerned about the effect of what we don't say as therapists. If we don't at least let clients know that we are willing to talk about their spiritual lives if they feel it would be helpful to therapy, then what we don't say is in effect telling them that it is not ok to talk about these things (ibid., p. 168).

However, while many of the respondents in the survey were well disposed to opening the door in therapy to a discussion of religious or spiritual matters, there is no indication that any would go as far as Rajski, above, whose own experiences of religious contemplation have inclined him to encourage clients to be silently contemplative during psychotherapy.

So far, we have been considering the negative and positive aspects of silence in the context of one-to-one therapeutic analysis. Silence also frequently arises as a relevant factor when group psychotherapy is in progress, on the part of a single member or sub-group, or even on the part of the group leader or whole group. Gans and the aptly named Counselman, his co-author at the Harvard Medical School, have identified five common sources of silence in group psychotherapy. They note (2000) that, "Silence can reflect defenses or indicate conditions favourable to intensified group work." They argue that, "Silence, sometimes mistaken for psychological inactivity, should be viewed as significant communication."

Inarticulacy

In considering the relationship between therapy and silence, it is appropriate to refer to the experiences of those for whom disabilities either prevent or grossly inhibit verbal articulation. In such cases, silence is not so much a particular form of expression as it is expression's prison. Taking time to hear the voices of people thus burdened may be a challenge that requires special patience and consideration, as well as the employment of therapeutic techniques and resources that are appropriate in specific circumstances.

For a person with a debilitating speech impediment, the spaces between words loom large. Watching old newsreels of King George VI (1895–1952) struggling to overcome his severe stammer as he addressed the people of Britain during wartime, one understands that the recent Oscar-winning film about his efforts might have been as aptly entitled "The King's Silence" as it is actually entitled *The King's Speech* (2010).

The category of those who are unable to talk because of a physical disability must be distinguished from that of the socially silenced. The latter, for particular cultural or political reasons, feel constrained from speaking their minds. Their excluded voices have been discussed in an earlier chapter. The former would speak if they physically could.

Christopher Nolan has told the story of one physically disabled person who overcame some of his difficulties. His autobiographical *Under the Eye of the Clock* was published when he was 21, and it won Britain's Whitbread Book of the Year Award. Deprived of oxygen, Nolan had almost died at birth. His injuries left him quadriplegic and unable to communicate in clearly formed words. For years, his mind burned to express his thoughts and ideas. Medication facilitated the movement of his neck muscles, and his mother patiently and painstakingly helped him to learn to work a keyboard by affixing a stick to his forehead. He also attended, in Dublin, the Central Remedial Clinic School and Mount Temple Comprehensive. Nolan's first book appeared in 1981, a collection of poetry that was appropriately entitled *Dam-burst of Dreams*. Six years later came *Under the Eye of the Clock*, in the introduction to which John Carey wrote of Nolan that,

> He plummeted into language like an avalanche, as if it were his one escape route from death—which, of course, it was. He had been locked for years in the coffin of his body, unable to utter. When he found words he played rapturously with them, making them riot and lark about, echoing, alliterating and falling over one another.

Another disability that can leave minds trapped in a kind of silence is autism. Here, too, stories have emerged from people who once might have been unheard. They include Sean Barron and Tito Mukhopadhyay and Donna Williams. It would be rash and even cruel to interpret their success as meaning that all autistic children can be enabled to write coherently, if only those closest to them try hard enough to help. The challenge is not that simple, not least because autism is a term used to cover a spectrum of disorders. Nevertheless, referring in a broadcast interview in 2003 to Tito Mukhopadhyay, Dr Mike Merzenich, who is a neuroscientist at the University of California at San Francisco, said (CBS) that, "Here we have a boy that largely through the empirical interaction of this boy with his mother, a way has been found into his ability, into his spirit .... I think there could be thousands, maybe tens of thousands of Titos out there." Tito has written hundreds of poems, including one that CBS watched him write from beginning to end.

A woman called Fini was the subject of a 1971 film documentary entitled *Land des Schweigens und der Dunkelheit* (*Land of Silence and Darkness*). Fini, aged 56, had been blind and deaf since her late teens. Having spent 30 years confined by her mother to her bed, she struggled to overcome her isolation and to help others similarly afflicted. Directed and produced by the great German filmmaker Werner Herzog, the documentary listens to one of those who have been silent because of disabilities that seem unbearable to many citizens. The struggle for such a person and for her or his family is formidable, as can be seen also from the earlier and better-known case of Helen Keller (1880–1968) of Alabama. Helped by her teacher Annie Sullivan, who was "a dark-haired Irish orphan raised in a poorhouse" (Herrmann, p. 3), Helen was the first deaf and blind person to be awarded an arts degree in the United States and her story was later dramatized in a 1959 Broadway play and a 1962 film, both starring Anne Bancroft and Patty Duke and both called *The Miracle Worker*.

Another person who has struggled against adversity has been Guido Nasi, an Italian student who came to Ireland to learn English. He was 17 years old and it was his first time living away from home. In 1999, he and his friends were playing football in Fairview Park. They were joined for a short while by some Dublin youths but, as these departed, Nasi realized that his wallet was missing. He chased and grabbed the youth whom he believed had stolen it. Two of the latter's acquaintances struck Nasi. As the confrontation continued, a man intervened and advised the boys to flee before the Gardai (the Irish police) arrived. As Nasi turned away, that same man hit him on the head with a bottle partly filled with lager. Nasi fell to the ground banging his head on the pavement. Nasi ended up almost totally paralyzed from the neck down. His attacker was caught and confessed. The court heard that the assailant, aged 29 at the time of the assault, was an alcoholic who had been drinking for most of the day of the attack. The court was told that the assault was "fuelled by drink and rage". A letter from Guido Nasi was read to the court. It had been prepared with great difficulty and with the assistance of others. Its tone captured the sense of loss and shock experienced by such victims. He asked,

> Why can't I read or write? Why can't I go to school, which I enjoyed so much and which gave me so much satisfaction? Why am I living such a monotonous life without all the activities of young people of my age which are my rights? Why, when my friends have finished university, will I be still waiting to finish school? Why will I always be separated from my friends when they go ahead and I stand still? Why me? Why?

During an unsuccessful appeal by the assailant against the length of that sentence, Mr Justice Hugh Geoghegan said that the phrase "a fate worse than death" came to mind when one contemplated Guido Nasi's condition. Two years after the attack, Guido Nasi was back in Dublin, in a wheelchair, to thank Irish people for the support that he had received. His condition had improved slightly following treatment at an Austrian clinic, yet he faced a bleak future. He was reported to have limited power in one hand but to have managed to complete a collection of poetry, entitled "Just look into my eyes: verses from a silent bed".

Another form of silence is that of persons who have learning difficulties. During the past 25 years there has been a much greater effort than before to engage such people. For example, in 1996, Tim and Wendy Booth of the Department of Sociological Studies at the University of Sheffield addressed the challenge of using narrative methods with people who have learning difficulties, focusing especially on the problems of inarticulateness and unresponsiveness. They have explained that a revival of academic interest in narrative methods inspired them to explore the value of such methods in respect of one group that was frequently in the past ignored by researchers, namely people with learning disorders. They acknowledge the fact that researchers have recently been talking and listening more than before to such people:

> For the most part, however, informants with learning difficulties have been regarded mainly as sources of data for researchers' narratives rather than people with their own stories to tell. This marks the crucial difference between narrative research and interview research. In the former it is the voice of the subject that determines the frame of reference of the narrative (Booth, p. 56).

In this context, it is worth asking ourselves how many times each of us has used research data principally to support our own narrative even where our informant has quite a different understanding of the meaning or significance of what he/she has told us.

Some inarticulacy derives from social oppression and is exacerbated by poverty and poor education. Whether principally social or principally personal, its manifestations include a limited ability to answer certain types of question, especially that open-ended style of question regarded as desirable in narrative research. Some informants also have difficulties in generalizing from experience, in giving meaning to the present by reflecting on and evaluating the past. A strong orientation on the present may also indicate that questions about time and frequency should be avoided as the informant may, for social reasons, "lack many of the milestones people use to order their past". These are all matters of relevance when considering the silence of the inarticulate:

> People who are able to express themselves easily give direction to the interview by what they say. With people who are not talkative the researcher has to be more attentive to what goes unsaid, and to learn to distinguish between an expressive silence (waiting to be broken) and a closed silence (waiting to be passed over).
>
> There are no easy rules for distinguishing these two types of silence, except that the researcher should not give up too quickly. The clues are usually personal and idiosyncratic, and are picked up only by getting to know the informant. For this reason, interviews with inarticulate subjects should normally be spread over several sessions, and where possible supplemented by time spent with the person in other settings and situations (Booth, pp. 56–57 and 63–64).

This is useful advice, but one wonders how many academics or journalists in our busy world of must-publish and publish quickly will be attracted to such painstaking preparation in order to hear what the inarticulate truly wish to say. Referring to the informant who is the principal object of consideration in their article, the Booths admit that,

> Danny Avebury's story represents meagre pickings for almost two-and-a-half hours of interview time. A Studs Terkel or Tony Parker would not make a living out of the Danny Aveburys of the world (p. 66).

Among researchers noted for their efforts to listen to those who often are regarded as inarticulate was Louis "Studs" Terkel (1912–2008), a US historian of poverty and war who gathered personal recollections across a broad spectrum of society. Tony Parker (1923–1996) was a foremost British interviewer of the marginalized.

CHAPTER EIGHT

Sacred silence

There is a special if seldom used word for someone who observes or recommends silence, especially from religious motives, or for an official whose duty is to command silence. That word is "silentiary". Whether official or unofficial silentiaries, there have always been those who bid silence or who practised silence for broadly spiritual purposes.

Egyptians

Priestly documents from Ancient Egypt and Mesopotamia are said to have "frequently" contained prescriptions of silence (McEvilley, p. 285). The Egyptian god Horus was depicted in statuettes as a somewhat cherubic child with a finger in, or to, his mouth. The Greeks came to regard him as the god of silence, naming him Harpocrates, whence it appears that the silent clown of the Marx Brothers comedy team was named Harpo. However, Plutarch writes,

> Nor are we to understand Harpocrates to be either some imperfect or infant God, or a God of pulse (as some will have him), but to be the governor and reducer of the tender, imperfect,

and inarticulate discourse which men have about the Gods.
For which reason, he hath always his finger upon his mouth, as
a symbol of talking little and keeping silence. Likewise, upon
the month of Mesore, they present him with certain pulse, and
pronounce these words: "The tongue is Fortune, the tongue is
God" (W. Goodwin, vol. 4, p. 125).

"Pulse" here indicates edible leguminous seeds, or the plants themselves from which such seeds come. They can include peas, beans,
and lentils. A "God of pulse" might be a primitive fertility deity.

Indians

In Indian literature of the late Vedic period, there is a striking
acknowledgement of the place of silence in religious ritual. This
occurs in the Satapatha Brahmana, which is regarded by some scholars as being the most significant of all the Brahmanas that were written down between about 800 and 600 BC (Tull, p. 7). The section of
this lengthy work in which the following passage occurs deals with
a complicated ritual concerning the construction of the Fire Altar.
One reason why that ritual is important is that, according to Eggeling, "There seems, indeed, some reason to believe that it was elaborated with a definite object in view, viz. that of making the external
rites and ceremonies of the sacrifical cult the practical devotional
expression of certain dominant speculative theories of the time"
(1897, p. xiv), which is to say that the Brahmana's description of the
ritual reflects a world-view that is more advanced and complex than
what preceded it. Eggeling explains that Pragapati is *the* god above
all other gods: "But Agni, the god of fire, is created by Pragapati, and
he subsequently restores Pragapati by giving up his own body (the
fire-altar) to build up anew the dismembered Lord of Creatures and
by entering into him with his own fiery spirit—'whence, while being
Pragapati, they yet call him Agni'" (1897, pp. xix–xxi). Agni is said
to be master and guest of every house (Winternitz, I, pp. 88–90 and
201). Eggeling also notes that,

> 28. These (verses) have one and the same explanation with
> regard to this (Agni-Pragâpati [= God]), how he may heal him,

and preserve him. They are anushtubh verses—the Anushtubh is speech, and speech is all healing medicine: by means of all healing medicine he thus heals him.

29. Now, then, regarding the defined and the undefined (ceremonies)—with prayer he yokes two oxen, silently the others; with prayer he ploughs four furrows, silently the others; silently he puts on the grass-bush, with prayer he makes a libation thereon; silently he pours out the jarfuls of water, with prayer he sows.

30. This Agni is Pragâpati, and Pragâpati is both the defined and the undefined, the limited and the unlimited. Now whatever he does with prayer thereby he restores that form of his which is defined, limited; and whatever he does silently, thereby he restores that form of his which is undefined, unlimited—verily, whosoever, knowing this, performs thus, restores this whole and complete Pragâpati. The outer forms are defined, and the inner ones are undefined; and Agni is the same as an animal: hence the outer forms of the animal are defined, and the inner ones undefined (1894, pp. 340–342).

When a new Indian temple was being built, silence might be enjoined throughout a whole city. This, writes, McEvilley, is a case of "euphemia" or ritual silence—"the prohibition against speaking when the gods are listening lest something ill-omened might be said" (p. 270).

Silence continues today to have an important place in Indian religious practice. Writing about the life of total renunciation to which the *sannyasi(n)* is committed, the French Benedictine monk known as Swami Abhishiktananda (1910–1973) stated that, "Always he will remember that his essential obligation is to silence, solitude, meditation (*dhyana*), and this he can never abandon" (pp. 46–47). He quoted from Mahatma Gandhi's letters to the Ashram:

> The sannyasi has renounced the society of men to live in silence and solitude. Even when he moves among men, he will not indulge in idle conversation …. Yet the sadhu's lack of interest in the personalities and events of the world does not at all mean that he is a self-centred egotist. Quite the reverse … (p. 8).

Jews

Silence was also being praised by Jewish sages who lived centuries before the birth of Christ. In the texts known as the Babylonian "Talmud" ("Teaching"), it is recorded that 120 elders had earlier drawn up prayers "in the proper order" and that Simeon the Takulite had reformulated them afresh when they were forgotten. Beyond these formulated prayers, it was "forbidden to declare the praise of the Holy One, blessed be He":

> For R[abbi]. Eleazar said: What is the meaning of the verse, *Who can express the mighty acts of the Lord, or make all his praise to be heard* [Psalms 106:2]? ... *Should a man [try to] say, surely he would be swallowed up* [Job 37:20. English Version, "*Or should a man wish that he were swallowed up*"]. R. Judah a man of Kefar Gibboraya, or, as some say of Kefar Gibbor Hayil, gave the following homily: what is meant by the verse, *For thee silence is praise* [Psalms 65:2. E. V., "*Praise waiteth for thee*"]? The best medicine of all is silence. When R. Dimi came, he said: In the West [Palestine] they say: A word is worth a *sela'*, silence two *sela's* (Epstein, at "Megillah" 18a, pp. 108–109).

A *sela'* is a silver coin from Tyre, weighing 14.34 grams and equivalent to a shekel (Funk & Wagnalls, xii, p. 485). While Cohen suggests (p. 106) that a modern saying, "Speech is silver, silence golden", has its "counterpart" in the older saying about *sela's*, it is going too far to attribute the modern version to the Talmud as Stevenson (*Proverbs*, p. 2108) and Flavell (p. 217) appear to do.

So what was the nature of these Jewish silences? The *Oxford Dictionary of the Jewish Religion* (1997, p. 644) suggests that, "Silent prayer seems to have been unknown in ancient times, when worshippers called on God with a loud voice or at least moved their lips" as Hannah did (1 Samuel 1:13). Yet, the Mishnah clearly indicates that silence long ago had some place in Jewish worship. This is evident from the passage from the Talmud just quoted above, and from this extract from the later "Tractata Berakoth" ("Benedictions"):

> None may stand up to say the *Tefillah* save in sober mood. The pious men of old used to wait an hour before they said the

> *Tefillah*, that they might direct their hearts towards God. Even if
> the king salutes a man he may not return the greeting; and even
> if a snake was twisted around his heel he may not interrupt his
> prayer.

The translator of this tract, Danby, remarks that such silence was
required in addition to the immersion prescribed for the purification of the men's particular major uncleanness (*Mishnah*, p. 5).
A. L. Williams states (p. 35) that the word in the passage quoted here
that is translated as "God" means literally "the Place" (p. 35).

People are prepared to wait in silence until those whom they consider to be wise speak (Wisdom 8:12). Being silent in the face of God
can be a sign of reverence or fear or of expectation that He is about to
communicate by word or deed, as He did when the Jewish prophet
Elijah emerged into silence at the cave on Horeb (1 Kings 19:12–13;
Zephaniah 1:7; Zechariah 2:13; Amos 8:3; Psalms 62:1 and 5; Psalms
65:7). For, "… the Lord is in his holy temple; let all the earth keep
silence before him!" (Habakkuk 2:19–20). The Lord's "word" may be
heard directly in the mind or heart of the believer.

Greeks

Silence was also an important aspect of the rites of popular mystery cults in the ancient world. Initiates were expected to keep their
mouths closed about what transpired on feast-days, and silence
itself was reverentially and symbolically incorporated into the
ceremonies. Writing in the early third century after Christ, (Saint)
Hippolytus recalled that,

> The Phrygians also say, however, that he ["the Perfect man"
> who has knowledge of man and God] is a "green ear of corn
> reaped"; and following the Phrygians, the Athenians when
> initiating (any one) into the Eleusian (Mysteries) also show to
> those who have been made epopts [initiated to a certain level]
> the mighty and wonderful and most perfect of mysteries for
> an epopt there—a green ear of corn reaped in silence [Cruice,
> p. 171 omits this second "green"]. And this ear of corn is also,
> for the Athenians, the great and perfect spark of light from the
> Unportrayable One (Legge, vol. 1, p. 138).

Sourvinou-Inwood speculates that the ear of corn was displayed in silence as the sign of the divine advent rather than, as Hippolytus thought, reaped in silence as a kind of radiant reflection of the divine that cannot be portrayed. Hippolytus, he believes, engaged in "a transformation, a reinterpretation through Christian filters" (pp. 35–37).

This symbolical display of the ear of corn was unsurprising, for Eleusis was the centre of the cult of Demeter, fertility goddess of farming communities, who was sometimes depicted crowned with an ear of corn. Lying about 20 kilometres west of Athens, Eleusis was perhaps second only to Delphi as a place of religious importance in ancient Greece. The fact that initiates were bound to silence means that we have scant information about aspects of the cult and its ceremonies, which ignorance is no bad thing so far as the Christian Gregory was concerned. He wrote sarcastically, "Eleusis knows these things, and so do those who were spectators of the things about which silence is kept and which are indeed worthy of silence" (cited at Sourvinou-Inwood, p. 29).

It is the case that this kind of silence or secrecy was also associated with the school of the Greek philosopher Pythagoras (c575–c495 BC), who trained in Egypt and whose pupils were later said to have kept "no ordinary silence". Its extraordinary nature appears to have extended beyond a certain respect for their teacher and beyond discretion about their group's proceedings to become a form of self-discipline for which they were respected. However, dressed only in worn cloaks and putting their property into common ownership—and using as sacrificial offerings humble dried figs, the pulp of pressed olives and cheese—these pious Pythagoreans also found themselves satirically characterized by the poet Alexis and others for their "eating little, filth, frost, silence, gloominess and being unwashed" (Riedweg & Rendall, pp. 39, 60, 62, 106, and 108). Plutarch observes that the Pythagoreans would not eat fish because they respected the fishes' silence, "and they thought silence to be divine, since the Gods without any voice discover their meaning to the wise by their works" (W. Goodwin, vol. 3, p. 422). And the silence of Pythagoras's pupils was said by Busiris to have earned them admiration greater than that bestowed on people who had the greatest reputation for speaking (C. H. Kahn, pp. 8, 12, and 83).

In a text associated with the Pythagorean School we find advice that, "gods should always be worshipped with pious silence". That this was not a universal requirement in Greek ceremonies is suggested by the fact that a character in one of Menander's plays recommends, in the context of Pan's ritual, that, "In silence, one ought never to approach this god, they say" (Allinson, p. 347).

Plutarch writes that the famous Greek general, Alcibiades, was once formally cursed and had his property confiscated for enacting a mockery of the ceremonies at Eleusis. Notwithstanding that, Alcibiades still appreciated the practical value of such Mystery ceremonies and, in 407 BC, led the solemn procession to Eleusis for the first time since the Spartan enemy had occupied Decelea:

> ... taking with him the priests and Initiates and the Initiators ["*Mystae*" and "*Mystagogi*"], and encompassing them with his soldiers, he conducted them with great order and profound silence; an august and venerable procession, wherein all who did not envy him said he performed at once the office of a high priest and of a general (Clough, vol. 2, pp. 26–27 and 44).

Mithra

It is clear that silence also had a significant place in the rituals of those being initiated into the liturgy of the popular cult of Mithra, which spread across the Roman world about the time of Christ. Initiates were told to expect to see the gods staring intently at them and rushing them, and were advised that they should then,

> Immediately lay your right finger on your mouth and say "Silence! Silence! Silence! Symbol of the living, imperishable God!" (Dieterich, p. 42).

Silence was invoked a number of times during this ceremony. Cumont, who worked extensively on Mithraic sources, notes that, at the ceremony of initiation ("*sacramentum*"), "The candidate engaged above all things not to divulge the doctrines and rites revealed to him ..." (p. 156). It appears that such secrecy also became part of the practice of some early Ophite heretics (Legge, pp. 132, 139, and 171; Cruice, pp. 160–161, 208, and 226).

In a discourse on "Talkativeness", Plutarch (c45–120) writes that,

> ... the gods teach us to be silent, silence being enjoined on us in the mysteries and in all religious rites. Thus Homer has described the most eloquent Odysseus, and Telemachus, and Penelope, and the nurse, as all remarkable for their taciturnity (1898, p. 221).

Plutarch also notes that, "... when there is dead silence in any assembly they say Hermes has joined the company" (1898, p. 215).

Ancient customs

It is clear that silence has played a role in the religious or sacred proceedings of many peoples, enhancing the experience by rendering it more efficacious. Whether or not one considers such silences sacred or magical is a matter of cultural perspective. Living among the Yucares people in the foothills of the Andes, in what is now central Bolivia, a Franciscan friar called Lacueva found in the early 1800s that the manufacture of pottery was not an everyday event there. There were special rituals to be observed when it was undertaken. The task was reserved for women who proceeded solemnly to look for the appropriate clay and to retreat to the most sequestered parts of the forest. There they built a hut: "While they are at work they observe certain ceremonies and never open their mouth, speaking to each other by signs, being persuaded that one word spoken would infallibly cause all their pots to break in the firing" (Lacueva MS, cited at Frazer, vol. 2, 204–205, from d'Orbigny).

At Cape Coast Castle, on 9 October 1844, a missionary named John Martin recorded details of an annual and very noisy festival that involved people driving out an evil spirit called Abonsam. The castle, situated in what is today the state of Ghana, had that same year become the centre of administration for the British colony of Gold Coast. It also long served as a centre of the slave trade and, for that reason, in 2009 Barack Obama and his family visited Cape Coast Castle during his first trip to Africa as US president. On the particular evening described in 1844, as soon as the 8 o'clock gun sounded at the castle, local residents started shouting and beating about their homes with sticks and firing muskets. This noise surely seemed all the louder because, as Martin noted,

> The custom is preceded by four weeks' dead silence; no gun is allowed to be fired, no drum to be beaten, no palaver to be made between man and man. If, during these weeks, two natives should disagree and make a noise in the town, they are immediately taken before the king and fined heavily. If a dog or pig, sheep or goat be found at large in the street, it may be killed, or taken by any one, the former owner not being allowed to demand any compensation. This silence is designed to deceive Abonsam, that, being off his guard, he may be taken by surprise and frightened out of the place. If any one die during the silence, his relatives are not allowed to weep until the four weeks have been completed (Tremearne, pp. 138–139).

It is said that a secular manifestation of ritual silence in this part of Africa was "silent trade", which reportedly occurred when Ghanaian merchants laid out goods for examination by miners who knew to leave gold in return if they wished to keep an item. Drums were used to signal stages in the transaction as each party to it withdrew (e.g., Collins, p. 6). However, de Moraes Farias questions the evidence for such "dumb barter".

Ancient European religious customs have also involved silence, as Frazer observed. He recorded the fact that at San Pietro in Calabria, southern Italy, for example, "… they plunge into the river on the night of Easter Saturday before Easter Sunday dawns, and while they bathe they never utter a word." In the villages on the River Leine in Germany, "… servant men and maids used to go silently on Easter night between the hours of eleven and twelve and silently draw water in buckets from the river." They mixed this water with animal fodder and washed in it, believing it to be especially good. They also believed that "at the same mysterious hour" the water turned into a kind of wine until the crowing of a cock could be heard, so they placed their tongues in the water and took gulps (vol. 10, pp. 29 and 123–124).

In some parts of Europe it was commonly believed that silently picking particular plants at Midsummer's Eve made them especially efficacious for certain purposes. For example, in Germany,

Thüringen peasants hold that if the root of the yellow *mullein* (Verbascum ["Our Lady's Flannel"]) has been dug up in silence with a ducat [gold coin] at midnight on Midsummer's Eve, and is worn in a piece of linen next to the skin, it will preserve the wearer from epilepsy (Frazer, vol. 11, p. 63).

Similarly, in the Prussian principality known as the Mark of Brandenburg, people kept silence on Midsummer's Eve while cutting a branch of hazel to serve as a divining rod. Elsewhere, those passing a ruptured or rickety child through a cleft tree or creeping through a hoop of willow as a cure kept silent (Frazer, vol. 9, p. 58, and vol. 11, pp. 67, 171 and 184).

Quakers

The Quakers have given silence a central place in their rituals, one related to the role of meditation in religious practice, as we shall see later. Their reason for doing so was explained in the 19th century by Caroline Stephen of York, an aunt of the novelist Virginia Woolf. She wrote that,

> It seems to me that nothing but silence can heal the wounds made by disputations in the region of the unseen. No external help, at any rate, has ever in my own experience proved so penetratingly efficacious as the habit of joining in a public worship based upon silence. Its primary attraction for me was in the fact that it pledged me to nothing, and left me altogether undisturbed to seek for help in my own way (Stephen, p. 54).

There were other benefits, too, as Stephen explained:

> And another result of the practice of silent waiting for the unseen Presence proved to be a singularly effectual preparation of mind for the willing reception of any words which might be offered "in the name of a disciple". The words spoken were indeed often feeble, and always inadequate (as all words must be in relation to Divine things), sometimes even entirely irrelevant to my own individual needs, though at other times profoundly impressive and helpful; but, coming as they

did after the long silences which had fallen like dew upon the thirsty soil, they went far deeper, and were received into a much less thorny region than had ever been the case with the words I had listened to from the pulpit (ibid., p. 55).

Irish

Some Irish Catholics themselves complain that their celebration of the liturgy is frequently a subdued affair, and compare the singing of hymns by their own congregations unfavourably with singing by members of the Anglican Church of Ireland. Explanations for any apparent lack of enthusiasm refer to centuries of colonial domination by a Protestant elite, the nature of a persecuted peasant church, the effective restriction on freedom of choice between modes of religious expression within traditional Irish Catholic communities, or simply differing cultural tastes. The silence may be a deliberate or semi-conscious holding-back from authority or a personal unwillingness to be noticed. Whatever the explanation, such an evident reluctance to sing can be unnerving for those from other places or traditions. One former Episcopalian priest who converted to Roman Catholicism in the United States (Marshall) has included among "strange and foreign elements that I still find uncomfortable" in his new environment, "the voiceless 'silent Irish' phenomenon that occurs during hymns at Mass"!

Sport

Given the fervour with which many people today approach sporting events, and the fact that some observers believe that sport fills a void in life for those to whom religion no longer appeals greatly, it is not suprising to find what in effect is a hymn to silence in sport, published on the back page of *The Times*. Writing on the eve of the English cricket team's efforts to regain "The Ashes" from Australia in 2009, that newsaper's chief sports writer reflected that,

> Some people think that the greatest moments in sport are the noisiest. They are wrong.
>   It is in silence that you find sport at its finest; that moment when thousands, utterly captivated by the same thing, cease to

speak, cease to think, cease to breathe. The match-point silence on Centre Court [Wimbledon], when you can hear the server bounce the ball on the grass; the B-of-the-bang silence before the start of the Olympic 100 metres; the pin-drop hush before the first ball of an Ashes series. All are silent. All are still .... All are waiting for a clue, perhaps for an omen; what will happen now? (Barnes)

While such silences may not precisely fulfil the same role as silences in liturgical or religious contexts, they are not entirely dissimilar from them.

The monastic rule

The ancient Indian "Bhagavadgita" refers to forms of good penance that include "calmness of mind, mildness, taciturnity, self-restraint and purity of heart" (ch. 17, s. 18, at *Bhagavadgita*, p. 119). The Hebrew scriptures remind us that there are occasions on which we should accept suffering with quiet composure:

> The Lord is good to those who wait for him,
>   to the soul that seeks him.
> It is good that one should wait quietly
>   for the salvation of the Lord.
> It is good for one to bear
>   the yoke in youth,
> To sit alone in silence
>   when the Lord has imposed it,
> To put one's mouth to the dust
>   (there may yet be hope),
> To give one's cheek to the smiter,
>   and be filled with insults (Lamentations 3:25–30).

Thus, at least for a while, Job did not open his mouth when he felt chastised by the Lord for his transgressions (Job 39:7–10).

The silence of students of Pythagoras, already discussed above, possibly extended in its nature beyond mere secrecy or reserve. McEvilley acknowledges that our understanding of the mystery cults, "or even knowledge of the Indian tradition of *mauna* or vowed silence", may prompt unwarranted assumptions about the motivation of followers of Pythagoras. Yet he finds reason enough to suspect that their practice of silence may well have involved an inner contemplative rumination on the teachings (pp. 178–179 and 182).

The association of taciturnity or silence with religious discipline was one that was recognized by early Christians. For example, during the century after the death of Christ. Ignatius of Antioch advised that,

> It is better for a man to be silent and be [a Christian], than to talk and not to be one. It is good to teach, if he who speaks also acts. There is then one Teacher, who spoke and it was done; while even those things which He did in silence are worthy of the Father. He who possesses the word of Jesus, is truly able to hear even His very silence, that he may be perfect, and may both act as he speaks, and be recognised by his silence (Roberts, Donaldson & Cleveland, at "Epistle to the Ephesians", ch. 15).

About the year AD 382, Gregory of Nazianzus was asked by a correspondent what his practice of silence signified. He replied that, "It means a right balance between talking and being silent." He told Eugenius that, "Fasting without measure is your philosophy. Mine is the discipline of silence. Let us exchange our particular gifts, and when we meet together, we shall sing to God, offering to Him the fruit of an eloquent silence, as well as of godly words" (Barrois, pp. 183–184). At the end of the fifth century, the Christian contemplative Julianus Pomerius described silence as one of the virtuous practices that could supplant vices, for "… only do vices depart if they are firmly cast out and made to give place to virtues. Otherwise, … these bide their time and return." So he advised,

> Therefore, let gentleness oppose cruelty in us; let resolute patience check anger; chastity overcome lust; calmness take away wrath; discreet silence repress loquacity; spiritual delight lessen carnal desires; the rigor of abstinence blunt the stings of the flesh … (p. 109).

The most important single document for an understanding of the spread of Christian monasticism is, after the Bible, probably the

Rule of Saint Benedict (c480–543). Benedict of Nursia in Umbria gave up his family's wealth and eventually presided over a large monastic settlement of his followers. His Rule came to be regarded as authoritative by later religious orders. Benedict vowed to serve God but also to support himself by his own labours and this self-sufficiency became a mark of his followers. His sixth rule for monastic order refers to "restraint of speech" and includes the following exhortation:

> Let us follow the Prophet's counsel: I said, I have resolved to keep watch over my ways that I may never sin with my tongue. I was silent and was humbled, and I refrained even from good words [*obmutui et humiliatus sum et silui a bonis*] (Psalms 38[39]: 2–3). Here the Prophet indicates that there are times when good words are to be left unsaid out of esteem for silence. For all the more reason, then, should evil speech be curbed so that punishment for sin may be avoided. Indeed, so important is silence [*propter taciturnitatis gravitatem*] that permission to speak should seldom be granted even to mature disciples, no matter how good or holy or constructive their talk, because it is written: *In a flood of words you will not avoid sin* (Proverbs 10:19); and elsewhere, *The tongue holds the key to life and death* (Proverbs 18:21). Speaking and teaching are the master's task; the disciple is to be silent and listen [*tacere et audire*] (Fry, p. 191).

The English word "taciturn" has something of an air of dourness as well as silence about it and, indeed, Benedict's seventh rule cautions against laughter. It states that,

> The ninth step of humility is that a monk controls his tongue and remains silent [*taciturnitatem habens*], not speaking unless asked a question, for Scripure warns, *In a flood of words you will not avoid sinning* (Proverbs 10:19), and, *A talkative man goes about aimlessly on earth* (Psalms 139[140]:12).
>
> The tenth step of humility is that he is not given to ready laughter, for it is written: *Only a fool raises his voice in laughter* (Sirach 21:23).
>
> The eleventh step of humility is that a monk speaks gently and without laughter, seriously and with becoming modesty,

briefly and reasonably, but without raising his voice, as it is written: "A wise man is known by his few words" [no source given] (ibid., p. 201. Also see p. 185, Rule 4).

Benedict cautions that if brethren are sent on a journey then, upon their return, "No one should presume to relate to anyone else what he saw or heard outside the monastery, because this causes the greatest harm" (ibid., p. 289, Rule 67). It is remarkable that Benedict's rule was composed for laymen. He was not instituting an order of clerics with clerical duties and offices but, as Ford says, "an organisation and a set of rules for the domestic life of such laymen as wished to live as fully as possible the type of life presented in the Gospel". Later, the Church imposed the clerical state on Benedictines and, with this, came a preponderance of clerical and sacerdotal duties.

In explaining the place of silence in the Rule of St Benedict, Wathen notes that,

> the term is primarily and exclusively related to silence from words and not to a broad concept of silence, a concept that would include inner tranquility and inactivity. This is not to say that these values are rejected. But they are not the primary concern (p. 14).

Wathen finds no appreciable difference between the meanings of the Latin words "*silentium*" and "*taciturnitas*" as used in the Rule to denote silence. He identifies three reasons for silence in the Rule. These are to avoid sin; for the sake of silence and gravity; and in order to listen. The listening that is encouraged by the rules is not so much the silent receptivity of Buddhist meditation but the hearing of God in "The Work of God" (offices), holy readings, and the teachings of the abbot (Wathen, pp. 26, 28, 39, 57, and 83). An even older monastic guide, "The Rule of the Master", asks and answers a germane question:

> "Why are you silent and sad and walking with a bowed head?" The monk responds: "Because I am fleeing from sin and fear God and I guard myself from all that God hates. For that reason I am always cautious" (Wathen, p. 82).

This particular "master" explains, in Chapter Eight of his Rule, that the root of man's life is his heart. Two branches rise up from the heart to the outside, one the eyes, the other the mouth. The soul looks out on the world through the eyes. It "emits sounds in the external world" through the mouth. The mouth is a gate, its teeth are the bars. If evil thoughts rise up and find the mouth shut then they are "turned back to the heart where they will be dashed to pieces" (Wathen, pp. 80–81).

The existence of such rules may create the impression that all Christian monks are dour and that their monasteries are glum places. This is by no means invariably the case. A certain joy can come to fill corridors as individual monks use the silence to cultivate spiritual values and to demonstrate charity to their neighbours and visitors, to whom they are allowed to speak when appropriate. In any event, the rules of most Christian monasteries today are considerably more relaxed than they used once to be.

Religious Christians were not alone in appreciating that a primary benefit of silence is the avoidance of troublesome speech. One of the central figures in the history of Tibetan Buddhism is Milarepa, whose story of hardship for the sake of spiritual enlightenment is often recounted and who is frequently depicted sitting in a meditative position while silently cupping his ear. Likewise, Samuel B. Meir (c1085–1174), a Jewish rabbi, recalled the old Jewish proverb that, "he who multiplies words occasions sins" and spoke of the Holy One's anger "at the sound of your many words, which are empty void, mere nothing, and damage and destroy your achievements, what you have accomplished, which is the essence of your deeds" (Japhet & Salters, ch. 5, 1 (2) and 5 (5)).

About 1441, Fra Angelico (c1390–1455), a Christian Dominican friar, undertook the task of decorating the convent of San Marco in Florence, Italy. Among the frescoes completed there by this great artist was an image of Peter Martyr with a finger to his lips, enjoining silence. This may still be seen on a lunette in the cloister. For her part, as we have seen Teresa of Avila (1515–1582), a Discalced Carmelite, strongly supported the practice of silence as an aid to avoiding sin. In the context of a particular transgression of the rules of her religious order, she wrote that,

> ... we must not talk about these things to one another. The
> devil could thereby gain greatly and manage to get the custom

of gossiping started. The matter should be discussed with the one who will benefit, as I have said. In this house, glory to God, there's not much occasion for gossip since such continual silence is kept; but it is good that we be on guard (Teresa, vol. 2, p. 296).

She accepted that there ought to be exceptions "in a time of some need or temptation. This rule of silence should not be understood to refer to a question and answer or to a few words, for such things can be spoken without permission." (Teresa, vol. 3, p. 320). Her co-founder of the Discalced Carmelite religious order, John of the Cross (1542–1591), was no less enthusiastic about silence. In 1587, he explained to the nuns of Beas Granada that his failure to write was not due to any unwillingness but to his belief that,

> ... enough has already been said and written for doing what is important; and that what is wanting, if anything is wanting, is not writing or speaking—rather these usually superabound— but silence and work. Furthermore, speaking distracts one, while silence and work recollects and strengthens the spirit. Once individuals know what has been told them for their benefit, they no longer need to hear or speak, but to put it into practice, silently and carefully and in humility and charity and contempt of self (p. 741).

He recommended that one suffer silence in the face of monastic annoyances and mortificiations (p. 726), believing that, "Wisdom enters through love, silence, and mortification. It is great wisdom to know how to be silent and to look at neither the remarks, nor the deeds, nor the lives of others ..." (p. 93). He thought that, "It is better to learn to silence and quiet the faculties so that God may speak" (p. 274). In 1590, as we have seen, he told a nun suffering from scruples that she should, "When something distasteful or unpleasant comes your way, remember Christ crucified and be silent" (p. 756). In the light of such examples, it is not surprising to find Barbour concluding recently that, "Communal silence integrates into community life the solitary's wariness about gossip, distraction and idle conversation" (p. 18).

Contrary to a popular misconception, even before the monastic rule was relaxed after the Second Vatican Council, there were always "seasonable hours" when monks could consort and speak with one another. Frequent condemnation of "murmuring" in the Rule of St Benedict itself suggests that, in practice, many monks also talked to one another when not strictly permitted to do so. Monks also engaged in solitary reading during the midday rest period, and during the Middle Ages this reading was probably not entirely silent but audible—yet restrained so as not to disturb those who were trying to rest (Wathen, pp. 15, 33–37, and 65).

The place of silence in the monastic tradition has had its critics, among whom was Samuel Johnson, the English author and Anglican. His biographer recorded that, one day in 1776,

> We talked of religious orders. He [Johnson] said, "It is as unreasonable for a man to go into a Carthusian convent for fear of being immoral, as for a man to cut off his hands for fear he should steal .... Their silence too, is absurd. We read in the Gospel of the apostles being sent to preach, but not to hold their tongues. All severity that does not tend to increase good, or prevent evil, is idle" .... I wondered at the whole of what he now said; because, both in his "Rambler" and "Idler", he treats religious austerities with much solemnity of respect (Boswell, pp. 436–437).

Johnson was sceptical not just of silence but of solitude, two states that are sometimes equated but which are not the same. One of his acquaintances reported his trenchant opinion that,

> Solitude ... is dangerous to reason, without being favourable to virtue: pleasures of some sort are necessary to the intellectual as to the corporeal health; and those who resist gaiety, will be likely for the most part to fall a sacrifice to appetite; for the solicitations of sense are always at hand, and a dram to a vacant and solitary person is a speedy and seducing relief. Remember ... that the solitary mind is certainly luxurious, probably superstitious, and possibly mad: the mind stagnates for want of employment, grows morbid, and is extinguished like a candle in foul air (Piozzi, p. 81).

In fact, the Christian monastic tradition is founded on community life, not simply because of the centrality of community responsibility in Christian teaching and tradition but precisely because of the psychological and other risks involved in an isolated pursuit of God in a hermitage or elsewhere. A regime of individual contemplative or meditative practice is certainly possible within the confines of community living, especially today when monks have a cell or room of their own, but was difficult in days when many shared a large sleeping space with thin or no partitions. The hermitage is an option only for the more mature, in exceptional circumstances. William Johnston (1925–2010) points out that, "… most religious traditions have sought to initiate their devotees into mystical silence rather than allowed them to wander freely into the deeper caverns of the mind" (p. 94). His belief, that the best norm for distinguishing the mystic from the neurotic is a person's adaptability both to community living by humble service and to the habits of hard work or even drudgery, is a common one among supervisors of spiritual practices.

When it comes to prayer generally, Hepher insists that religious silence is not merely the absence of speech: "It is no failure of vocal prayer. Rather it is prayer gathering itself into an intensity of concentration in which it lays firmer hold of God, and that for which it intercedes." He feels that silence allows one the freedom to concentrate on a particular need and to somehow commune, "by a steadfast and deliberate act of compassion and love", with the object for which one is interceding, while also realizing the presence of God:

> Silence facilitates those acts of the soul by which it attains to the realisation of the divine Presence and makes fast its hold on God. Silence enables imagination and memory to do their work of quickening into actuality and power the love and faith that underlie all intercession. The moving panorama, in which one object of prayer after another passes and is gone, gives but little chance for the intercessor to take them into his heart in any deep way (p. 134).

Paradoxically, the silence of monastic life may come to enrich the value of the spoken word, as the writings of Thomas Merton testify. Moreover, believes Vest, there are words which we can speak that exist in "rhythmic congruence" with silence. Herself a Benedictine oblate, she notes that the Rule of St Benedict "sought to minimise noise and maximise 'Word' (including the human words formed in the silence of God's presence)" (p. 15). However, she warns, being silent in such a constructive manner is not as easy as it may seem:

> Strangely enough, we moderns, who experience so little silence, often think that silence is easy. We who are so noise-addicted believe that silence is something anyone can claim readily—until we try it. Being silent is an art to be learned, much like playing basketball or speaking a language (p. 17).

Meditation

Meditation takes various forms. Sitting in silence and kneeling in silence are two of them. Within that silence, there may be inner turmoil or peace; there may be a simple watching of the natural breath pattern or the adoption of some special breathing techniques; there may be a letting go of words and concepts or the repetition and even dwelling upon a mantra or prayer or object. The terms "contemplation" and "meditation" are each found being used on some occasions to indicate active reflection on a particular text or image, and on other occasions to indicate the releasing of any train of thought. A meditator who does not adopt a mantra or prayer to repeat during meditation may simply observe the arising and passing of emotions and thoughts while maintaining psychological equilibrium. This kind of "sitting" is frequently what is meant today by "meditation" when that term is used in Western societies. To some people such meditation is a way of getting closer to their God. To others it is a way of calming the mind and seeing all things more clearly. Some regard such personal outcomes as sufficient, not least for their mental health, while others insist that meditation is also a fundamental step towards the necessary recognition, development, and expression of compassion for our fellow beings.

When understood as a form or method of mind-training and awareness, meditation may be practised at all times, even in very noisy situations. However, it is common to learn and usual to practise meditation quietly. Moreover, many people believe that silence is conducive to one's communion with benign forces that are natural or divine.

John Henry Breasted of the University of Chicago has written of the significance of such silence in the worship of ancient Egypt, more than a thousand years years before Christ. He found that, "in the opinion of the sages ... the most effective means of gaining the favor of God is contemplative silence and inner communion". To support his opinion he quoted from two ancient texts of the 21st or 22nd dynasty (pp. 355–356). The first comprises some instructions of the scribe Any of the palace of Queen Nefertari, "meant for the average man", and it states,

> Be not of many words, for in silence shalt thou gain good .... As for the precinct of God, his abomination is crying out; pray thou with a desiring heart whose every word is hidden, and he will supply thy need and hear thy speech and receive thy offering (Lichtheim, 1975, p. 135).

Breasted says that it is with such an attitude as this that the worshipper turns to his god as a source of spiritual refreshment. He quotes from the second text: "Thou sweet Well for him that thirsteth in the desert; it is closed to him who speaks, but it is open to him who is silent. When he who is silent comes, lo, he finds the well" (p. 356). Breasted remarks that,

> This attitude of silent communion, waiting upon the gracious goodness of God, was not confined to the select few, nor to the educated priestly communities. On the humblest monuments of the common people, Amon is called the god "who cometh to the silent", or "the lord of the silent" (pp. 349–351).

In this context, "the silent" need not be assumed to be a reference to the dead.

Silverman writes that the cobra goddess Meretseger was known as "she who loves silence" (p. 163). And "The instruction of Amenemope", an Egyptian text from the 12th or 13th century before Christ, is thought to have influenced the author of the Hebrew Book of Proverbs. The text states:

> The truly silent, who keeps apart,
> He is like a tree grown in the meadow.
> It greens, it doubles its yield,
> It stands in front of its lord.

> Its fruit is sweet, its shade delightful,
> Its end comes in the garden (Lichtheim, 1976, p. 151).

In the Upanishads of ancient India it was said that true spiritual freedom may be achieved by abstinence. This abstinence includes, according to the Khandogya-Upanishad,

> What people call the vow of silence (mauna), that is really absti-nence [of one type], for he who by abstinence has found out the Self, meditates (manute) (Müller, 1879, p. 131).

A writer of the ancient *Babylonian Talmud* believed that, "... a charm against suffering is silence and prayer" (p. 410). Down the centuries, many people have found meditation to have beneficial physical effects. At the very least it is a form of relaxation. Thus, the practice of silence may be valued for both material and spir-itual reasons.

As noted above, Jews were silent in anticipation of a religious experience. One writer tells us that,

> For God alone my soul waits in silence;
>   from him comes my salvation (Psalms 62:1).

Elsewhere, the Lord God bids us, "Be still, and know that I am God" (Psalms 46:10). Jesus himself spent much of his life out of the public gaze. When he did begin to teach, he also took time to retreat to the desert. And Matthew tells us that when Jesus gave us that great prayer, that became known as "The Lord's Prayer" or "Our Father", he advised,

> Beware of practising your piety before men in order to be seen by them; for then you will have no reward from your Father who is in heaven .... And when you pray, you must not be like the hypocrites; for they love to stand and pray in the syna-gogues and at the street corners, that they may be seen by men. Truly, I say to you, they have received their reward. But when you pray, go into your room and shut the door and pray to your Father who is in secret; and your Father who sees in secret will reward you.

And in praying do not heap up empty phrases as the Gentiles do; for they think that they will be heard for their many words. Do not be like them, for your Father knows what you need before you ask him. Pray then like this: Our Father who art in heaven, Hallowed be thy name. Thy kingdom come. Thy will be done, On earth as it is in heaven. Give us this day our daily bread; And forgive us our debts, As we also have forgiven our debtors; And lead us not into temptation, But deliver us from evil. For if you forgive men their trespasses, your heavenly Father also will forgive you; but if you do not forgive men their trespasses, neither will your Father forgive your trespasses (Matthew 6:1–15).

One early Christian who was not averse to "uttering a lot of words" when explaining his life and when teaching others what he believed was Augustine of Hippo (354–430). However, he also clearly recognized the limitations of speech. He writes in his *Confessions* (bk. 9, ch. 10) of how he sat at a window with his mother not long before her death, both of them looking out into the garden of the house that they had taken at Ostia on the River Tiber, near Rome. He recounts how he recognized then the benefits of silence when preparing to hear God's Word, which he says is not uttered by a tongue of flesh nor an angel nor the sound of thunder but by God himself in a way that we may hear without the aid of such things when we have silenced the body. Sceptics may regard his experience as an example of fanciful projection or wishful thinking but believers are convinced that such insights cannot be merely dismissed as self-deception.

In his 26th oration, Gregory of Nazianzus (C325–389) expressed the opinion that, "It is an exercise of great value … to speak of God, but there is one that is worth much more, namely to purify one's soul before God in silence" (Hastings, p. 512). Three centuries later, Maximus the Confessor indicated that a person may, through "a silence that speaks rich in tone", summon "the silence of the unseen and unknown call of the deity much hymned in the innermost sanctuaries". This has inspired Davies, who responds that, "Liturgy *is* the meeting of silence with silence, and the span between the divine and human silence is the measure of the liturgical moment" (2006, pp. 215–216, referring to the *Mystagogy*, ch. 4).

In a Palestinian commentary on the Hebrew Book of Leviticus that is thought to date from slightly later than the fifth century after Christ, we are reminded that,

> R[abbi]. Joshua b. Levi said: A word is worth a sela', but silence is worth two [sela'im], even as we have learnt in the Mishnah [Abot I, 17 (18)]: Simeon his son used to say: "All my life I grew up among the Wise, and I found nothing better for a person than silence" (*Midrash Rabbah: Leviticus*, p. 207).

Earlier in the Midrash this saying is extended somewhat ambiguously to read, "A word for a *sela'*, but silence for two *sela'*s;—like a precious stone." One might reasonably assume that "silence" is here being compared to a precious stone, for the word "silence" in this saying is closer to the words "precious stone" than is the word "word". Indeed, Charles Taylor added in brackets simply "it is" before "like a precious stone" (p. 25, n. 38). However, Cohen added in brackets, after the dash, "Let your words be" (*Midrash Rabbah: Ecclesiastes*, p. 133).

The words of Jesus when reciting the "Our Father" were echoed over a millennium later by Rabbi Samuel Ben Meir (c1082–c1160), who lived in northern France and who was one of the outstanding Jewish figures of the Middle Ages. He wrote,

> When you pray before him do not be hasty in your prayer, by uttering a lot of words before the Holy One. For he is in heaven; therefore you should fear him if you multiply words before him. Let there be few words lest you err by means of your many words (Japhet & Salters, ch. 5, 1. 2).

The meeting of silence with silence that occurs in meditation often occurs when an individual is alone and is not usually described as liturgical. The joy of such private silence was famously celebrated by the Spanish mystic, John of the Cross. In stanzas 14 and 15 of his "Song of the Soul Praising her Beloved, as Bride and Bridegroom", for example, he wrote (p. 525) of

> My Beloved, the mountains,
> And lonely wooded valleys,

strange islands,
and resounding rivers,
the whistling of love-stirring breezes,

the tranquil night
at the time of the rising dawn,
silent music,
sounding solitude,
the supper that refreshes, and deepens love.

In a commentary, he explains his use of the term "silent music" by saying (pp. 535–536),

In that nocturnal tranquility and silence and in knowledge of the divine light the soul becomes aware of Wisdom's wonderful harmony and sequence in the variety of her creatures and works. Each of them is endowed with a certain likeness of God and in its own way gives voice to what God is in it. So creatures will be for the soul a harmonious symphony of sublime music surpassing all concerts and melodies of the world. She calls this music "silent" because it is tranquil and quiet knowledge, without the sound of voices. And thus there is in it the sweetness of music and the quietude of silence. Accordingly, she says that her Beloved is silent music because in him she knows and enjoys this symphony of spiritual music. Not only is he silent music, but he is also sounding solitude.

This is almost identical with silent music, for even though that music is silent to the natural senses and faculties, it is sounding solitude for the spiritual faculties.

John of the Cross also writes that, "The Father spoke one Word, which was his Son, and this Word he speaks always in eternal silence, and in silence must it be heard by the soul" (p. 92). He believed that, "… the knowledge of God is received in divine silence" (p. 88), and was one of many mystics in various religious traditions to find that language is inadequate to match such experience (p. 439). In stanza 39 of "The Spiritual Canticle" he states that, "In contemplation God teaches the soul very quietly and secretly, without its knowing how, without the sound of words, and without the help of any bodily or spiritual faculty, in silence and quietude, in darkness to all sensory and natural things" (p. 626). For him, silence can open one to a special kind of spiritual influence: "… the blessings this silent communication and contemplation impress on the soul, without its then experiencing them, are inestimable …" (p. 689).

It is clear then that silence has long been a part of the monastic tradition. However, in writings of early or medieval Christians the occurrence of occasional passages praising it ought not to mislead us into believing that it preoccupied the Church in general. Church organizations were actively engaged in evangelization and good works, and the practices of contemplation and meditation were intended to be secondary to and supportive of such engagement. As a random measure of the perceived status of silence, one may note that it is listed in the index of just four of the 35 volumes of works of the ancient Christian writers (or "fathers") that were published by The Newman Press and Longmans, Green & Co. between 1945 and 1965, and in one of those works its single use is entirely inconsequential. There are, also, very few index entries for silence in more than two dozen volumes of the *Library of Christian Classics* published by SCM Press in London between 1953 and 1957.

Secular poets

It is notable that the experience of a monastic meditator such as John of the Cross appears in some ways to be shared by secular poets such as Coleridge and Keats at least as much as it is by some Christians. Thus, for example, in "The Rime of the Ancient Mariner" (1798), Samuel Taylor Coleridge sketched that sailor's vision of benign but voiceless spirits: whose "silence sank / Like music on my heart". And in a poem called "There Was a Boy" which was first published in 1800, William Wordsworth refers to that very boy's "mimic hootings to the silent owls" that induces them to raise an echoing din around the cliffs and islands of Lake Windermere in north-western England:

> … when there came a pause
> Of silence such as baffled his best skill:
> Then, sometimes, in that silence, while he hung
> Listening, a gentle shock of mild surprise
> Has carried far into his heart the voice
> Of mountain-torrents;

John Keats (1795–1821) wrote in his "Ode to a Grecian Urn" that,

> Heard melodies are sweet, but those unheard
> Are sweeter: therefore, ye soft pipes, play on;
> Not to the sensual ear, but, more endeared,
> Pipe to the spirit ditties of no tone.

Thomas Carlyle, that great admirer of silence, remarked that,

> Under all speech that is good for anything there lies a silence
> that is better. Silence is deep as Eternity; speech is shallow as
> Time. Paradoxical does it seem? Woe for the age, woe for the
> man, quack-ridden, bespeeched, bespouted, blown about like
> barren Sahara, to whom this world-old truth were altogether
> strange (vol. 4, p. 190).

In 1872, George Eliot proclaimed strikingly in *Middlemarch* that,

> If we had a keen vision and feeling of all ordinary human life,
> it would be like hearing the grass grow and the squirrel's heart
> beat, and we should die of that roar which lies on the other side
> of silence. As it is, the quickest of us walk about well wadded
> with stupidity (p. 162).

Her words will seem familiar to fans of the rock-band U2, whose song "Breathe" includes a line referring to "The roar that lies on the other side of silence". Another beautiful expression of the experience of silence that meditators and poets share is found in "The Habit of Perfection", a poem by Gerard Manley Hopkins (1844–1889). The first two words of these verses later provided a title for the abbreviated edition of Thomas Merton's autobiography, *The Seven Storey Mountain*, that was published in England:

> Elected Silence, sing to me
> And beat upon my whorlèd ear,
> Pipe me to pastures still and be
> The music that I care to hear.
>
> Shape nothing, lips; be lovely-dumb:
> It is the shut, the curfew sent

From there where all surrenders come
Which only makes you eloquent.

Silent night

One of the most evocative compositions referring to silence is the popular and well-known carol "Silent Night". Written in the early 19th century by Josef Mohr, an Austrian priest, it manages to express succinctly the expectant joy of sacred silence. Jacob believed that, in general, "... it is not simply God's absolute vastness but his nearness which is so silencing a thought" (p. 3). However, there is a danger that believers will profess such nearness while continuing to reach beyond it noisily. Andrews thought that many modern Christians risked paying "a very terrible price" by their failure to pause quietly or retreat: "He will seek entrance and the door of our hearts and our ears will be too occupied with the din and noise of the world to hear His pleading" (p. 27). This last is a reference to that message from Jesus Christ that an angel ostensibly brought to John for the Church in Laodicea: "Behold, I stand at the door and knock. If anyone hears my voice and opens the door, I will come in to him and eat with him, and he with me" (Revelation 3:20).

Earlier, we saw how Quakers value silence when they assemble. However, as Caroline Stephen also wrote,

> It is not only the momentary effect of silence as a help in public worship that constitutes its importance in Quaker estimation. The silence we value is not the mere outward silence of the lips. It is a deep quietness of heart and mind, a laying aside of all pre-occupation with passing things—yes, even with the workings of our own minds; a resolute fixing of the heart upon that which is unchangeable and eternal. This "silence of all flesh" appears to us to be the essential preparation for any act of true worship. It is also, we believe, the essential condition at all times of inward illumination. "Stand still in the light," says George Fox again and again, and then strength comes—and peace and victory and deliverance, and all other good things. "Be still, and know that I am God." It is the experience, I believe, of all those who have been most deeply conscious of His revelations of Himself, that they are made emphatically to the "waiting" soul—to the spirit

which is most fully conscious of its own inability to do more than wait in silence before Him. The possibilities of inward silence can be but distantly referred to in words. The clearness of inward vision which sometimes results from it must be experienced to be fully understood; the things revealed to that vision are rather to be lived in than uttered .... They soon began to exercise a strangely subduing and softening effect upon my mind. There used, after a while, to come upon me a deep sense of awe, as we sat together and waited—for what? In my heart of hearts I knew in whose Name we were met together, and who was truly in the midst of us. Never before had His influence revealed itself to me with so much power as in those quiet assemblies (pp. 56–57).

Stephen's description of the experience of silent meditation is one to which people of more than one faith may assent. A remarkable Anglican friar, Henry Earnest Hardy (1869–1946), compared the importance of giving people space in which to be silent to the need for lovers to be undisturbed, so that the soul may by degrees come to God. There is, firstly,

> ... the threshold of silence, which is the cessation of speech; then that inner silence of the mind, which ceases from distracting thoughts; so reaching on to the silence of the will, that wonderful silence to which our Lord Himself only came through the agony and prayer in the Garden, the silence which can say quite simply, "Thy will be done" (Andrew, p. 5).

Another author has worried that, "... there appear to be many people who have reached the state where noise, at least in the background, has become a necessity .... What possible appeal can they find in the psalmist's injunction 'be still and know that I am God'? What sense can the silence of a church arouse in them save that of embarrassment?" (E. Morgan, p. 19). In the mid-20th century, the Trappist monk Thomas Merton wrote about the appeal of silence:

> Then, in the deep silence, wisdom begins to sing her unending, sunlit, inexpressible song: the private song she sings to the solitary soul. It is his own song and hers—the unique, irreplaceable

song that each soul sings for himself with the unknown Spirit, as he sits on the door-step of his own being, the place where his existence opens out into the abyss of God. It is the song that each one of us must sing, the song God has composed Himself, that he may sing it within us. It is the song which, if we do not listen to it, will never be sung. And if we do not join with God in singing this song, we will never be fully real: for it is the song of our own life welling up like a stream out of the very heart of God (p. 24).

Frère Roger (1915–2005), the founder and prior of the ecumenical monastic community of Taizé who was killed brutally in old age, wrote,

Jesus Christ is the Word of God, and we have to be passive and attentive if we want to hear him. We have to forget ourselves and our little kingdoms, and listen attentively. That is the way to be beautiful with the only beauty that he sees. Strange as it may seem, it is in the silence that we can speak to him best: in the silence of meditation, when we respond to him; in questioning silence, when we wait for him to explain to us what it is he wants us to do or know; in troubled silence, when we know that we are confronted with our Judge, and our whole life is lit up and we see it for what it is, and God invites us to change our ways; in the silence which is a cry for help, when we see that we cannot possibly do what he is asking us, and realize that it is only he who can give us the strength; and in awed silence, when we see him as he allows himself to be seen, and we quail at our own nothingness, and then discover that he is asking us to live as his sons and daughters. We need times of outward silence, if we are to know the inward sort. Some lucky ones can always find it, but all must be on the look-out for the silent moment that is possible, when no one and nothing can get at them; and it nearly always is possible to find it some time or somewhere (pp. 60–61).

Elected silence is, of course, not the exclusive preserve of contemplatives and poets such as Brother Roger or Thomas Merton. Each of us may swim in that stream. We can benefit from devoting time to being silent. Runcorn believes that, "... in all the varied encounters of our lives of whatever the nature, silence is part of an inner response that invites us to *deepen* the moment" (p. 4).

Supervised silence

On becoming silent, we are liable to think about ourselves and our circumstances. This is one of the reasons why not only Christian authorities but also Buddhist teachers encourage people to seek informed guidance when attempting to meditate frequently. Ideas and emotions can arise that are disturbing. It may be noted, for example, that "while gentle silence enveloped all things" and God's "all-powerful word leaped from heaven", it did so in the form of "a stern warrior" that produced "apparitions in dreadful dreams". These "greatly troubled" people, "and unexpected fears assailed them" (Wisdom 18:14–17). For another reason, also, William Johnston is sceptical if not cynical about meditation outside a structured religious context. He wonders if contemporary mankind, "having secularized art, music, poetry, education and politics, has finally decided to do the job properly and secularize prayer". He writes that the Japanese have attempted radically secularized meditation for generations, insofar as Zen, which originated in China as a religious exercise, "was quickly used in Japan, first by Samurai, then by suicide pilots, and finally by business tycoons .... And now the West, which knows a good thing when it sees it, follows suit" (p. 19). If meditation practices are undertaken to bolster the ego, either consciously or unconsciously, then the consequences will not be good.

Although the feelings that we experience when meditating are not always pleasant, people who find silence therapeutic or enabling believe that the effort involved is worth it. One of those who has found silence useful is Frances Adeney of Louisville Presbyterian Theological Seminary, Kentucky. She writes,

> The experience of entering silence has allowed me to explore the deeper reaches of myself, gaining insights into areas of suppressed pain and anger and aiding me in finding direction in my life. I do not know why or how this happens, but it seems to me an experience that Buddhists and Jungians, as well as Jews

and Christians, agree can spring from developing a habit of practising silence (p. 18).

Adeney is correct about the cross-cultural appreciation of silence. It was noted 90 years ago that, "Silence, as an aid to worship or as a method of preparing the soul for spiritual experiences, has been practised among larger or smaller groups in almost all periods of religious history and in almost all parts of the world" (Jones, pp. 512–513). That idea has been elaborated upon by William Johnston who, as we shall see in the final chapter, translated a notable Japanese novel concerned with the apparent silence of God. Johnston, a Jesuit, long worked at Sophia University in Tokyo and was an authority on Eastern religion in general and on meditation in particular. He remarks that, in the meditation of the great religions,

> one makes progress by going beyond thought, beyond concepts, beyond images, beyond reasoning, thus entering a deeper state of consciousness or enhanced awareness that is characterised by profound silence. This is the *silentium mysticum*. It is a state of consciousness in which there may be no words or images (p. 55).

Once more, Johnston draws attention to the fact that silence is not always easy: "Frequently this state of silent unification will be filled with peace; but it may at times be dry and even painfully filled with anguish. It is a silence that probably differs considerably according to the faith of the meditator ..." (ibid). These words are a corrective to views of silence and meditation that are romantically unrealistic.

Moreover, it is worthwhile distinguishing not only between cultures and their specific understanding of silence but even between different kinds of silence that are regarded as enjoyable or beneficial within any particular culture. And so Kelsey distinguishes between Christian and other types of meditation: "The basic difference between the two is whether one sees ultimate reality as a Lover to whom one responds, or as a pool of cosmic consciousness in which one seeks to lose identity" (p. 1). However, in practice, the distinction between traditions may not be as clear-cut as he seems to think it is.

Thus, for example, there is a way of understanding one old Christian practice that may seem quite familiar to Tibetans who clutch their prayer beads, for an author writes of the Christian rosary,

> When you say the rosary aloud, it may be that after a time your mind no longer rests in the words, nor yet in one of the myteries (if that is your way), nor in anything else you could name.
>
> It is likely that your mind is resting largely in the silence which is beyond the words, which is God (Llewelyn, p. 32).

Llewelyn regards the person who reaches this state as being engaged in contemplation, although some might describe the same state as meditative. He himself deploys the latter term purposefully, referring to "meditations on the fifteen mysteries" and writing that, "Meditation is a preliminary stage preparing us for the deeper relationship God has in store" (pp. vii–viii). Such usage of language serves to remind us of the need to be aware of the particular meaning that each author intends when using the word "meditation".

Llewelyn was chaplain of the Julian Shrine at Norwich in England. He notes that the rosary has been described in recent times as "merely a monotonous and boring relic of past ages", but adds that it has in fact been, for many, "a way in to silent prayer. The silence of the heart before God is of the essence of the prayer life" (pp. ix–x).

Experiencing such silence may well be pleasant but, for the world's great religions, feelings of equilibrium or bliss achieved in contemplation or meditation are by no means an end in themselves. They may even be a distraction from the true objective of spiritual practice. Abhishiktananda reminds us that,

> Meditation helps towards concentration and the quieting of the mind and leads to that interior silence, without which nothing can be achieved. Yet meditation and silence should never be confused with the end itself, which is equally beyond both silence and non-silence (p. 102).

That end in turn is not, at least for many Hindu and Buddhist and Christian meditators, some kind of quietistic self-annihilation but is the location of one's ego within a framework of understanding in which the care of others is recognized as a compassionate and moral obligation upon which spiritual liberation and fulfilment depend.

Jim Cotter has provided some practical advice to those who want to incorporate more silent moments of prayer into their lives. He advises, "Start with silence, and let the words rise out of the depths of silence and fall back into silence." He believes that we can thus leave behind our isolation and "the awful experience of uttering words that seem meaningless, dry and exhausted …. We become aware of the extraordinary connecting web or network that the universe seems to be." Unfortunately, in a busy world, some people find themselves pressed for time to be silent. For example, visiting a workshop in the Louisville Center for Spiritual Living, Christopher Hall reported that, "Dana Bryant [said] she didn't have enough time in her schedule to meditate the way she has in the past. 'I'm most curious to see what else I can do that would be meditative—and fast,' she said"!

Personal narratives

There is a long line of individuals who, outside any formal religious framework, have set out on a personal odyssey that entails being silent by choice for significant periods of time. Such individuals are sometimes inspired or informed by the example or words of spiritual teachers but they remain, even perhaps as hermits in the woods or city, part of the secular world. Inspired or eccentric, they are found in every culture. John Francis, for example, gave up motorized transport in response to a massive oil spill in San Francisco Bay. Soon afterwards, Francis, the son of working class, African-American parents in Philadelphia, also gave up speaking and remained mute for 17 years. He communicated by means of some signs and notes. He took his vow of silence partly "because, man, I just argued all the time". As he later explained,

> I realized that I hadn't been listening, it was as if I had locked away half of my life. I just hadn't been living half of my life. Silence is *not* just not talking. It's a void. It's a place where all things come from. All voices, all creation comes out of this silence. So when you're standing on the edge of silence, you

hear things you've never heard before, and you hear things in ways you've never heard them before. And what I would disagree with one time, I might now agree with in another way, with another understanding (Hertsgaard).

Sara Maitland, feminist and writer and mother, found herself living alone in her late forties. She became intrigued and attracted to silence and set out to explore her new love by reading about it and by spending time in retreat in Scotland and elsewhere. Her account of her growing silence was published in 2008. It includes delving into fairytale and myth, as well as into other cultural and historical aspects of silence. Hers is an engaging and enjoyable account. She recalls her experience of that mysterious "song" or "sound of silence" but writes that, "There is a problem describing it, because it does feel like an aural experience, you do hear it, but I think it is in fact the absence of anything to hear" (p. 197). At times quite lyrical, she also writes of "the dark side" of solitude when silence and isolation can induce disorientation and even madness. Especially intriguing are her accounts of the trying experiences of some of those who have attempted to sail single-handed around the world, particularly in the period prior to constant electronic communications.

Another and more disturbing tale of solitude and silence is the story of Chris McCandless. He was a young and troubled man who headed into the Alaskan wilderness, where he became lost and met his death. His story has been told in a book (Krakauer) and film (2007), both entitled *Into The Wild*. His fate is a reminder of the benefits, if not necessity, of having a mature and informed guide or "soul-friend" when embarking long-term upon the path of deliberative or meditative silence, especially if that path is also one of solitude.

CHAPTER NINE

The silence of God

Three centuries before Christ, the Greek playwright Menander (c342–290) reflected on the fact that divine beings, if they act at all, act in mysterious and inscrutable ways. "In silence, God brings all to pass," he wrote (Allinson, p. 533).

Divine silence has frequently frustrated or even terrified the faithful, who continue to pray notwithstanding what appears to be divine indifference in the face of adversity and cruelty. At the same time, that very silence confirms for atheists their belief in the absence of any God. Yet, even for atheists, there are aspects of reality that elude or transcend everyday language. These aspects cannot simply be dismissed as insignificant. The silence that surrounds us and permeates our world seems to be challenging us.

Was there silence before anything? Can we say in any meaningful sense that there was silence before "The Big Bang", or before phenomena became manifest in this universe?

And if one believes that there is a God, and if communications are part of his Creation, then why is he apparently silent on so many occasions when he might be expected to speak up? Where was God's voice at Auschwitz, or during recent Asian tsunamis? Where was he when a friend's son died young, or when so many children were

231

being abused? Does God's failure to be heard mean that he does not care or does not exist? Are silence and absence the same thing in this case? Might an existing God conceivably answer our prayers in obscure and seemingly perverse ways, or even refuse to listen to our pleas, as implied by some passages in the Old Testament? These include a complaint to God in the Book of Lamentations that, "You have wrapped yourself with a cloud so that no prayer can pass through" (Lamentations 3:43. See also Ezekiel 20:3). Perhaps the only logical conclusion is that his silence does indeed signify his absence. The sort of blind faith that simply avows that there is a God and then goes looking for reasons to back up that avowal is not for everyone. As one young doctor wrote, "I do not wish to talk with myself and to imagine to myself that it is God who is talking to me. God does not talk. There is the silence of God" (Dewailly, p. 294). Yet many believers claim to have had deep experiences of his love that contradict such a conclusion. They hear his words in their hearts, discern his word in Creation.

The Word

John, writing his Christian gospel during the first century, began his account by declaring that,

> In the beginning was the Word,
> and the Word was with God,
> and the Word was God (John 1:1).

"In the beginning was the Word." Now how can *that* be, John? Surely in the beginning there was actually silence before any words, even if by "word" we mean idea or creative force rather than speech? One big long silence until God suddenly decided "Let there be light." Or silence at least until "The Big Bang"? In one of the apocryphal books, God threatens that the world shall be turned back to "primeval" or "primordial" silence for seven days, "as it was at the first beginnings, so that no one shall be left" (2 Esdras 7:2). The same text also states that on the first day of creation "darkness and silence embraced everything" (6:38). However, it may be noted that the account of Creation in the Book of Genesis itself makes no reference to silence.

The Gilgamesh epic, which is said to be 3,000 years old and which recounts the tale of a catastrophic flood in the Tigro-Euphrates region, has Utnapishtim recalling that when he opened a window, "I looked upon the sea [or "at the weather"], (all) was silence. All mankind had turned to clay" (Heidel, Tablet 11, lines 132–133). There are clear parallels here with the biblical story of Noah and his ark. Apocalyptic silence features in the Book of Revelation: "When the Lamb opened the seventh seal, there was silence in heaven for half an hour" (Revelation 8:1). This silence signifies awe and reverence. One of the best-known films of Sweden's Ingmar Bergman takes its title from this passage. *The Seventh Seal* (1957), as we saw, is set during a plague and famously features a chess match between a returning knight and taciturn death, with the silence of God as its motif.

The Big Bang or Word had to arise somewhere, most likely in a silence that pre-existed it or that was born at the same time. But if there was nobody present to hear noise or to appreciate silence, then how can we say that there really was a bang? What is the sound of one hand clapping? Our language fails us. Hilaire Belloc observed (p. 12) that, "All will discover, on examining their memories, that Silence, like his brother Darkness, is enhanced and framed by slight exceptions." Darkness to be experienced must be that type of abysmal gloom of Hell that John Milton described as "darkness visible" (*Paradise Lost*, Book 1, line 73). So, also, silence is framed and underlined by the least sounds accompanying it.

It seems that Richard Dawkins and his deist counterparts agree on one thing—that there was sound right at the start of the universe. Word or bang. In the beginning was communication. Before time was reckoned we were promised. A relevant Semitic term used in the Bible was "*miltha*": in Aramaic, this can mean "word, saying, sentence, precept, utterance, message, command, a communication" (Erico & Lamsa, pp. 9–10).

Any silence before the first sounds in the universe would have had to have been as old as God, because silence, insofar as it is merely the absence of sound, does not depend on creation. Silence has no essence. It is not a thing. You cannot cut or bottle it, or pick it up on a radio receiver. Silence was then latent, part of a void, becoming apparent only when a listener existed to distinguish it from sound. We cannot say when the first sound occurred but recent discoveries indicate that, contrary to a common misconception, it would not have depended on the existence of air in the earth's atmosphere. Our ears need air to carry the sounds that we can hear but other kinds of sound travel through space in what is ostensibly but not completely a vacuum. In 2003, for example, astronomers were reported to have detected "the deepest note ever generated in the cosmos". It was "a B-flat flying through space like a ripple on an invisible pond. No human will actually hear the note, because it is 57 octaves below the keys in the middle of a piano ... a note that is more than a million billion times deeper than what you can hear" (Britt). The note, originating from a black hole, was picked up by the Chandra X-ray Observatory and appears to be part of a veritable music of the spheres that is only discernible by human beings indirectly through technological equipment.

Silence as we humans know it is like the dark side of the moon, while sound is the bright side. You cannot have one without the other, because both depend on our observation. They are not opposites but complement, or depend on, each other. Silence is always ready to return and engulf us, like the waters that engulfed Utnapishtim and Noah.

So why did John not write in his gospel that, "In the beginning was the Word *and Silence*"? Because for John the term that is translated in the Bible as "Word", commonly spelt with a capital "W", signified a fuller manifestation of Creation than simply speech or sound. Boman advises a clear distinction between "the Word" and "the Voice of God", in that "Voice signifies the sound of speech, Word means the utterance or what is said" (pp. 60 and 68). When God says "Let there be light," these words represent a creative act. The actual words and deeds of the prophets and of Jesus later support and make sense of that creative act or Word. Language in such instances is seen to flow closely from the act of creation, as Blaser indicates (passim). Jesus is not just a talker of words. He is regarded as "The Living Word", who teaches by the example and fact of his life. The community of his true followers and his spoken words are extensions or expressions. Put more theologically,

> ... this word is not simply external utterance or solely intellectual discourse, but the efficacious self-communication of God to the world and to humanity. The Hebrew word *dābār* of the OT [Old Testament] means not only "spoken word", but also event, affair, act (Komonchak et al., p. 1096).

Not only Jews but Hindus too had a conception of the creative "word" (Panikkar, pp. 165–166). The Christian John tells us that, in the beginning, "the Word" was with God "and without him nothing came to be". Nothing. "What came to be through him was life, and this life was the light of the human race," says John. Just as sound exists in relationship to silence, so light exists in relationship to darkness. However, God ("Wisdom") takes precedence over all (Wisdom 7:29; John 1:5 and 12:35). Indeed, the idea that God takes precedence over everything, including silence, was an important one for early Christians.

Gnostic silence

As Chrisians struggled to agree on an understanding of God, some interpretations of the divine came to be condemned as heresies. The latter included the beliefs of a group known as "Gnostics", who held complex views within which they appear in some cases to have invested silence with a type of essential divine property. Thus, according to the student of Valentinus named Ptolemy,

> Within invisible and unnamable heights there was—they say—a preexistent, perfect, eternity; this they call also prior source, ancestor, and the deep. And it existed uncontained, invisible, everlasting, and unengendered. Within infinite eternal realms it was in great stillness and rest.
>
> And with it coexisted thought, which they also call loveliness and silence.
>
> And eventually the aforementioned deep ... deposited [an] emanation that it had thought to emit, like sperm, in the womb of the silence that coexisted with it. And the latter received this sperm, conceived, and brought forth intellect, which was like and equal to the emitter and was the only being that comprehended the magnitude of its parent. And this intellect they call also only-begotten ... (Layton, p. 281).

The Gnostic tradition was deemed to treat God as a dyad, "consisting, in one part, of the Ineffable, the Depth, the Primal Father; and in the other, of Grace, Silence, the Womb, and 'Mother of All'". Some Gnostics prayed to this mystical eternal silence. Some appear to have regarded Silence as existing prior to the emergence of a creative and productive Mind (Pagels, pp. 50–54). It is said that while some Gnostics in fact regarded the first principle as a solitary monad, developing all derived existence from itself alone, "others, following the analogy of natural generation, by the union of male and female, assigned to the first principle a consort called Σιγή (Sigé) or Silence". The first principle was Βυθός (Buthos) or Depth (Mansel, pp. 86, 88, and 169–171). One Gnostic document that gives a flavour of the complex texts and of the place of silence in divine order is "The Gospel of the Egyptians". This includes references to:

> the Father of the silence …. Three powers came forth from him; they are the Father, the Mother, (and) the Son, from the living silence, what came forth from the incorruptible Father. These came [forth from] the silence of the unknown Father ….
> (Böhlig & Wisse, p. 209).

In one of two versions of a creation myth in the Jewish Book of Genesis, God is said to have created both man and woman "in his own image and likeness" (Genesis 1:26–28). Therefore, it is reasonable for Christians to attribute to God features that are traditionally associated with either the male or female personality or both. To do so is not necessarily to assert that God is more than what Christianity recognizes as The Trinity (of Father, Son, and Holy Spirit). Early Christians appear to have believed that Gnostics went further and saw God as co-existing with some other entity or force such as silence, or as consisting of two or more intrinsic entities. While treating God as male and female may have implications for those who defend the dominant male order in Jewish and Christian traditions, allowing the possibility of more than a single and undivided ultimate creator is downright heresy.

The theology of Gnosticism seems labyrinthine. No less an authority on Vedic writings than Eggeling has bracketed it unfavourably with aspects of that ancient India corpus. Referring to those particular aspects, he wrote that, "For wearisome prolixity of exposition, characterised by dogmatic assertion and a flimsy symbolism rather than by serious reasoning, these works are perhaps not equalled anywhere; unless, indeed, it be by the speculative vapourings of the Gnostics" (1882, p. ix)! However, in reacting against the place of silence in Gnostic thought, it is possible that some Christians themselves tended to downplay or overlook the value of both silence and the feminine. A receptive and quiet Virgin Mary, who scarcely utters words in the gospels and whom God made pregnant with his Son, may have filled the place of Gnostic silence for some Christians.

In any event, silence and darkness remain aspects of our experience no matter how one understands them. They are not measured in themselves but are defined by their relationship to phenomena. We cannot imagine silence without ears to notice it, or think of darkness without eyes to register it.

Elijah's sheer silence

If God transcends words, if there is more to Him than meets the eye or ear within Creation, it seems from the Bible that silence itself may somehow be a portal through which we access Him. But are we to try to interpret His silence, or just listen to it receptively in the expectation or hope that we will pick up a clear signal— perhaps like one of those radio telescopes slowly combing the universe for signs and sounds that are not capable of being perceived directly by our bodily senses?

The association of God with silence, in some primeval sense, is evident in the story of Elijah, the last surviving prophet of his day. He is said in Hebrew scriptures to have had a memorable encounter at Horeb, "the mountain of God" (where the Lord had also revealed his law to Moses and which is also known as Sinai). Elijah fled there in fear of his life, under threat from Jezebel, and spent the night in a cave. Then, "the word of the Lord" came to him and said (as translated in the New Revised Standard Version of the Bible),

> "Go out and stand on the mountain before the Lord, for the Lord is about to pass by." Now there was a great wind, so strong that it was splitting mountains and breaking rocks in pieces before the Lord, but the Lord was not in the wind; and after the wind, an earthquake, but the Lord was not in the earthquake; and after the earthquake a fire, but the Lord was not in the fire; and after the fire a sound of sheer silence. When Elijah heard it, he wrapped his face in his mantle and went out and stood at the

> entrance of the cave. Then there came a voice to him that said,
> "What are you doing here, Elijah?" (1 Kings 19:9–15).

Elijah is a man in terror of death. On his way to Horeb he had already had an angel appear to him and address him. Then "the word of the Lord" directed him and now, finally, "a voice" came to him after he "heard" the "sheer silence" mentioned here. "Sheer" is a word used in English to describe cliffs that fall vertiginously and dizzyingly into the sea. It is indeed awesome, clearly more awesome for Elijah than is an earthquake or fire or wind that split mountains. In Assyria and Babylon the Divine Word appeared ordinarily as a strong wind (Boman, p. 60), but here no word came until after the wind had subsided.

This account in the first Book of Kings is so striking that the quotation is used as a key production device to set the stage for the depiction of life in a Carthusian monastery in Philip Gröning's acclaimed German documentary, *Die Grosse Stille* (2005, English release title *Into Great Silence*). Yet the concept of some kind of pure or sheer or great silence is not a common one in the Hebrew scriptures, and we shall see in practice that the language used by the original author has challenged translators. For this reason, we bear in mind Žižek's assertion, quoted earlier above, that, "The first creative act is therefore to *create silence*—it is not that silence is broken, but that silence itself breaks, interrupts the continuous murmur of the Real, thus opening up a space in which words can be spoken." This idea may help to explain why some translators of the passage employ English terms such as "murmuring" or "whispering" here rather than blank "silence".

The Hebrew word for silence that is found in the passage above about Elijah's experience occurs just three times in the Old Testament, the other occasions being in Job and Psalms. Before considering the significance of that particular term it may be said that references by means of any Hebrew word to what we might translate into English as "silence" are not very common in the Old Testament. Moreover, seemingly irreconcilable translations of the passage relating to Elijah in the Book of Kings diverge on the very concept of "sheer silence".

The Hebrew original of the New Revised Standard Version's "sheer silence", in the passage reproduced above, is rendered quite differently in the New American Bible (NAB) as "a tiny whispering sound". Perhaps even more striking is the variation between that "sheer silence" of the New Revised Standard Version (NRSV) and the translation of the same Hebrew words as "a still small voice" in both the Revised Standard Version (RSV) and the King James Version (KJV): the NRSV historically flows from the RSV and the KJV, yet this striking change in translation is not explained in any footnote, and this is despite the fact that the NRSV editors promise guidance "where it is evident that the text has suffered in transmission and that none of the [earlier] versions provides a satisfactory restoration" (Metzger & Murphy, pp. ix–xi). Runcorn, who himself renders the Hebrew words as "a small thin silence", complains that "the traditional 'still small voice' is not the most helpful reading" (p. 9). A footnote that *is* given in the NRSV for 1 Kings 19:12, but that ignores the change in translation from the RSV, further muddies the water by asserting that, "The sound of sheer silence was the demanding voice of God" (Metzger & Murphy, pp. 455–456). Auld notes correctly that, "The end of v. 12 does not actually say that the Lord was in 'the still small voice' [KJV version]" (p. 127).

However well one understands Hebrew (and the present author does not understand it at all), it seems difficult to square the RSV, NRSV, and NAB options, which are the fruit of years of work by teams of highly qualified scholars! Any sound, no matter how tiny or whispering, literally cannot be any kind of silence, especially sheer silence. This kind of difference or fudge is disheartening for those who like to turn to the Bible for a personal interaction with what one assumes is a close translation in letter and spirit of the original text. Another example, if not quite as stark but yet disturbing, occurs at Wisdom 18:14 where "gentle silence" in the NRSV is given as a "peaceful stillness" in the NAB. Apart from the present interest in possible contrasts between different types of silence ("sheer" and "gentle"), simpler questions about the intended meaning of the original arise. For it is the case that birds might be singing beautifully or musicians strumming on lyres and harps in a "peaceful stillness" but surely not in a "silence". Indeed, absolute silence appears to be allowed by the NSRV but not by the NAB.

The RSV and NSRV both descend from the 1611 King James version, which is regarded as an influential masterpiece of the language and literature of England. Translations may tell us as much about the perspectives and cultural milieus of the societies from which they arise as they do about any ancient Hebrew understanding of reality in general or of silence in particular. At the very least, they provide a perspective on how various kinds of silence have been differentiated and understood by those believers who translated the texts. Gloer writes that, "Thirty-one appearances of 'silence' and 'silent' in the RSV Old Testament represent several Hebrew words with differing nuances of meaning and usage" (vol. 4, pp. 509–510).

The Hebrew word for silence that is used in the passage relating to Elijah is *d-m-m* and Davies notes that on each of the three occasions that this noun appears in the Old Testament, "… it is closely associated with the presence and speech of God":

> The translation of this term has given difficulty over the ages. It appears in the LXX [Septuagint] as [a Greek word pronounced "aura"], meaning "breeze" or "puff of wind" and in the Vulgate similarly as "aura", in all three places (pp. 207–208).

Davies believes that the contrast here between silence on the one hand and wind, earthquake, and fire on the other is significant in distinguishing the Jewish God from deities of the elements. The former transcends elements. However, Davies also acknowledges an "unresolved interplay" between silence as absence of noise and silence as a mode of God's speech, "since the God who inhabits the silence is a God who speaks".

Indeed, only on one of the two other occasions that *d-m-m* is found in the Old Testament is it actually translated in either the NRSV or the New American Bible version as "silence". On that occasion, the NRSV gives words that Eliphaz the Tremanite spoke to Job as,

> … dread came upon me, and trembling,
>   which made all my bones shake.
> A spirit glided past my face;
>   the hair of my flesh bristled.
> It stood still,
>   but I could not discern its appearance.
> A form was before my eyes;
>   there was silence, then I heard a voice: (Job 4:15–16).

Looking across a range of translations at the three occurrences of this Hebrew word d-m-m in the Old Testament, we find that it is given in the case of 1 Kings (referring to Elijah's experience) as "a whistling of a gentle air" (DRA), "a still small voice" (KJV), "a tiny whispering sound" (NAB), "a light murmuring sound", "sheer silence" (NRS) and "a still small voice" (RSV). Other translators give "a still small voice" or "a light whisper", the latter being described by Montgomery and Gehman (p. 314) as "... Burney's excellent rendering, although the translation of AV [Authorized Version], 'a still small voice', remains classical". Montgomery and Gehman themselves, for good measure, proceed to refer to it also as "the Zephyr-like whisper". Brueggemann (p. 89) cites also Gray's "a sound of thin silence" and Ferrein's "the sound of utmost silence". In the case of the occurrence of this word at Job 4:16, we find it rendered as "a gentle wind" (DRA), "still[ness]" and "silence" (KJV, NJB, NRS, RSV). Each of these translations in this particular context also refers to a voice, with DRA notably attributing the voice directly to the wind by giving "the voice as it were of a gentle wind", while NAB somewhat similarly turns the noun into an adjective descriptive of the voice, i.e. "a still voice". The other four translations distinguish between the silence and the subsequent voice. In the case of Psalms 107:29 we find a word other than silence used to translate d-m-m: "he turned the storm into a breeze: and its waves were still" (DRA), "he maketh the storm a calm, so that the waves thereof are still" (KJV), "he hushed the storm to a murmur; the waves of the sea were stilled" (NAB), "he reduced the storm to a calm, and all the waters subsided" (NJB), "he made the storm be still, and the waves of the sea were hushed" (NRS and RSV).

Metzger and Murphy remind us that, "During the years following the publication of the Revised Standard Version [in 1952], twenty-six other English translations and revisions of the Bible were produced ..." (p. x). I am grateful to Brother Lawrence of the Abbey of Gethsemani for his assistance in locating some of the translations given above.

Oliver Davies says that Hebrew words for silence, however translated into English, "are characteristically linked with notions of stupefaction, stillness and rest". He contrasts this with the Greek view that associates silence with the mind and with transcendence.

He deals also with a number of other subtle distinctions in the use of words designating silence in a number of languages. However, while such Hebrew words may be linked with notions of "stupefaction, stillness and rest", it seems significant that on the three occasions being considered here the word *d-m-m* is found in a narrative context where it is preceded by considerable disturbance before being followed by a voice in two cases and by entry to a metaphorical harbour in Psalm 107. In the Book of Kings there had been earthquake, fire, and wind, while in Job there had been dread, trembling, and some kind of spirit that made Job's hair stand on end, and in Psalm 107 there was a storm. Furthermore, in the case of Elijah, his location in a cave and his wrapping himself in a cloak when he encounters the silence suggest not so much "stupefaction" as the expectant stillness that is appropriate to awe. This reminds one of Moses at Mount Horeb (Exodus 33:17–23), or of Plato's contemplation of the nature of shadows within a cave, or of Mohammed being folded in a cloak when he received visions in the cave at Hira (Surah 73, i; 74, i.). One is also reminded of Žižek's image of the vase, quoted earlier, and his contention that,

> The primordial fact is not Silence (waiting to be broken by the divine Word) but Noise, the confused murmur of the Real in which there is not yet any distinction between a figure and its background. The first creative act is therefore to *create silence*—it is not that silence is broken, but that silence itself breaks, interrupts the continuous murmur of the Real, thus opening up a space in which words can be spoken (p. 224).

The original authors of the Old Testament were struggling to find a way to express a mystical paradox where immersion in or exposure to silence and stillness may give rise within it to a sensation of immanent and directional presence so that the silence is not only pregnant but moving towards the birth of—or a harbour for—some inner realization or voice that will in turn be expressed in spoken words of the prophet. The inadequacy of even the most poetic language to express this experience which transcends concepts and words is exacerbated at the translation stage, because not even the best translator can get entirely inside the head, soul, or muse of the original inspired author—regardless of whether or not that translator has an acute personal sense of the spiritual experience being indicated in the original passages (which may not always be the case). Language in its very dualistic nature divides silence from sound and so cannot capture the non-verbal stimulus or communication that occurs prior to the prophet necessarily attempting to relate to the realization or the prompt in a verbalized or conceptualized manner. Even the best original accounts cannot have a silence and voice at the same time (as voice negates silence unless described as "an inner voice", which may of course be what is signified if not expressly articulated in these cases). However, unless stated explicitly to be "an inner voice" (or equivalent term) the writer will have to have the voice proceeding out of or following immediately after silence (perhaps from a bush (Exodus) or a whirlwind (Job 40:6) or a devouring fire *and* mighty tempest (Psalms 50:3)). Just as poetry must sometimes defy logic to express truth, so the prophetic voice cannot always be adequately understood by reference merely to the structure of the narrative or language deployed to express it. The position is complicated further in the case of silence as there is seldom if ever heard an absolute silence, not least because our own blood-flow or heart-beat may be faintly audible to us and signals the sometimes whispering life force: thus the concept of silence is itself suggestive unless clearly intended to designate some kind of void or abyss or primeval silence. Romantically, one contemporary author has proclaimed that, "Heaven is the song that God sings to the world out of his silence" (Russell, p. xiv).

Brueggemann gives some useful guidance in respect to Elijah's experience, when he writes,

> This is a famous passage giving special nuance to the way of God's presence. But not too much should be made of the famous "still small voice" [Authorised Version]. John Gray suggestively renders it, "a sound of thin silence". Samuel Ferrein has it "the sound of utmost silence" which "can be cut with a knife". This is not the voice of conscience but of *awe*, not romantic whisperings but overriding *majesty*. God's inscrutable holiness is not packaged in utilitarian ways. For all his graciousness, God stays free of any grasping Elijah may want to do of him. In this drastic moment, Elijah becomes freshly aware that it is Yahweh and none other and not himself, who is God. All his fears are set in

proper place. There is now only one to fear, the same who must
be obeyed (p. 89).

Not all Christians have an experience of God's voice that is as majes-
tic as that of Elijah. Some hear the voice of silence in small, weak
places. Jean Vanier, who worked closely with the disabled, felt:

> … in some mysterious way that there is a calling, the silent cry-
> ing out of misery, tears of silence, and in my deepest being I hear
> the call, a sort of whispering that life has meaning (p. 42).

The striking contrasts between various translations of the Hebrew
description of Elijah's experience serve to remind us of the ways
in which we may understand a word in our own language without acknowledging that the meaning of the word as well as any
associations with it that we take for granted may be culturally and
personally determined and not be as straightforward as we assume.
There are many implications of this fact. For example, when he
or she today approaches the stories of the "desert fathers" or the
practice of Buddhist meditation, what is a Westerner's assumption
about the nature of silence? Is such silence regarded as, for example,
passive or active?

Keeping silent

On occasion, the silence of God himself is a puzzle to the Jewish
writers. Habakkuk asks "… why … are [you, Lord] silent when the
wicked swallow those more righteous than they" (Habakkuk 1:13).
Isaiah, surveying the misfortunes of his people, cries out, "After all
this will you restrain yourself, O Lord? Will you keep silent, and
punish us so severely?" (Isaiah 64:12). Isaiah consoled himself that
God would ultimately deal with evildoers, for although the Lord
"kept silent" and closed his eyes to idolaters yet the Lord noted their
behaviour and not even their good deeds could save them (Isaiah
57:11–12). God may not finally speak until the last days; even then
he may prefer to express himself through actions rather than words
alone, as has been promised (Isaiah 65:6):

> See, it is written before me:
> I will not keep silent, but I will repay;

> I will indeed repay into their laps
>> their iniquities and their ancestors' iniquities
>> together.

It is hard for people to cope with God's silence. Not all can remain quiet in the face of God's apparent failure to respond to our pleas. He has, after all, proclaimed that "For Zion's sake I will not keep silent" and has, on the walls of Jerusalem, posted sentinels: "all day and all night they shall never be silent" (Isaiah 62:1 and 6:2; Esdras 15:8). He "will not keep silence" when it comes to impressing Job with his divine power over Leviathan (Job 41:12). However, God makes no promise to reveal himself as we might wish, even when others dishonour him and his followers. In a passage that is regarded as being prophetic of events when Jesus would later stand before Pilate, it was written (Isaiah 53:7),

> He was oppressed, and he was afflicted,
>> yet he did not open his mouth:
> Like a lamb that is led to the slaughter,
> And like a sheep that before its shearers is silent,
> So he did not open his mouth.

In the Psalms we see mankind at its most vulnerable, calling out to God for vindication and relief, for a sign that he hears us (Psalms 28:1 and 35:22):

> To you, O Lord, I call;
>> my rock, do not refuse to hear me,
> for if you are silent to me,
>> I shall be like those who go down to the pit.

A man reaches up to heaven from out of his misery and cries, "O God, do not keep silence; do not hold your peace or be still" (Psalms 83:1), and again "Do not be silent, O God of my praise" (Ps. 109:1). The Psalms are a sort of dialogue with the self, in which the singer calls on God to answer and then discerns God's answer in Creation (e.g., "The voice of the Lord breaks … the cedars of Lebanon" (Ps. 29:5)), or in the misfortune of his enemies, or in his own recovery of confidence (e.g., "O Lord, you … restored me to life …" (Ps. 30:5), "so that my soul may praise you and not be silent"

(Ps. 30:12). Voices in the psalms are plaintive, at times bordering on despair, but recurrently hopeful. The 150 psalms are well over two thousand years old and have been loved by monks and others since the early Christian period. The psalms are sung day-in, day-out in monasteries in celebration of the unvarnished reality of a world where paradise may be promised to mankind but it is never present on this earth. They are poetry, prayer, and theology, words to voice in the silence that surrounds us. There is nothing neat or final about the psalms, yet they are wonderfully reassuring at some deep human level. It is hard to see how anyone familiar with their rhythms and refrains could conclude that the question of God may be answered neatly or glibly. The fact that they have served Jews and Christians so well and for so long forcefully struck one Zen master during a week spent at the Trappist Abbey of Gethsemani in Kentucky. Norman Fischer was astonished by the violence and bitterness expressed in them and, stirred by his own Jewish background, he essayed a new Buddhist-inspired rendering. Even if Westerners such as himself practise as mindful Buddhists, he says, "We find that there is still sometimes a need to call out, to sing, to shout, to be heard, to answer" (p. xv).

Jesus and silence

Silence is an experiential reality rather than an abstract concept in the Bible, and this reality is no more obvious than in the four gospels that tell the story of Jesus Christ. Indeed, the noun "silence" is absent from the RSV translation of the life of Christ. Yet, silence is part of the story of Jesus. On some occasions, he deliberately silences his apostles, instructing them to keep to themselves until after his death and resurrection their knowledge of him as Messiah or their experience of his transfiguration on the mountain. He also bids some of those whom he cures to remain quiet about what he has done (Green, McKnight & Marshall, pp. 521–522).

Pilate confronts the great silence of Jesus. For Jesus simply chooses not to answer the questions of those who interrogate and will ultimately crucify him. The scene is remarkable and the silence is stunning. It is as if Jesus is on another wavelength, speaking another language, moving inexorably towards his destiny. Nothing that he could say at this point would reach the Romans or their Jewish supporters in the way that he wishes to reach people. "If I tell you, you will not believe; and if I question you, you will not answer," he says to his tormentors (Luke 22:67). So when asked by Pilate to confirm that he is "the King of the Jews" he replies simply "You say so" and then says nothing more. He also makes no response when Pilate asks, "What is truth?" (John 18:38). It falls back on the authorities to make their decisions. Pilate is "greatly amazed" by the silence of Jesus (Matthew 27:11–14; Mark 15:1–5). Herod too gets no answer, even though he "was hoping to see him [Jesus] perform some sign" (Luke 22:66–23:8). Signs and words at this point might have enabled Jesus to escape crucifixion, but for Christians miracles and words are not God's primary concern in our encounter with the divine.

The decision on his fate having been made, Jesus is led away to be crucified. Indeed, at this point, he himself appears to be suffering the torment of those many people who have cried out to God but who have not had the immediate response for which they had hoped. From his anguished vigil in the Garden of Gethsemani until his death on the cross, Jesus pleads with his heavenly Father. He asks without avail for the bitter cup of his fate to pass from his lips. Some ancient authorities do say that, as his sweat became like great drops of blood, an angel appeared and strengthened him (NRSV, Luke 22:43–44). However, hung on the cross and dying, he cries out in apparent despair, "My God, My God, why have you forsaken me?" (Matthew 27:46; Mark 15:34). He echoes here the opening verse of Psalm 22,

> My God, my God, why have you forsaken me?
> Why are you so far from helping me, from the words of my groaning?
> O my God, I cry by day, but you do not answer;
> and by night, but find no rest.

On the part of the authors of the gospels themselves, there is at least one particular great silence and some lesser silences that deserve to be mentioned. The former is the absence of any account of how Jesus passed the years before he began his great public mission. Was he quietly working with Joseph, viewed by the mothers of local girls as an eligible young man and later perhaps as someone who was a little odd because of his lack of interest in any long-term relationship? Did he know women friends in his twenties? Did he travel away, perhaps going to India to learn from the wisdom traditions there? We have no idea, and we have no clear idea why this was deemed so irrelevant as not to rate a mention. However, Dewailly has suggested that "the silences of His hidden life" are significant. These include his quiet listening and his period in the desert.

> In fact, Jesus Christ multiplied silences. The Incarnate Word was not one of those "untiring" preachers who are constantly producing discourses and explanations in private as well as in public .... The secret of God which is the Word is incommunicable. In God word and silence call to and need one another, rather than exclude one another (pp. 287 and 289).

A full consideration of the place of silence in the Bible would of course have to take into account not just the occurrence of the word "silence" but other words that indicate its presence, words such as "listen" or "hear" or "give ear" that may merely flag passages of speech or action but that in some cases suggest periods of silent waiting. Words such as "stillness" may also imply silence. It has been sufficient here to note the variety of silences that are acknowledged by the writers or translators of scripture.

The Bible is a lengthy collection of sacred scriptures written over many centuries. It reflects a religious tradition that deals in words, where prophets pour out warnings, where people argue and plead with God for signs or for relief, where Jesus is continually engaged in debate and discussion, where early Christian communities are embroiled in heated disputes and where even God himself is sometimes heard "having a word". In this context it is not surprising to find relatively little attention paid to silence and to see that the explicit references to it are, in nearly all cases, quite insignificant or incidental. Indeed if one chooses a translation other that the RSV one may find silence mentioned even less. It is possible that such differences in translation are due to ambiguities in the original languages of the Bible or reflect the fact that silence as we conceive it was conceived differently by others—perhaps being thought of as indistinguishable from stillness, for example. Yet there seems no doubt that, while they may be heard pleading long and hard for God to respond to them, those who plead with him in the Bible or who patiently await a sign are confident that they will hear from him eventually. They do not fundamentally doubt his existence.

Eternal silence

Among the early Christians we find that Ignatius of Antioch is noted for his references to silence. Ignatius (c50–c107) is tradition- ally believed to have received teachings directly from the apostle St John. Ramsay thinks that the Antioch man's understanding of silence partly reflects the fact that he and some other non-Jewish converts to Christianity had prior experience of cultic mysteries such as those at Eleusis or those of Mithraism (pp. 158–166). In any event, for whatever reason, and as we partly saw earlier, Ignatius wrote to the Ephesians that,

> It is better to be silent and to be, than loquacious and not be. It is good to teach, if one does what one says. There is, therefore, one Teacher [Christ], who spoke and it was done; but what he did silently was worthy of God. He who possesses the word of Jesus, is truly able to hear His silence, so that he is perfect [Kleist, p. 66 adds "he will act through his speech and be under- stood through his silence"], so that what he says he does, so that by being silent he is known. Nothing is hidden from God; even that which we conceal is near Him. (Lightfoot, vol. 2, p. 68, n. xv and vol. 3, p. 27, par. 15)

Also, in his epistle to the Ephesians, Ignatius speaks of the virgin- ity of Mary and the birth and death of Jesus as "three mysteries for crying out that were wrought in the silence of God" (Lightfoot, vol. 2, pp. 76–78 and vol. 3, p. 28, par. 19. Richardson (p. 93) gives "crying to be told"). Elsewhere, in his epistle to the Magnesians (par. 8), Ignatius appears to write of God as having manifested Himself through his Son, who is His Word "proceeding from Silence". However, the extant text which was for long the most common had two additional words, "eternal, not", inserted before these three words so that they asserted that Jesus was "eternal, *not* proceeding from Silence"! Lightfoot argues strongly that the extant text is wrong and that the negative was interposed because tran- scribers feared that the affirmative lent itself to certain Gnostic and other heretical interpretations (Lightfoot, vol. 2, pp. 126–128, n. 8 and vol. 3, pp. 170–172, n. 28; Ramsay, p. 440). Hammond Bammel (p. 75) agrees with him. Lake, who follows "recent editors" including Lightfoot, says that there was "a doctrinal emendation due to fear of Gnostic theories in which σιγή [Sigé: Silence] and θεός [Theos: God] were the original pair from which λόγος [Logos: Word] emanated" (vol. 1, p. 204). We considered earlier above the significance of this dualism. Lightfoot's belief that the two words were added to distort the original appears to be in accord with the reading of Ignatius by Severus, patriarch of Antioch in the early sixth century. The latter explained the words of Ignatius quoted above, as follows,

> That then he proceeded from Silence is this, that He was ineffa-
> bly begotten of the Father, and as the word is incomprehensible
> whatever it be or the mind; therefore it is right that He should be
> honoured in silence, and not that his divine and unprecedented
> birth should be inquired into (Cureton, pp. 30–31).

Richardson perceives an influence other than that of Gnosticism. He describes Ignatius as being "hospitable to quite a few phrases and ideas familiar from Hellenistic religion and alien to the general stream of Biblical thought", including that God is Silence, and sums up the saint's thinking about God as being that, "God's essential character was that of silence—a silence broken only by the incarna-tion, and even then with reserve and modesty" (pp. 78–80).

St Augustine of Hippo (354–430) says of God that, "He made all things through His Word; and His Word is Christ Himself, in whom the angels and all the most pure heavenly spirits rest in holy silence" (Christopher, p. 57). Augustine also looks forward to joining other believers after death in the holy city of God, "that we may no longer shout … a profession of faith expressed in babble of words, but may absorb this by most pure and fervent contemplation in that heavenly silence" (ibid., p. 79). Like the earlier psalmists, Augustine calls out to God to speak so that he may hear. In the opening sections of his *Confessions*, he pleads that his heart is listening and begs God not to hide his face from the unworthy man who is longing for revelation (bk. 1, ch. 5). "This straining of his ears, the ears even of his heart," writes Taylor (p. 40), "is the painful longing which pulsates through the entire *Confessions*." She observes that Augustine yearns for revelation rather than self-revelation, despite his *Confessions* being frequently invoked as the prototype of modern autobiography. However, the distinction between knowing God and knowing oneself is not clear-cut when one believes that we are made in God's image and likeness.

Fear of silence

With or without God, the very idea of silence or darkness as an everlasting state is terrible. This is so not least because we know that all phenomena that are evident to our ears or eyes must by their nature eventually pass away. Sounds and light emanate from objects that will fade and die. The terror of contemplating this prospect was famously expressed by Blaise Pascal (1623–1662), the French scientist and mathematician, who wrote in his *Pensées* (s. 3, no. 206) that, *"Le silence éternel de ces espaces infinis m'effraie"* (The eternal silence of these infinite spaces frightens me).

Matthew Arnold, in his poem "Self-Dependence", recalls standing at the prow of a ship and gazing up to the stars. He admires their apparent detachment or indifference:

> Unaffrighted by the silence round them,
> Undistracted by the sights they see,
> These demand not that the things without them
> Yield them love, amusement, sympathy.

However, the apparent indifference of God can also be terrifying. Where is there clear communication from that source whom we are told exists and with whom we may have a personal relationship? Chesterton (1874–1936) thought that ostensible absence was worse than any concept of divine vengeance or punishment. He wrote (Chapter Eight), "For it is not the activeness of tyranny that maddens, but its passiveness. We hate the deafness of the god, more than his strength. Silence is the unbearable repartee." But believers claim that God is not really absent. He is evident from his creation, and his word may be heard through the scriptures and in other ways.

One of the most poignant accounts of the struggle to come to terms with God's apparent indifference and silence has been written by Reynolds Price, who was confined for life to a wheelchair.

It is poignant because it is his reply to a young medical student who himself seeks meaning when he is diagnosed with terminal cancer, and who will die without seeing Price's considered response. Price's ability as a professor of English to compose succinct and clear prose is matched by his honesty as a doubting believer. He writes that,

> You'll have gathered then that, in recent years, I've come more and more to wish that the scriptures of Judaism and Christianity— and a great many more modern clergy and counsellors—had forthrightly confronted the silence at the very heart of any God we can worship and that they'd observed it more unflinchingly with us, not dimming our view with rose-coloured screens and sweet-voiced chatter that are certain to smash or go cold-dumb at the first touch of heat, not to mention the scalding breath of terror at the sight of pained death (p. 74).

Price's opinion is by no means glib. He shares the view of those believers who think that God's silence is not indifference, that we are answered in ways that are appropriate to our lot as beings with free will. Yet the scriptures themselves demonstrate that the absence of clear evidence of benign intervention by God has long bothered even believers who were as staunch as Job. Indeed, the extent to which the authors of the psalms repeatedly refer to the suffering inflicted by enemies suggests that there has long been an underlying insecurity and doubt about God hearing us or caring about us. The lament of the person who seems forsaken by God is itself a theme of the psalms. More than two thousand years later, spiritual seekers are still asking, "If God exists then why does s/he not speak up?" What, if anything, lies outside the text that is Creation? Can a divine s/he or it communicate with and help us?

We live in an epoch that can grasp in unprecedented ways just how vast and relatively empty is space. It is far greater than Pascal imagined even in his most frightened moments. If there are gods and angels they are nowhere to be seen, and we know that some of those who believe that they hear them talking or see them appear are simply psychologically disturbed. Even our ability to talk about the possibility of a God is problematic, as modern philosophers and theologians grapple with the limitations of language and the senses when it comes to describing aspects of existence. Nevertheless, people continue to have faith, even if that faith is blind. Is it admirable or meaningless? Can they by dint of prayer and reflection grasp some ultimate truth that transcends relative existence, or are they engaged in self-delusion and wishful thinking?

The Japanese novel *Silence*, by Shusahu Endo (1923–1996), treats imaginatively the grinding down of faith by force of negative experience. It takes as its theme the attempted conversion of Japan to Christianity. Jesuit priests found themselves working in a culture where their ostensible achievements turned out to be far more ambiguous than they had thought. Not for the first time in the case of Christians encountering an old culture, it happened that such local people as adopted Christianity did so in ways that folded their new beliefs back into their former ways of viewing the world. While missionaries wondered what kind of faith was taking root, they found themselves facing persecution by authorities that regarded them as meddling, foreign intruders. Burdened by doubts about the underlying progress of their mission and by the torture and killing of colleagues, they turned to God for guidance but experienced "the feeling that while men raise their voices in anguish God remains with folded arms, silent" (Endo, p. 105). As that early mission fell apart, some priests apostasized and "went native". Others died miserably while their colleagues called on God:

> Stop! Stop! Lord, it is now that you should break the silence.
> You must not remain silent. Prove that you are justice, that you are goodness, that you are love. You must say something to show the world that you are the august one.
> A great shadow passed over his soul like that of a bird flying over the mast of a ship (Endo, p. 266).

The story also touches on the suffering of Christ himself when facing death, and the relevance of his death to that of some local martyrs who had recently been drowned in Japan:

> On that night had that man [Christ], too, felt the silence of God? Had he, too, shuddered with fear? ... The sea into which those bodies wrapped in straw matting had dropped straight down! This sea stretched out endlessly, sadly; and all this time, over the sea, God simply maintained his unrelenting silence. "*Eloi, Eloi,*

lama sabacthani!" [Aramaic: "My God, My God, why have you forsaken me?", at Mark 15:34]. With the memory of the leaden sea, these words suddenly burst into his consciousness. *"Eloi, Eloi, lama sabacthani!"* It is three o'clock on that Friday; and from the cross this voice rings out to a sky covered with darkness. The priest had always thought that these words were that man's prayer, not that they issued from terror at the silence of God (Endo, pp. 222–223).

One person who says that he has read Endo's novel "countless times" is the film director Martin Scorsese, who has been working on an adaptation of it for the screen. He sees it as the tale of one who begins on the path of Christ but ends up replaying the role of Judas, but he still discerns in this story of silence the ultimate presence of God in a world of free will (Foreword to Endo). Endo was interested in the Jesuits not least because these men were educated believers, and certainly not unthinking or credulous when it came to spiritual formation or religious tradition. He himself was also writing in a century that had seen a most ferocious assault on a religious people in the form of the Nazi liquidation of Jews. Yet many Jews continued to believe despite such terrible and sustained suffering, no doubt fortified by the fact that their Hebrew scriptures showed clearly that this was not the first such deadly assault on their nation. That they took comfort from their scriptures is evident in the fact that, even as they were being gassed, some sang the psalms. A people who had composed the psalms knew very well that God does not respond instantly to our cries for help, and that a people may be long ground down before relief arrives.

Indeed, the silence of some gods has been more sustained than that of the Christian God in Japan or the Jewish God in Auschwitz, for in neither of those cases was a whole people's fate ultimately sealed by silence. Christians came to be tolerated in Japan, and Jews have survived the Holocaust as a distinct nation. Yet, during the past two centuries, many native religions have passed away or all but passed away. Colonization and "progress" and modernity, or simply the basest forms of liquidation, obliterated them. While it is common to describe such beliefs as "primitive", many of those who held them supported communal lifestyles that appear to have been admirable in their respect for members of the group and for their gods and for nature. If the diversity of their languages and belief systems is lost, what of the realities that they attempted to describe?

Claude Lévi-Strauss commented on the silence of those histories of which we are unaware. Referring to the possibility of intense cultural and economic activity by peoples on both the Asiatic and the American coasts of the Pacific long before Columbus set sail from Europe, he warned that we may have fallen into an error, namely,

> ... that of thinking that for twenty thousand years America was cut off from the rest of the world, simply because, during that time, she was cut off from western Europe. Everything points, on the contrary, to the hypothesis that, while the Atlantic remained in total silence, a humming as of innumerable bees could be heard all around the periphery of the Pacific (p. 246).

Apophatic theology and empty phrases

Philosophers allow for the possibility of forms of existence that we do not yet glimpse or understand—as one might well expect any open-minded intellectual to do in the absence of evidence of an absence. For its part, the branch of theology that wrestles with the angel of the void is known as "apophatic theology". This has been succinctly defined thus:

> Negative theology, that is, theology which is so conscious that God transcends all created conceptions that it limits itself to statements about what God is not rather than making any claims to know God in himself (Komonchak et al., p. 48).

While Davies and Turner observe that, "... it can seem defeatist, at best, to preach a God of the gaps to half-empty pews rather than a God who is Lord and Creator of all" (p. 1), the fact is that much of what is asserted in churches about God today seems empty and false to an educated mind. Language and iconography that served earlier generations may now be a hindrance on the spiritual path. Indeed, Muers explores how the silences of Christ himself can speak to us meaningfully.

The discovery of apophatic theology is a liberating experience for some people. This tradition is particularly associated with Eastern Christianity, going back to Clement of Alexandria and Origen:

> Using the symbol of the divine darkness which Moses entered on Mount Sinai [also known as Horeb and the place where Elijah encountered "sheer silence"] when he went to meet God, Gregory [of Nyssa] makes it clear that only within this darkness, after intellectual and sense impressions have been stripped away, does the soul come as close to God as it can, by faith (*The Westminster Dictionary of Christian Theology*, p. 32).

The apophatic tradition does not dispense with the requirement that seekers use their brains as best they can to know as much as they can about Creation and about God's presence in it, and to develop moral codes. A mystical, still less mystifying silence, is no alternative to illumination and purification. So cataphatic theology, which contemplates God as he may be known in the world, complements apophatic theology. Papanikolaou has recently examined two divergent views on how apophaticism can influence the conception of God even within one Church.

Thomas Aquinas is sometimes derided for advancing certain positive "proofs" of God, as though God might be proved by evidence adduced in a court of law. However, his proofs were more in the nature of preliminary skirmishes in the struggle to know God. They point to a mystery and he was aware of their limitations (Turner; McCabe). Respect for the rational and for science is part of a mature Western Christian tradition, as it is too of some other mystical paths. Panikkar asks,

> Have we perhaps betrayed the message of the Buddha by seeking to render it intelligible through words and concepts? Ought we to have respected its silence, and made no attempt to interpret its meaning on a rational level? But the suspension of the intellect entails the risk of falling into the opposite excess, irrational pietism. The Buddha—to repeat—declares himself equally far from either extreme. The renunciation of philosophy as a vehicle incapable of carrying us to the goal because it is too weak, is an extreme as pernicious as the pretension to a wish to understand all (p. 170).

Thus, apophatic or "negative" theology has affinities with other ways of seeing reality that highlight the limits of conceptualization, including with Buddhism and philosophical deconstructionism. A modern critical mind that has fed on the thoughts of Derrida, Foucault, and Lacan will understand such a theological method. It holds open the door for radical encounters with the divine while maintaining intellectual standards in relation to the dangers of personal self-delusion and emotionalism, and at the same time anchors negation in liturgical and ecclesiastical practices. Silence then becomes not simply what there was before people spoke or wrote but also what remains of reality after they have exhausted their resources attempting to define and describe it. Dewailly observes that negative theology,

> ... refuses to affirm anything about God which would run the risk of overstepping the bounds of what is actually known. The attitude is to be found outside Christianity—in the Jewish apologetics against idolatry and mythology, in Gnosticism, Hinduism, and Taoism .... Even in the New Testament we find the use of privative adjectives. The judgements of God are "inscrutable", his ways are "unsearchable" (Romans 11:33) (pp. 294–295).

Both the theologian and the philosopher may advance by stripping away the accumulated undergrowth of theories that were idolatrous or totalitarian in their absolute assumptions and certainties. Suddenly there is space to breathe again, even if the primeval silence of that space is alarming. For that reason, for example, Buddhists are frequently reminded of the need for an experienced teacher to help one avoid pitfalls.

Absence of evidence is not evidence of absence. Philosophers such as Heidegger, Derrida, Merleau-Ponty, and Habermas concede that there is more to reality than can or will be expressed in words or grasped logically by our limited human minds. The *Oxford English Dictionary* currently defines "ineffable" as that which "cannot be expressed or described in language; too great for words; transcending expression; unspeakable, unutterable, inexpressible". Funk comments on the intrinsic inadequacy of language that, "Prattle closes off understanding, idle talk indicates that language has been split off from its grounds." As a result, we no longer know the need to keep silent, to listen, to hearken. He adds that, "... as phenomenology is concerned with the silence that surrounds language, it attends to the silence which permeates language itself" (pp. 44, 230, and 234).

Might silence then sometimes speak as, or even more, eloquently of the ineffable than sound does? This matters because deafening silence is not merely an intellectual challenge for philosophers and theologians, it is a terrifying reality for people who must live with its reproach and for whom the question is not simply academic. The poet Marianne Moore, herself once a very lonely adolescent (her father died insane when she was 14), may have spoken for many people when she flashed, "Professional theologians know nothing about a silent God!" (Terrein, pp. 388–389).

The question of how we might move from the limitations of our present language and knowledge to know the silent spaces beyond them in any way is more complex, with the religious insisting that there are ways of grasping ultimate truth outside conceptualization and through centred prayer or silent meditation. Jesus said,

> I thank you, Father, Lord of heaven and earth, because you have hidden these things from the wise and the intelligent and have revealed them to infants .... No one knows the Son except the Father, and no one knows the Father except the Son and anyone to whom the Son chooses to reveal him (Matthew 11:25–27).

Indeed, as noted earlier above, in teaching us the greatest of Christian prayers—known as "The Lord's Prayer"—Jesus specifically cautioned against "heaping up empty phrases as Gentiles do; for they think that they will be heard because of their many words. Do not be like them, for your Father knows what you need before you ask" (Matthew 6:7). It may be noted that his followers appear not always to follow his advice in that respect.

For the believer, asking men or women to attempt to know God and to explain him is a bit like asking your dog to report back to you on the workings of the jet engine. Language is our creation, comes from our experience, and only expresses what we are capable of knowing. The dog can bark but he will never explain why aircraft fly. To a terrier such knowledge is part of the abyss that lies outside his range, part of a silence which he can never fathom. He is condemned by his nature to a cycle of barking. According to philosophers such as Derrida, men and women appear to be in a similar predicament. Grace may somehow allow us to escape the predicament and to "know" what is in the silence but language can never do so. Plato must stay in his cave and watch shadows reflected on its wall, but Elijah goes to the mouth of the cave and finds that he can hear the voice of God. On 9 February 1841, Henry Thoreau wrote in his journal, "I have been breaking silence these twenty-three years, and have hardly made a rent in it. Silence has no end. Speech is but the beginning of it" (Blake, p. 358).

When Derrida said there is nothing knowable outside the text ("*il n'y a pas de hors texte*"), he was referring to the limitations of the logical mind that must try to understand by means of concepts or words. The mind cannot do otherwise, no matter how sublime its ideas. Prayer may well be an attempt to be heard by God, but usually on our own conceptual terms. Indeed, insofar as all language struggles to make sense of reality and to place us adequately in relationship to it, making language has itself been described by Norman Fischer as making prayer:

> Our utterances, whether silent or voiced, written or thought, distinct or vague, repeated or fleeting, are always essentially prayer, even though we seldom realize it. To speak, to intone, to form words with mouth and heart and spirit, is to reach out and reach in. What we're always reaching out and in to, even when we don't know that we are, is the boundless unknowable, the unnameable (p. xix).

Our minds are not broad enough to encompass the entire universe and so silence remains. God may be regarded as unnameable because to attempt to name him by word or to represent him in an image is a travesty of his boundless nature. Hence the earliest Christians did not depict Jesus visually as a man. The image of Jesus hanging on a cross became common only later. Early Buddhists too avoided iconography. The Jews even avoided pronouncing their word for God, and when they wrote it omitted the vowels in "Yahweh". Most Muslims refrain from depicting God or their prophet in an image. Such silences are sacred.

What some apophatic theologians and some atheists have in common is that they both reject explanations for God that are entirely verbal. Atheists may also, especially if they are deconstructionists, reject any explanation of the material world that is entirely verbal, given the intrinsic limitations of language. Both acknowledge a certain intrinsic mystery, a sort of "cloud of unknowing" that obscures reality, even if believers sense a divine presence in it while "unbelievers" have no experience of any such presence and are unable or unwilling to accept on faith that such a mysterious presence exists. The apophatic theologian may have more respect for an honest atheist than for a high-sounding churchman whose very verbosity becomes a kind of idolatry that presumes to present God in the form of an ultimately knowable being or as a neat formula. Living with the limitations of concepts and words is a challenge. Reality eludes any fixed and final definitions. As the opening words of a great Taoist text assert,

> The Tao that can be trodden is not the enduring and unchanging Tao. The name that can be named is not the enduring and unchanging name.
> (Conceived of as) having no name, it is the Originator of heaven and earth; (conceived of as) having a name, it is the Mother of all things (Lao-Tse, section 1).

Comfort

It may be comforting for people to be promised that that they can know God in a personal way rather than simply as an idea or through words. One of the ways in which believers try to communicate with God is through silent prayer, not the silences of Hannah whose lips shaped words even as she remained quiet, but the silence of not heaping up any words deliberately and of remaining mindul, present, and disposed towards the divine, who knows what we need without our asking (Matthew 6:32). At the heart of Zen koans there is likewise a recognition of the limitations of logic and language when it comes to understanding Creation. Jesus himself, not just his words or what is written about him in the gospels, is "the way, the truth and the light". Once again we see that there is a dimension of reality that is not merely the opposite or absence of words but that is beyond words.

Yet, the manner in which some people purport to know God and his will is quite unconvincing. In February 2009 I flew into New York City. On my mind as my aircraft descended were two very recent crashes. In the first incident, when jet engines failed on take-off at La Guardia and the captain "miraculously" managed to land his plane on the Hudson River, nobody died. In the second, when a Continental flight out of Newark went down while approaching Buffalo, everyone perished. On my next day in Manhattan I happened to catch a TV broadcast by one of America's leading televangelists. Dressed slickly in a suit, he was holding forth to a massive and packed auditorium about how God had saved those passengers in the Hudson. You could see God's hand in the fact that the pilot was so experienced, that he was an expert in gliding, and so on and so on. There was not one word about the other crash. It seems that God opted for one group to be saved and for the other to die.

A believer in God has suggested that, "While guesses and speculation may distract from the pain, ignorance stands ready to mock the inquirer." He notes that the researcher or theologian may have any number of theories but suspects that, "… it is only in the silence of faith and the peace of trust that God's answer can be heard" (Garrison, p. 85). Lines from "A Lancashire doxology" come to mind:

> He opens and He shuts His hand,
> But why, we cannot understand:
> Pours and dries up His mercies' flood,
> And yet is still All-perfect Good (Craik, p. 603).

It is an awkward fact that God's interventions appear to be arbitrary. Some people get cured, some do not. Some hear from God or an angel or a saint, some do not. And it may be that the people who do not get saved or helped as they would like have prayed the hardest. To say that the Lord works in mysterious ways in not just an understatement. It is glib. The silences of God suggest that, whether you believe in an omnipotent God or not, you cannot count on him to intervene directly even if you are being mugged or raped or gassed. We are abandoned in our humanity no more and no less than was Jesus in the last hours before his crucifixion. The fact that many of us like Reynolds Price (pp. 50–51) have felt a helpful presence or intervention on some occasions, or that rational people think that praying to a holy man like Padre Pio can result in miracles, simply highlights the divine inconsistencies and apparent injustices. They are the sort of injustices about which the authors of the psalms cried out to heaven. Their cries are still being repeated today, as witnessed for example by the fact that Rabbi Kusher's *When Bad Things Happen to Good People* has been a best-seller internationally.

The problem of evil presents priests and pastoral helpers with a special difficulty when they are faced with counselling victims of violence, especially in the case of children. One minister has admitted frankly that, "My belief in God's presence has on some occasions been little more than a small knot tied at the end of a threadbare rope" (Duke, pp. 5 and 53). Not all stories about the silence of God have as neat an ending as does that of old Job.

"Out of the depths I cry to you, O Lord," is the prayer of Psalm 130. They are the depths of pending despair in the face of silence. Many other psalms also open with pleas in the face of apparent indifference. The silence of heaven seems to be long-standing and it mocks our limited knowledge of the universe, whether we are believers wrestling with angels or non-believers struggling with language. But it is a silence that is as real as any sound. It was there in the beginning, is there now, and will be there at the end of time when, as Hilaire Belloc put it (p. 13),

> ... the sea will recover all its heritage of silence: the works of
> Man will have ceased, and the rattle of his metal contrivances.
> Then the Silence of the Sea will return.

EPILOGUE

Iam standing alone in a field. It is late and almost dark, and the crows no longer call from the old wood across the River Nore. Tonight is warm, for Ireland. No breeze disturbs the scent of summer flowers. No car moves. Venus shines brightly in the southern sky.

We know this neighbouring planet now. Two dozen spacecraft have travelled millions of miles to probe its clouds and map its surface. Copernicus remained silent about aspects of its brightness that did not suit his theory of the solar system. Our silence reaches out into space.

My gaze tonight goes beyond Venus and is lost in deepening darkness. Far away a star explodes, but no one will hear it. Here is infinity. The sky is crossed by the sound of an invisible aircraft, high above Ballilogue, making its way from America to some city in Europe or Asia.

Now there is silence as complete as any can be in this country. An animal shuffles and stomps its hoof on hard ground. A distant dog barks. It is peaceful again. The very silence is an invitation to thought, to speech.

BIBLIOGRAPHY

Abhishiktananda (Le Saux, H.) (1975). *The Further Shore*. Delhi: ISPCK.

Adeney, F. S. (2003). How I, a Christian, have learned from Buddhist practice, or "The frog sat on the lily pad ... not waiting". In: Gross, R. M. & Muck, T. C. (Eds.), *Christians Talk about Buddhist Meditation: Buddhists Talk about Christian Prayer* (pp. 15–19). New York: Continuum.

"A. E." (Russell, G. W.) (1913). The Silence of Love. In: *Collected Poems by A. E.* London: Macmillan.

Aeschylus (2006). *Suppliant Maidens, Persians, Prometheus, Seven against Thebes*. Smyth, H. W. (Trans.). Cambridge, MA: Harvard University Press.

Ali, A. Y. (1999). *The Meaning of the Holy Qur'an*. Beltsville, MD: Amana Publications.

Allinson, F. G. (Ed.) (1921). *Menander: The Principal Fragments*. London: W. Heinemann.

(Father) Andrew, SDC (1947). *In the Silence: Four Retreats*. London: Mowbray.

Andrews, C. P. (1933). *Christ in Silence*. London: Hodder & Stoughton.

Annual Register, or a View of the History, Politics and Literature for the Year 1791. New ed. (1824). London: Baldwin, Cradock & Joy.

Anon (1993). Silence: the resounding experience. *American Journal of Psychotherapy, 47*(2): 167–170 (editorial).

Anon (2003). Obituary of Maurice Blanchot. London: *The Daily Telegraph*, March 11.

Aristophanes (1925). *Lysistrata*. Lindsay, J. (Trans.). Sydney: Fanfrolico Press.

Armstrong, K. (1993). *The End of Silence: Woman and the Priesthood*. London: Fourth Estate.

Asch, S. E. (1953). Effects of group pressure upon the modification and distortion of judgments. In: Cartwright, D. & Zander, A. (Eds.), *Group Dynamics; Research and Theory* (pp. 151–162). New York: Row, Peterson.

Ashworth, G. (1999). The silencing of women. In: Dunne, T. & Wheeler, N. (Eds.), *Human Rights in Global Politics* (pp. 259–276). Cambridge: Cambridge University Press.

Asjad, N. (2004). High cost of Pakistani women's silence. London: BBC, November 29. At: http://news.bbc.co.uk/2/hi/south_asia/4043321. stm (4/2/11).

Augustine of Hippo (1960). *The Confessions*. Ryan, J. K. (Trans.). New York: Image.

Auld, A. G. (1986). *1 and 2 Kings*. Daily Study Bible Series. Philadelphia, PA: Westminster Press.

Babylonian Talmud: Tractate Berakot (1921). Cohen, A. (Trans.). Cambridge: Cambridge University Press.

Bacon, F. (1645). *De dignitate et augmentis scientiarum libri IX*. Lugd. Batavorum (now Leiden, Netherlands): Moyardum & Wijngaerde.

Bair, D. (1978). *Samuel Beckett*. London: Jonathan Cape.

Baker, S. (1955). The theory of silence. *Journal of General Psychology, 53*: 145–167.

Banes, S. & Lepecki, A. (Eds.) (2006). *The Senses in Performance*. London: Routledge.

Barbour, J. D. (2004). *The Value of Solitude: The Ethics and Spirituality of Aloneness in Authobiography*. Charlottesville, VA: University of Virginia Press.

Barker, W. W. (2001). *The Adages of Erasmus*. University of Toronto Press.

Barnes, S. (2009). One moment of silence, then summer roars into life. London: *The Times*, July 8.

Barrois, G. A. (1986). *The Fathers Speak: St Basil the Great, St Gregory of Nazianzus, St Gregory of Nyssa*. Crestwood, NJ: St Vladimir's Seminary Press.

Barron, S. (1992). *There's a Boy in Here*. New York: Simon & Schuster.

Basso, K. H. (1972). "To give up on words": silence in Western Apache culture. In: Giglioli, P. P. (Ed.), *Language and Social Context* (pp. 67–68). Harmondsworth, UK: Penguin.

Basso, K. H. (1990). *Western Apache Language and Culture: Essays in Lingustic Anthropology*. Tucson, AZ: University of Arizona Press.

Baules, G. & Klein, R. D. (Eds.) (1983). *Theories of Women's Studies*. London: Routledge.

Bauman, R. (1983). *Let Your Words be Few: Symbolism of Speaking and Silence among Seventeenth-century Quakers*. Long Grove, IL: Waveland Press.

Beckett, S. (1975). *The Unnamable*. London: Calder & Boyars.

Belloc, H. (1941). The silence of the sea. In: Belloc, H. *The Silence of the Sea and Other Essays* (pp. 9–13). London: Cassell.

Benjamin, O. (2003). The power of unsilencing: between silence and negotiation in heterosexual relationships. *Journal for the Theory of Social Behaviour, 33*(1): 1–19.

Bergin, A. E. & Jensen, S. P. (1990). Religiosity of psychotherapists: a national survey. *Psychotherapy, 27*: 3–7.

[The] *Bhagavadgita* (1882). Telang, K. T. (Trans.). In: Müller, M. *Sacred Books, 8*.

Bianco, R. (2005). Unforgivable trespass: incessant commentary. McLean, VA: *USA Today*, April 10.

Bindeman, S. L. (1981). *Heidegger and Wittgenstein: The Poetics of Silence*. Lanham, MD: University Press of America.

Birrell, A. (1887). *Obiter dicta* (2nd series). London: Eliot Stock.

Blackmore, R. D. (1872). *The Maid of Sker*. Edinburgh: Blackwood.

Blanchot, M. (1989). *The Space of Literature*. Smock, A. (Trans.). Lincoln, NE: University of Nebraska Press.

Bland, R. (1814). *Proverbs Chiefly Taken from the Adagia of Erasmus, with Explanations*. 2 vols. London: Egerton.

Blake, H. G. (Ed.) (1888). *Winter: From the Journal of Henry D. Thoreau*. Boston: Houghton Mifflin.

Blaser, R. (1989). Poetry and positivism: high muck-a-muck or "spiritual ketchup". In: Blodgett, E. D. & Coward, H. G. (Eds.), *Silence, the Word and the Sacred* (pp. 21–50). Calgary, Alberta: Wilfrid Laurier University Press.

Bock, P. K. (1976). I think but dare not speak: silence in Elizabethan culture. *Journal of Anthropological Research, 32*: 285–294.

Bogarde, D. (1983). *An Orderly Man*. London: Chatto & Windus.

Böhlig, A. & Wisse, F. (1996). Translation of "The Gospel of the Egyptians". In: Robinson, J. M. (Ed.), *The Nag Hammadi Library in English: The Definitive New Translation of the Gnostic Scriptures, Complete in One Volume* (pp. 208–220). Leiden, Netherlands: Brill.

Boman, T. (1960). *Hebrew Thought Compared with the Greek*. Philadelphia, PA: Westminster.

Boomer, D. S. (1965). Hesitation and grammatical encoding. *Language and Speech, 8*(3): 148–158.

Booth, T. & Booth, W. (1996). Sounds of silence: narrative research with inarticulate subjects. *Disability & Society, 9*(1): 55–69.

Boswell, J. (1823). *The Life of Samuel Johnson.* 4 vols. London: Richardson.

Boyd, C. (2006). Report of email from Athol Fugard, February 4. Posted by *The Morning After: Performing Arts in Australia,* at http://chrisboyd. blogspot.com/2006/02/power-without-power-athol-fugards.html (4/2/2011).

Breasted, J. H. (1912). *Development of Religion and Thought in Ancient Egypt.* London: Hodder & Stoughton.

Brereton, P. (2005). *Hollywood Utopia: Ecology in Contemporary American Cinema.* Bristol, UK: Intellect.

Brislin, R. W. & Kim, E. S. (2003). Cultural diversity in people's understanding and uses of time. *Applied Psychology: An International Review, 52*(3): 363–382.

Britt, R. R. (2003). Sounds in space: silencing misconceptions (September 22). At: http://www.space.com/scienceastronomy/mystery_monday_030922.html (4/2/2011).

Brockopp, B. W. & Lester, D. (1973). The silent caller. In: Lester, D. & Brockopp, D. (Eds.), *Crisis Intervention and Counseling by Telephone* (pp. 199–205). Springfield, IL: Charles C. Thomas.

Bromiley, G. W. (1953). *Zwingli and Bullinger.* London: SCM.

Brown, A. & Coupland, C. (2005). Sounds of silence: graduate trainees, hegemony and resistance. *Organisation Studies, 26*(7): 1049–1069.

Bruce, V. R. (1970). *Movement in Silence and Sound.* London: Bell, G.

Brueggemann, W. (1982). *1 Kings.* Knox Preaching Guides. Atlanta, GA: John Knox Press.

Bruller, J. ("Vercors") (1942). *Le Silence de la Mer.* See Vercors.

Bruneau, T. J. (1973). Communicative silences: forms and functions. *Journal of Communications, 23*(1): 17–46.

Bruneau, T. J. (2008). How Americans use silence and silences to communicate. *China Media Research, 4*(2): 77–85.

Burke, E. (1857). *The Speeches of the Right Honourable Edmund Burke on the Impeachment of Warren Hastings. To Which is Added a Selection of Burke's Epistolary Correspondence.* 2 vols. London: Bohn, H. G.

Burke, E. (1887). *The Works.* 12 vols. London: Nimmo.

Bushnell, R. W. (1988). *Prophesying Tragedy: Sign and Voice in Sophocles' Theban Plays.* Ithaca, NY: Cornell University Press.

Bushnell, R. W. (1998). Speech and silence: Oedipus the King. In: Bushnell, R. W. *Prophesying Tragedy: Sign and Voice in Sophocles' Theban Plays,* ch. 4. Ithaca, NY: Cornell University Press.

Bushnell, R. W. (2005). *A Companion to Tragedy*. Oxford: Blackwell.

Cacoullos, A. R. & Sifianou, M. (Eds.) (1998). *Anatomies of Silence: Selected Papers, Second HASE International Conference on Autonomy of Logos: Anatomies of Silence*. Athens, Greece: University of Athens School of Philosophy.

Cage, J. (1954). For a speaker. In: J. Cage, *Silence* (pp. 146–193).

Cage, J. (1958). Composition as process: lecture iii, Communication. In: Cage, J. *Silence* (pp. 41–57).

Cage, J. (1959a). Lecture on nothing. In: Cage, J. *Silence* (pp. 109–127). First in *Incontri musicali*, August 1959.

Cage, J. (1959b). Lecture on something. In: Cage, J. *Silence* (pp. 128–145). First in *It is* (P. Pavia, Ed.), 1959.

Cage, J. (1973). *Silence: Lectures and Writings*, Middletown, CT: Wesleyan University Press.

Cage, J. (1981). *For the Birds: John Cage in Conversation with Daniel Charles*. Boston: Marion Boyars.

Caranfo, A. (2004). Silence as the foundation of learning. *Educational Theory*, 54(2): 211–230.

Carbaugh, D. (Ed.) (1990). *Cultural Communication and Intercultural Contact*. Hillsdale, NJ: Lawrence Erlbaum.

Cardullo, B. (2004). The space of time, the sound of silence: on Ozon's *Under the Sand* (2000, France) and Tsai's *What Time is it There?* (2001, Taiwan). In: Cardullo, B. *In Search of Cinema; Writings on International Film Art* (pp. 215–231). Montreal: McGill-Queen's University Press.

Carlson, T., Kirkpatrick, D., Hecker, L. & Killmer, M. (2002). Religion, spirituality, and marriage and family therapy: a study of family therapists' beliefs about the appropriateness of addressing religious and spiritual issues in therapy. *American Journal of Family Therapy, 30*: 157–171.

Carlyle, T. (1840). *Chartism*. London: James Fraser.

Carlyle, T. (1846). *Sartor resartus: The Life and Opinions of Herr Teufelsdröckh*. New York: Wiley & Putnam.

Carlyle, T. (1860a). *Critical and Miscellaneous Essays*. 4 vols. Boston, MA: Brown & Taggard.

Carlyle, T. (1860b). *Oliver Cromwell's Letters and Speeches*. 2 vols. New York: Harper.

CBS News (2003). Breaking the silence (July 16). Report on autism. At http://www.cbsnews.com/stories/2003/01/14/60II/main536416.shtml (4/2/2011).

Chesterton, G. K. (1906). *Charles Dickens*. London: Methuen.

Cheung, K. (1993). *Articulate Silences: Hisaye Yamamoto, Maxine Hong Kingston, Joy Kogawa*. Ithaca, NY: Cornell University Press.

Cheung, K. (1994). Attentive silence in Joy Kogawa's *Obasan*. In: Hedges, E. & Fishkin, S. (Eds.), *Listening to Silences: New Essays in Feminist Criticism* (pp. 113–129). New York: Oxford University Press.

Choong, P. (2002). New Zealand Chinese women: a hyphenated identity of East and West. MA thesis, University of Auckland. Chapter at http://www.stevenyoung.co.nz/chinesevoice/women/pepedec03. htm (4/2/2011).

Chow, M. W. (2003). Coping with silence: comparative analysis on post-abortion grief in Japan and the United States. Thesis for the Department of International Relations, Tufts University, Medford, MA.

Christopher, J. P. (1946). *St Augustine: the First Catechetical Instruction*. Westminster, MD: Newman Press and London: Longmans, Green & Co.

Clough, A. H. (Ed.) (1872). *Plutarch's Lives: Translation Called Dryden's*. 5 vols. Boston, MA: Little, Brown.

CNN (2002). Composer pays for piece of silence (September 23). At http://archives.cnn.com/2002/SHOWBIZ/Music/09/23/uk.silence/ (4/2/2011).

Cohen, A. (1932). *Everyman's Talmud*. London: J. M. Dent.

Collins, R. F. (1999). *Sacra Pagina: First Corinthians*. Collegeville, MN: Liturgical Press.

Collins, R. O. (1990). *Western African History*. Princeton, NJ: Markus Wiener.

Cook, J. (1964). Silence in psychotherapy. *Journal of Counseling Psychology*, 11: 42–46.

Cooper, C. & Theobald, T. (2004). *Shut up and Listen!* London: Kogan Page.

Corcoran, M. P. & O'Brien, M. (Eds.) (2005). *Political Censorship and the Democratic State: The Irish Broadcasting Ban*. Dublin: Four Courts Press.

Cosmopoulos, M. B. (2003). *Greek Mysteries: The Archaeology and Ritual of Ancient Greek Secret Cults*. London: Routledge.

Cotter, J. (2006). *Out of the Silence ... Into the Silence: Prayer's Daily Round*. Aberdaron, UK: Cairns Publications.

Cotterill, J. (2005). "You do not have to say anything ...": instructing the jury on the defendant's right to silence in the English criminal justice system. *Multilingua*, 24(1–2): 7–24.

Coupland, J. (Ed.) (2000). *Small Talk*. London: Longman.

Cronin, M. (2002). Silenced by sound. *Journal of Music in Ireland*, 3(1): 5–7.

Cruice, P. (Ed.) (1860). *Philosophumena*. Paris.

Cumont, F. (1956). *The Mysteries of Mithra* (2nd ed.). New York: Dover.

Cureton, W. (Ed.) (1845). *The Ancient Syriac Version of the Epistles of St Ignatius ... Collected with the Writings of Severus (et al.)* London: Rivington.

Danielsen. S. (1999). Welcome to my nightmare [interview with Tim Roth]. *Sight & Sound,* 9(8): 8–10.

Dante Alighieri (1867). *Paradiso.* H. W. Longfellow (Trans.). 3 vols. London: Routledge.

Dauenhauer, B. P. (1980). *Silence: The Phenomenon and its Ontological Significance.* Bloomington, IN: Indiana University Press.

Dauphin, G. (2003). Review of McWhorter. *Black Issues Book Review,* 5(1): 53–54.

Davies, J. G. (1965). *A Select Liturgical Lexicon.* London: Lutterworth Press.

Davies, O. (2006). Cosmic speech and the liturgy of silence. In: Rashkover, R. & Pecknold, C. C. (Eds.), *Liturgy, Time, and the Politics of Redemption* (pp. 215–228). Grand Rapids, MI: William B. Eerdmans.

Davies, O. & Turner, D. (Eds.) (2002). *Silence and the Word: Negative Theology and Incarnation.* Cambridge: Cambridge University Press.

Davies, P. (2010). *The Eerie Silence: Are We Alone in the Universe?* London: Allen Lane.

Deleuze, G. (1998). The greatest Irish film (Beckett's *Film*). In: Delueze, G. *Essays Critical and Clinical,* Smith, D. W. & Greco, M. A. (Trans.) (pp. 23–26). London: Verso.

De Moraes Farias, P. F. (1974). Silent trade: myth and historical evidence. In: *History in Africa, 1:* 9–24.

DePauw Theatre (2006). In the silence you don't know. Beckett production promotion. At: http://www.depauw.edu/univ/arts/theatre/former_seasons/season0506/samuel.asp (4/2/2011).

Dewailly, L. W. (1964). The silence of the Word. In: Kennedy, R. A. F. (Ed.), *The Word: Readings in Theology* (pp. 286–297). New York: P. J. Kennedy.

Dieterich, A. (1903). *Eine Mithrasliturgie.* Leipzig: Teubner. For Marvin Meyer's 1976 translation and notes see http://www.hermetic.com/pgm/mithras-liturgy.html (4/2/2011).

Dillard, A. (1995). *Mornings Like This.* New York: HarperCollins.

Dolin, T. (Ed.) (1998). *Under the Greenwood Tree,* by Thomas Hardy. Harmondsworth, UK: Penguin.

d'Orbigny, A. (1844). *Voyage dans l'Amérique Méridionale, iii.* Paris: Pitois-Levrault and Strasbourg: Ve. Levrault.

Du Bois, B. (1983). Passionate scholarship: notes on values, knowing and method in terminal-social science. In: Baules, G. & Klein, R. D. (Eds.), *Theories of Women's Studies* (pp. 105–116). London: Routledge.

Duke, H. O. (1991). *Where is God When Bad Things Happen*. St Meinrad, IN: Abbey Press.

Dunne, J. (2001). Review of *Silence Silence Silence* (production). *New York Times*, March 20.

Dunne, T. & Wheeler, N. (Eds.) (1999). *Human Rights in Global Politics*. Cambridge: Cambridge University Press.

Durham, J. (1964). *Directed Silence*. London: Faith Press.

Durnan, K. (2008). Dallas area bicyclists ride in silence at White Rock Lake. Dallas, TX: *The Dallas Morning News*, May 2.

Dworkin, A. (1996). Against the male flood: censorship, pornography and equality. In: Weisberg, D. K. (Ed.), *Applications of Feminist Legal Theory to Women's Lives: Sex, Violence, Work, and Reproduction* (pp. 28–36). Philadelphia, PA: Temple University Press.

Eggeling, J. (Ed. & Trans.) (1882–1897). *The Satapatha Brahmana*, pt. 1 (1882), pt. 3 (1894), pt. 4 (1897). In: Müller, M. (Ed.), *Sacred Books of the East*, xii, xli and xliii respectively. Oxford: Clarendon Press.

Eliot, G. (1868). *The Spanish Gypsy*. Edinburgh: Blackwood.

Eliot, G. (1871–1872). *Middlemarch*. Ware, UK: Wordsworth Classics, 2000.

Eliot, G. (1879). *Impressions of Theophrastus Such* (4th ed.). Edinburgh: Blackwood.

Emerson, R. W. (1841). *Essays and Lectures*. Porte, J. (Ed.). New York: Library of America. 1983.

Endo, S. (Ed.) (2007). *Silence*. W. Johnston (Trans.), with a foreword by Martin Scorsese. London: Peter Owen.

Eng, D. L. (1967). The value of silence. *Theatre Journal*, 54(1): 85–94.

Ephratt, M. (2008). The functions of speech. *Journal of Pragmatics*, 40(11): 1909–1938.

Epictetus (1807). *All the Works of Epictetus, Which Are Now Extant: Consisting of his Discourses, Preserved by Arrian, in Four Books, The Enchiridion, and Fragments* (4th ed.). Carter, E. (Trans.). 2 vols. London: Rivington.

Epstein, I. (Ed.) (1938). *The Babylonian Talmud: Seder Mo'ed*. London: Soncino Press.

Erico, R. A. & Lamsa, G. M. (2002). *Aramaic Light on the Gospel of John*. Smyrna, Georgia: Noohra Foundation.

Farr, J. (1962). How to communicate with silence. *Nation's Business, 50*: 96–97.

Farrar, F. W. (1879). *The Silence and the Voices of God*. London: Macmillan.

Faulkner, W. (1968). *Lion in the Garden: Interviews with William Faulkner, 1926–62*. Meriwether, J. B. & Millgate, M. (Eds.). New York: Random House.

Fermor, P. L. (1988). *A Time to Keep Silence*. Harmondsworth, UK: Penguin.

Fink, B. (2007). *Fundamentals of Psychoanalytic Technique: A Lacanian Approach for Practitioners*. New York: W. W. Norton.

Fischer, N. (2002). *Opening to You: Zen-inspired Translations of The Psalms*. New York: Viking Compass.

Flavell, L. & Flavell, R. (1993). *Dictionary of Proverbs and Their Origins*. London: Kyle Cathie.

Folsom, H. W. (2003). *Ah, Those Irish Colleens: Heroic Women of Ireland*. Nashville, TN: Cumberland House.

Ford, H. (1907). [Saint] Benedict [of Nursia]. In: *The Catholic Encyclopedia, ii*. New York: Robert Appleton.

Francis, J. (2008). *Planetwalker: 22 Years of Walking. 17 Years of Silence*. Washington, DC: National Geographic Society.

Frank, D. H., Leaman, O. & Manekin, C. H. (Eds.) (2000). *The Jewish Philosophy Reader*. London: Routledge.

Frankel, Z., Levitt, H. M., Murray, D. M., Greenberg, L. S. & Angus, L. (2006). Assessing silent processes in psychotherapy: an empirically derived categorisation system and sampling strategy. *Psychotherapy Research, 16*(5): 627–638.

Frayling, C. (2006). *Spaghetti Westerns: Cowboys and Europeans from Karl May to Sergio Leone* (revised ed.). London: Tauris.

Frazer, J. G. (1911–15). *The Golden Bough: A Study in Magic and Religion* (3rd ed.). 12 vols. London: Macmillan.

Freud, S. (1905e). Fragment of an analysis of a case of hysteria. *S. E., 7*. London: Hogarth.

Freud, S. (1926e). The question of lay analysis. *S. E., 20*. London: Hogarth.

Freud, S. & Breuer, J. (1955). Studies on hysteria. In: *S. E, 2*. London: Hogarth.

Fry, T. (Ed.) (1981). *The Rule of St. Benedict: in Latin and English with Notes*. Collegeville, MN: The Liturgical Press.

Fujio, M. (2004). Silence during intercultural communication: a case study. *Corporate Communications, 9*(4): 331–338.

Fuller, T. (1732). *Gnomologia: Adagies and Proverbs; Wise Sentences and Witty Sayings, Ancient and Modern, Foreign and British*. London: Barker.

Fuller, V. G. & Crowther, C. (1998). A dark talent: silence in analysis. *Journal of Analytical Psychology, 43*(4): 523–543.

Funk, R. W. (1966). *Language, Hermeneutics and the Word of God*. New York: Harper & Row.

Funk & Wagnalls (1901–1906). *Jewish Encyclopaedia*. 12 vols. New York: Funk & Wagnalls.

Gann, K. (2010). *No Such Thing as Silence: John Cage's 4'33"*. New Haven, CT: Yale University Press.

Gans, J. S. & Counselman, E. F. (2000). Silence in group psychotherapy: a powerful communication. *Journal of Group Psychotherapy, 50*(1): 71–86.

Garrison, R. (2000). *Why Are You Silent Lord?* Sheffield, UK: Sheffield Academic Press.

Gerson, J. & Peiss, K. (1985). Boundaries, negotiations, consciousness: reconceptualising gender relations. *Social Problems, 32*(4): 317–331.

Gibbons, L. (1996). The politics of silence: Anne Devlin, women and Irish cinema. In: L. Gibbons, *Transformations in Irish Culture* (pp. 107–116). Cork, Ireland: Cork University Press. Also (1998) Indiana, IN: University of Notre Dame Press.

Giglioli, P. P. (1972). *Language and Social Context*. Harmondsworth, UK: Penguin.

Gikandi, S. (Ed.) (2003). *Encyclopedia of African Literature*. London: Routledge.

Gill, A. (2004). Voicing the silent fear: South Asian women's experiences of domestic violence. *The Howard Journal, 43*(5): 465–483.

Gillan, M. (1995). *Where I Come From*. Toronto: Guernica Editions.

Gillan, M. (2003a). Shame and silence in my work. *PoetryMagazine.com, 8*(6). At http://www.poetrymagazine.com/archives/2003/Fall2003/gillan_shame.htm (4/2/2011).

Gillan, M. (2003b). *Greatest Hits 1972–2002*. Johnstown, OH: Pudding House Publications.

Glasser, P. & Pastore, R. (1999). China: right and wrong way to do things. In: *CIO* ("The resource for information executives"), March 29. Sydney: IDG Communications. At http://www.cio.com.au/article/107021/china_right_wrong_ways_do_things (4/2/2011).

Gloer, W. H. (1988). Silence. In: Bromiley, G. W. (Ed.), *The International Standard Bible Encyclopaedia*, iv: 509–510). 4 vols. Grand Rapids, MI: Eerdmans.

Glynn, C., Herbst, S., O'Keefe, G. & Shapiro, R. (1999). *Public Opinion*. Boulder, CO: Westview Press.

Gooch, P. W. (1996). *Reflections on Jesus and Socrates: Word and Silence*. New Haven, CT: Yale University Press.

Goodwin, J. (2003). *Price of Honour: Muslim Women Lift the Veil of Silence on the Islamic World*. New York: Plume.

Goodwin, W. (Ed.) (1878). *Morals, by Plutarch*. "Translated from the Greek by several hands". 5 vols. Boston: Little, Brown.

Gorbman, C. (2000). Music in *The Piano*. In: Margolis, H. (Ed.), *Jane Campion's The Piano* (pp. 42–58). Cambridge: Cambridge University Press.

Goytisolo, J. (1994). Algeria in the eye of the storm. *New Statesman & Society, 7*(316): 22–25.

Green, J. B., McKnight, S. & Marshall, I. H. (1992). *Dictionary of Jesus and the Gospels: A Compendium of Contemporary Biblical Scholarship.* Downers Grove, IL: InterVarsity Press.

Gröning, P. (2005). Information notes for *The Great Silence*, with clips of the documentary. At: http://www.diegrossestille.de/english/ (4/2/2011).

Gross, R. M. & Muck, T. C. (2003). *Christians Talk about Buddhist Meditation: Buddhists Talk about Christian Prayer.* New York: Continuum.

Gudykunst, W. B. (2003). *Bridging Differences: Effective Intergroup Communication.* Thousand Oaks, CA: Sage.

Gudykunst, W. B., Ting-Toomey, S. & Nishida, T. (1996). *Communications in Personal Relationships across Cultures.* Thousand Oaks, CA: Sage.

Gunning, T. (1994). *D. W. Griffith and the Origins of American Narrative Film: The Early Years at Biograph.* Champaign, IL: University of Illinois Press.

Gupta. R. (Ed.) (2003). *Homebreakers to Jailbreakers: Southall Black Sisters.* London: Zed Press.

Haan, W. (1999). Een Universiteit zonder Muziek is een Dode Plek: Afrikaanse lessen voor de westerse "kijk-mens". *de Marge, 8*(3): 21–26. Translated on the website of the Blaise Pascal Institute as "A university without music is a dead place: African lessons for the western 'eye-people'". At: http://www.bezinningscentrum.nl/teksten/wim_eng/africanmusic.htm (4/2/2011).

Hackett, D. C. (1996). *The Silent Dialogue: Zen Letters to a Trappist Monk.* New York: Continuum.

Haliburton, T. C. (1855). *Nature and Human Nature.* 2 vols. London: Hurst and Blackett.

Hall, C. (2009). Meditation workshop opens minds at center. Louisville, KY: *Courier-Journal*, March 30.

Hall, E. (1959). *The Silent Language.* New York: Doubleday.

Hammond Bammel, C. P. (1982). Ignatian problems. *Journal of Theological Studies, 33*(1): 62–97.

Hannay, M. (Ed.) (1985). *Silent But For The Word: Tudor Women as Patrons, Translators and Writers of Religious Works.* Kent, OH: Kent State University Press.

Hardy, T. (1999). *Under the Greenwood Tree.* Oxford: Oxford University Press.

Harper, M. S. & Welsh, D. P. (2007). Keeping quiet: self-silencing and its association with relational and individual functioning among adolescent romantic couples. *Journal of Social and Personal Relationships, 24*: 99–116.

Harries, L. (Trans.) (1962). *Swahili Poetry.* Oxford: Oxford University Press.

Harrison, D. (2005). *The End of Mind: The Edge of the Intelligible in Hardy, Stevens, Larkin, Plath and Glück*. Abingdon, UK: Routledge.

Harrison, K. (1997). *The Kiss: A Memoir*. New York: Avon.

Hass, A., Jasper, D. & Jay, E. (Eds.) (2007). *The Oxford Book of English Literature and Theology*. Oxford: Oxford University Press.

Hastings, J. (Ed.) (1920). *Encyclopaedia of Religion and Ethics*. Edinburgh: T. & T. Clark.

Hazlitt, W. & Horne, R. H. (1837). *Characteristics: In the Manner of Rochefoucault's Maxims*. London: J. Templeman.

Hedges, E. & Fishkin, S. F. (1994). *Listening to Silences: New Essays in Feminist Criticism*. Oxford: Oxford University Press.

Hedges, I. (1991). Film writing and the poetics of silence. In: Hedges, I. *Breaking the Frame: Film Language and the Experience of Limits* (pp. 18–31). Bloomington, IN: Indiana University Press.

Hedrick, C. W. (2000). *History and Silence: Purge and Rehabilitation of Memory in Late Antiquity*. Austin, TX: University of Texas.

Heidel, A. (Ed.) (1949). *The Gilgamesh Epic and Old Testament Parallels*. Chicago: University of Chicago Press.

Hepher, C. (1915). *The Fruits of Silence: Being Further Studies in the Common Use of Prayer Without Words, Together with Kindred Essays in Worship*. London: Macmillan.

Hepher, C. (Ed.) (1915). *The Fellowship of Silence*. London: Macmillan.

Herrman, D. (1999). *Helen Keller: a Life*. Chicago: University of Chicago Press.

Hertsgaard, M. (2005). John Francis, a "planetwalker" who lived car-free and silent for 17 years, chats with *Grist* (May 10). At: http://www.grist.org/article/hertsgaard-francis/ (4/2/2011).

Heyn, D. (1992). *The Erotic Silence of the American Wife*. New York: Signet.

Heywood, J. (1906). *Proverbs, Epigrams and Miscellanies*. Farmer, J. S. (Ed.). London: Early English Drama Society.

Hill, C. E., Thompson, B. J. & Ladany, N. (2003). Therapist use of silence in therapy: a survey. *Journal of Clinical Psychology*, 59(4): 513–524.

Hobson, H. (1969). Paradise lost (review of Pinter's *Silence*). London: *The Sunday Times*, July 6. At: http://www.haroldpinter.org/plays/plays_silence.shtml (4/2/2011).

Hodgken, L. V. (1915). The colour of silence. In: Hepher, C. (Ed.), *The Fellowship of Silence* (pp. 213–222). London: Macmillan.

Holland [Lady] (1869). *A Memoir of the Rev. Sydney Smith by his Daughter* (new ed.). London: Longmans, Green, Reader & Dyer.

Horne, C. F. (1917). *The Sacred Books and Early Literature of the East, 2: Egypt*. New York: Parke, Austin & Lipscomb.

Hu, Y. & Fell-Eisenkraft, S. (2003). Immigrant Chinese students' use of silence in the language arts classroom: perceptions, reflections, and actions. *Teaching & Learning, 17*(2): 55–65.

Hull, S. (1982). *Chaste, Silent and Obedient: English Books for Women 1475–1640.* San Marino, CA: Huntington Library.

Huxley, A. (1939). *After Many a Summer.* London: Chatto & Windus.

Jack, D. C. (1991). *Silencing the Self: Women and Depression.* Cambridge, MA: Harvard University Press.

Jacob, J. A. (1875). *Building in Silence, and other Sermons.* London: Macmillan.

Jaffres, L., Neuendorf, K. & Atkin, D. (1999). Spirals of silence: expressing opinions when the climate of opinion is unambiguous. *Political Communication, 16*(2): 115–131.

Japhet, S. & Salters, R. B. (1985). *The Commentary of R. Samuel Ben Meir Rashbam on Qoheleth* (Ecclesiastes). Jerusalem: Magnes Press.

Jaworski, A. (1993). *The Power of Silence: Social and Pragmatic Perspectives.* London: Sage.

Jaworski, A. (1997). *Silence: Interdisciplinary Perspectives.* Berlin: Mouton de Gruyter.

Jaworski, A. (Ed.) (2005). *Multilingua: Journal of Cross-cultural and Inter-language Communication, 24*(1–2). Special issue on silence in institutional and intercultural contexts.

Jaworski, A. & Sachdev, I. (1998). Beliefs about silence in the classroom. *Language and Education, 12*(4): 273–292.

Jenkins, S. & Parra, I. (2003). Multiple layers of meaning in an oral proficiency test: the complementary roles of nonverbal, paralinguistic, and verbal behaviors in assessment decisions. *The Modern Language Journal, 87*(1): 90–107.

Jensen, J. V. (1973). Communicative functions of silence. *ETC, 30*: 249–257.

Jervis, A. L. (1995). 1 Corinthians 14.34–35: a reconsideration of Paul's limitation of the free speech of some Corinthian women. *Journal for the Study of the New Testament, 17*(58): 51–73.

Johannesen, R. L. (1974). The function of silence: a plea for communication research. *Western Speech, 38*(1): 25–35.

John of the Cross (1991). *The Collected Works of St. John of the Cross.* Kavanagh, K. & Rodriguez, O. (Trans.). Washington, DC: ICS Publications.

John, M. E. & Nair, J. (Eds.) (1998). *A Question of Silence? The Sexual Economies of Modern India.* New Delhi: Zubaan.

Johnson, D. (2003). Maurice Blanchot: enigmatic French writer committed to the virtues of silence and abstraction. London: *The Guardian,* March 1 (obituary).

Johnston, I. (2009). Quietly booming, the silent disco scene. London: *The Sunday Telegraph*, September 6.

Johnston, W. (1974). *Silent Music: The Science of Meditation*. New York: Harper & Row.

Jones, R. M. (1920). Silence. In: *Encylopaedia of Religion and Ethics, xi*. Edinburgh: T. & T. Clark.

Joyce, J. (1992). *A Portrait of the Artist as a Young Man*. Ware, UK: Wordsworth Editions.

Joyce, J. (2000). "The dead". In: *Dubliners*. Oxford: Oxford University Press.

Kahn, C. H. (2001). *Pythagoras and the Pythagoreans: A Brief History*. Indianapolis, IN: Hackett Publishing.

Kahn, D. (1997). John Cage: silence and silencing. In: *The Musical Quarterly, 81*: 556–598.

Kauffmann, S. (1993). A new Spielberg; and others [including a review of Jane Campion's *The Piano*]. *The New Republic, 209*(24): 30–31.

Kelly, F. (1998). *Guide to Early Irish Law*. Dublin: Institute for Advanced Studies.

Kelsey, M. T. (1977). *The Other Side of Silence: A Guide to Christian Meditation*. London: SPCK.

Kenny, C. (2005). *Moments That Changed Us*. Dublin: Gill & Macmillan.

Kenny, O. (2004). The Boulevard du Temple and the Palais-Royal: changes in nineteenth-century Paris before Haussmann. MA thesis, University College Dublin.

King, K. (2003). *The Gospel of Mary Magdala: Jesus and the First Woman Apostle*. Santa Rosa, CA: Polebridge Press.

King, M. L. (1967). A time to break silence. In: Washington, J. M. (Ed.), *A Testament of Hope: The Essential Writings and Speeches of Martin Luther King, Jr.* (pp. 231–244). New York: HarperCollins, 1986.

Kirk, K. E. (1918). *A Study of Silent Minds: War Studies in Education*. London: SCM.

Kleist, J. A. (1946). *The Epistles of St Clement of Rome and St Ignatius of Antioch*. Westminster, MD: Newman Press, and London: Longmans, Green & Co.

Knowlson, J. (1996). *Damned to Fame: The Life of Samuel Beckett*. London: Bloomsbury.

Komonchak, J., Collins, M. & Lane, D. (Eds.) (1987). *New Dictionary of Theology*. Wilmington, DE: Michael Glazier.

Krakauer, J. (1996). *Into the Wild*. New York: Villard.

Krell, D. F. (Ed.) (1978). *Martin Heidegger: Basic Writings*. London: Taylor & Francis.

Kurzon, D. (1995). The right to silence: a socio-pragmatic model of interpretation. *Journal of Pragmatics, 23*: 55–69.

Kusher, H. S. (1981). *When Bad Things Happen to Good People*. New York: Schocken.

Labalme, P. (Ed.) (1980). *Beyond Their Sex: Learned Women of the European Past*. New York: New York University Press.

Lacan, J. (1958). The direction of the treatment and the principles of its power. Paper given at the Royaumont Colloquium. B. Fink (Trans). In: Lacan, J. *Écrits* (pp. 489–542). New York: W. W. Norton, 2006.

Lacout, P. (1970). *God is Silence*. London: Friends Home Service Committee.

Lake, K. (1912). *The Apostolic Fathers*. 2 vols. London: Heinemann.

La MaMa Experimental Theater Club, New York (2001). *Silence Silence Silence*. Publicity. At: http://www.lamama.org/archives/2001_2002/SilenceSilenceSilence.htm (4/2/2011).

Lane, R. C., Koetting, M. G. & Bishop, J. (2002). Silence as communication in psychodynamic psychotherapy. *Clinical Psychology Review*, 22(7): 1091–1104.

Lang, B. (1996). *Heidegger's Silence on The Jewish Question*. London: The Athlone Press.

Lao-Tse (1891). *Tao Teh King* (Way of Virtue). James Legge (Trans.). In: Müller, *Sacred Books of the East*, 39. Oxford: Clarendon Press. See for a comparative context: http://www.yellowbridge.com/onlinelit/daodejing.php (4/2/2011).

Latham, B. K. & Pazdro, R. J. (Eds.) (1984). *Not Just Pin Money: Selected Essays on the History of Women's Work in British Columbia*. Victoria, BC: Camosun College.

Laurence, P. I. (1991). *The Reading of Silence: Virginia Woolf in the English Tradition*. Palo Alto, CA: Stanford University Press.

Layton, B. (Ed.) (1987). *The Gnostic Scriptures*. New York: Doubleday.

Lebra, T. S. (1987). The cultural significance of silence in Japanese communication. *Multilingua*, 6(4): 343–357.

Leclerc-Madlala, S. (2000). Silence, AIDS and sexual culture in Africa. An 'Aids Bulletin'. In: *Women's International Network* [WIN] *News, 27* (1), 2001: 20–22.

Lee, Li-Young. (2001). *Book of My Nights*. Rochester, NY: BOA Editions.

Legge, F. (Trans.) (1921). *Philosophumena: Or the Refutation of All Heresies, Formerly Attributed to Origen, but now Hippolytus, Bishop and Martyr, who Flourished About 220 A.D.* 2 vols. London: SPCK.

Lehtonen, J. & Sajavarra, K. (1985). The silent Finn. In: Tannen, D. & Saville-Troike, M. (Eds.), *Perspectives on Silence* (pp. 195–196). Norwood, NJ: Ablex.

Leonard, T. (2004). *Access to the Silence: Poems and Posters 1984–2004*. Exbourne, UK: Etruscan Books.

Leong, W. K. (2000). The silent majority. Singapore: *The Straits Times*, August 15.

Lester, D. & Brockopp, D. (Eds.) (1973). *Crisis Intervention and Counseling by Telephone*. Springfield, IL: Charles C. Thomas.

Lévi-Strauss, C. (1961). *Tristes Tropiques*. J. Russell (Trans.). New York: Criterion.

Levitt, H. M. (2002). The unsaid in the psychotherapy narrative: voicing the unvoiced. *Counselling Psychology Quarterly*, 15(4): 333–350.

Lewandowski, J. (2000). Speaking in the language of silence. Buffalo, NY: *University of Buffalo Reporter, 32*, November 16.

Lhalungpa, L. P. (Trans.) (1977). *The Life of Milarepa*. New York: Dutton.

Lichtheim, M. (1975). *Ancient Egyptian Literature, i: The Old and Middle Kingdoms*. Berkeley, CA: University of California Press.

Lichtheim, M. (1976). *Ancient Egyptian Literature, ii: A Book of Readings: The New Kingdom*. Berkeley, CA: University of California Press.

Liegner, E. (1976). The silent patient. *Psychoanalytic Review*, 61: 229–245.

Lien, B. (2004). Cross-cultural differences in the use of silence—a study of Irish and Chinese attitudes. MA thesis, Dublin City University.

Lightfoot, J. B. (1889). *Apostolic Fathers, pt. II. S. Ignatius S. Polycarp*. 3 vols. London: Macmillan.

Llewelyn, R. (1987). *A Doorway to Silence: The Contemplative Use of the Rosary*. London: Darton, Longman and Todd.

Lobell, J. (1979). *Between Silence and Light: Spirit in the Architecture of Louis I. Kahn*. Boston: Shambhala.

Loevlie, E. (2003). *Literary Silences in Pascal, Rousseau and Beckett*. Oxford: Oxford University Press.

London, J. (1996). *The Son of the Wolf: Tales of the Far North*. Oxford: Oxford University Press.

Longfellow, H. W. (1902). The theologian's tale: Elizabeth, pt. iv. In: Longfellow, H. W. *Complete Poetical Works*. Boston: Houghton Mifflin.

Lorde, A. (1984). The transformation of silence into language and action. In: Lorde, A. *Sister Outsider: Essays and Speeches* (pp. 40–44). Santa Cruz, CA: Crossing Press.

Luckyj, C. (2002). *"A Moving Rhetoricke": Gender and Silence in Early Modern England*. Manchester: Manchester University Press.

Madan, A. C. (1903). *Swahili-English Dictionary*. Oxford: Clarendon.

Maier, H. O. (2004). The politics of the silent bishop: silence and persuasion in Ignatius of Antioch. *Journal of Theological Studies, n.s., 55(2)*: 503–519.

Maitland, S. (2008). *A Book of Silence*. London: Granta.

Malcolm, J. (1990). *The Journalist and the Murderer*. New York: Knopf.

Malraux, A. (1954). *The Voices of Silence*. S. Gilbert (Trans.). London: Secker & Warburg.

Malraux, A. (1967). *Museum without Walls*. S. Gilbert & F. Price (Trans.). New York: Doubleday, and London: Secker & Warburg.

Mandelstam, N. (1999). *Hope Against Hope*. M. Hayward (Trans.). London: Harvill Press.

Mannikka, E. (undated). Review of Anne Devlin (1984). At: http://movies. nytimes.com/movie/83770/Anne-Devlin/overview (24/3/11).

Mansel, H. L. (1875). *The Gnostic Heresies of the First and Second Centuries*. London: John Murray.

Manson, P. (2004/5). A Glasgow "this". Review of Leonard, T., *Access to the Silence. Poetry Review*, 94(4): 70–72.

Margolis, H. (Ed.) (2000). *Jane Campion's The Piano*. Cambridge: Cambridge University Press.

Marshall, T. (2006). My Canterbury trail to Rome. Blog, May 18. At: http://cantuar.blogspot.com/2006/05/my-canterbury-trail-to-rome.html (4/2/2011).

Martyres, G. (1995). On silence: a language for emotional experience. *Australian and New Zealand Journal of Psychiatry*, 29(1): 118–123.

Matsumoto, M. (1998). *The Unspoken Way: Haragei—Silence in Japanese Business and Society* New York: Kodansha International.

Matthews, G. (2002). The healing silence: Thomas Merton's contemplative approach to communication. *The Merton Annual, 15*: 61–76.

McCabe, H. (2002). Aquinas on the Trinity. In: O. Davies & D. Turner (Eds.), *Silence and the Word: Negative Theology and Incarnation* (pp. 76–93). Cambridge: Cambridge University Press.

McCroskey, J. D. & Richmond, V. P. (1991). *Quiet Children and the Classroom Teacher*. Bloomington, IN: ERIC Clearinghouse on Reading and Communication Skills, and Annandale, VA: Speech Communication Association.

McDaniel, M. (2005). Silence golden for Pope's funeral. Houston, TX: *Houston Chronicle*, April 8.

McDermott, R. P. (1988). Inarticulateness. In: Tannen, D. (Ed.), *Linguistics in Context: Connecting Observation and Understanding* (pp. 37–68). Norwood, NJ: Ablex.

McDonald, R. (2005). Strategies of silence: colonial strains in short stories of the Troubles. *The Yearbook of English Studies*, 35(1): 249–263.

McEvilley, T. (2002). *The Shape of Ancient Thought*. New York: Allworth.

McGill, W. J. (2003). *Poets' Meeting: R. S. Thomas, George Herbert and the Argument with God*. Jefferson, NC: McFarland.

McLeish, R. (1981). *The Technique of Radio Production: A Manual for Local Broadcasters*. London: Focal.

McWhorter, J. (2003). *Authentically Black: Essays for the Black Silent Majority*. New York: Gotham.

Merleau-Ponty, M. (1964). Indirect language and the voices of silence. In: M. Merleau-Ponty, *Signs* (pp. 39–83). McCleary, R. C. (Trans.). Evanston, IL: Northwestern University Press.

Merleau-Ponty, M. (1966). *Phenomenology of Perception*. Smith, C. (Trans.). London: Routledge.

Merton, T. (1956). *Silence in Heaven: A Book of the Monastic Life*. New York: Studio Publications with Thos. Crowell.

Merton, T. (2001). *Dialogues with Silence: Prayers and Drawings*. Montaldo, J. (Ed.). New York: HarperCollins.

Metzger, B. M. & Murphy, R. E. (1994). *New Oxford Annotated Bible: New Revised Standard Version*. Oxford: Oxford University Press.

Michelakis, P. (1999). The spring before it is sprung: visual and non-verbal aspects of power struggle in Aeschylus' *Myrmidons*. Conference paper at http://www2.open.ac.uk/ClassicalStudies/GreekPlays/Conf99/michelakis.html (4/2/2011). Revised, with bibliography on silence in Greek literature and theatre, in Michelakis, P., *Achilles in Greek Tragedy* (pp. 22–57). Cambridge: Cambridge University Press, 2002.

Midrash Rabbah: Ecclesiastes (1939). Cohen, A. (Trans.). London: Soncino Press.

Midrash Rabbah: Leviticus (1929). Israelstam, J. & Slotki, J. J. (Trans.). London: Soncino Press.

Miller, J. (1902). *The Complete Poetical Works of Joaquin Miller*. San Francisco: The Whitaker & Ray Co.

Milton, J. (1642). An apology for Smectymnuus. In: Griswold, R. W. (Ed.), *The Prose Works of John Milton: With a Biographical Introduction* (i). 2 vols. Philadelphia, PA: John W. Moore, 1847.

[*The*] *Mishnah* (1933). Danby, H. (Trans.). Oxford: Oxford University Press.

Mitchell, M. & Franklin, A. (1984). When you don't know the language, listen to the silence: An historical overview of Native Indian women in BC [British Columbia]. In: Latham, B. K. & Pazdro, R. J. (Eds.), *Not Just Pin Money: Selected Essays on the History of Women's Work in British Columbia* (pp. 17–35). Victoria, BC: Camosun College.

Montaigne, M. de. (1958). *The Complete Essays of Montaigne*. Frame, D. M. (Trans.). Palo Alto, CA: Stanford University Press.

Montgomery, J. A. & Gehman, H. S. (1951). *The International Critical Commentary: A Critical and Exegetical Commentary on The Books of Kings*. Edinburgh: T. & T. Clark.

Montiglio, S. (2000). *Silence in the Land of Logos*. Princeton, NJ: Princeton University Press.

Moore, M. (1951). *Collected Poems*. London: Faber and Faber.

Moran, R. T. (1985). *Getting Your Yen's Worth: How to Negotiate with Japan, Inc.* Houston, TX: Gulf Publishing.

More, C. (1828). *The Life of Sir Thomas More.* London: Pickering.

Morgan, E. (1964). Foreword. In: J. Durham, *Directed Silence.* London: Faith Press.

Morisset, V. (2006). Crossing the threshold to the invisible: from blue to three colours. Exhibition notes, *Yves Klein: Body, Colour, Immaterial*, Pompidou Centre, Paris, 2006–2007. At: http://www.centrepompidou.fr/education/ressources/ENS-klein-EN/ENS-klein-EN.htm#haut (4/2/2011).

Morton, N. (1985). *The Journey is Home.* Boston: Beacon.

Morton, T. (2002). The Turner Prize: everyone's a winner. In: *Tate*, 2. At: http://www.tate.org.uk/magazine/issue2/tp_everywinner.htm (4/2/2011).

Motley, J. L. (1908). *Motley's Dutch Nation: Being the Rise of the Dutch Republic (1555–1584).* W. E. Griffis (Ed.). New York: Harper.

Muers, R. (2004). *Keeping God's Silence: Towards a Theological Ethics of Communication.* Oxford: Blackwell.

Mukhopadhyay, T. (2003). *The Mind Tree: A Miraculous Child Breaks the Silence of Autism.* New York: Arcade Publishing.

Müller, M. (Ed.) (1879–1910). *Sacred Books of the East.* 50 vols. Oxford: Clarendon Press. Available at www.sacred-texts.com/sbe/index.htm (4/2/2011).

Müller, M. (Ed.) (1879). The Upanishads, pt. 1. In: Müller, *Sacred Books*, 1.

Mullins, M. (1998). Esther's smile: silence and action in Hisaye Yamamoto's "Wilshire bus". *Studies in Short Fiction*, 35: 75–82.

Munter, M. (1993). Cross-cultural communication for managers. *Business Horizons*, 36(3): 69–78.

Murray, P. (1955). Noh: The Japanese Theatre of Silence. *Icarus* (Dublin), 4: 102–107.

Mynors, R. A. (Ed.) (1992). *Collected Works of Erasmus: Adages II vii 1 to III iii 100.* Toronto: University of Toronto Press.

Nabokov, V. (1944). *Three Russian Poets: Selections from Pushkin, Lermontov and Tyutchev in New Translations.* Norfolk, CT: New Directions. For a recording of Nabokov reading Tyutchev's Russian "*Silentium!*" and his own English translation of it go to Penn State University's http://www.libraries.psu.edu/nabokov/nabokr3.htm (4/2/2011).

Nakane, I. (2007). *Silence in Intercultural Communication: Perception and Performance.* London: John Benjamins.

Neruda, P. (2003). *On the Blue Shore of Silence.* Reid, A. (Trans.). New York: Rayo/HarperCollins.

Neuwirth, K. (2007). The spiral of silence and fear of isolation. *Journal of Communication*, 57(3): 450–468.

Niebylski, D. C. (1993). *The Poem on the Edge of the Word: The Limits of Language and the Uses of Silence in the Poetry of Mallarme, Rilke, and Vallejo*. New York: Peter Lang.

Nietzsche, F. (1907). *Beyond Good and Evil*. Zimmern, H. (Trans.). In: Levy, O. (Ed.), *The Complete Works of Friedrich Nietzsche*. 18 vols. Edinburgh: Foulis, 1909–1913.

Nishida, T. (1996). Communication in personal relationships in Japan. In: Gudykunst, W. B., Ting-Toomey, S. & Nishida, T. *Communications in Personal Relationships across Cultures* (pp. 102–121). Thousand Oaks, CA: Sage.

Nixon, R. M. (1969). The great silent majority of my fellow Americans (November 3). In: Perlstein, R. (Ed.), *Richard Nixon: Speeches, Writings, Documents* (pp. 170–190). Princeton, NJ: Princeton University Press, 2008.

Noe, D. (1996). The mute speak—the writing of disabled authors Stephen Hawking, Christopher Nolan and Ruth Sienkiewicz-Mercer. *Humanist*, 56(2): 13–16.

Noelle-Neumann, E. (1993). *The Spiral of Silence: Public Opinion—Our Social Skin* (2nd revised ed.). Chicago: University of Chicago Press.

Nolan, C. (1981). *Dam-burst of Dreams*. London: Weidenfeld & Nicolson.

Nolan, C. (1987). *Under the Eye of the Clock*. London: Weidenfeld & Nicolson.

Nwoye, G. (1985). Eloquent silence among the Igbo of Nigeria. In: D. Tannen & M. Saville-Troike (Eds.), *Perspectives on Silence* (pp. 185–191). Norwood, NJ: Ablex.

O'Donovan, J. (Ed.) (1851). *The Tribes and Territories of Ancient Ossory*. Dublin: O'Daly.

Olsen, T. (2003). *Silences*. New York: Feminist Press at City University of New York.

O'Malley, M. P. (2005). Silence as a means of preserving the status quo: the case of ante-natal care in Ireland. *Multilingua: journal of cross-cultural and interlanguage communication*, 24(1–2): 39–54.

O'Rourke, K. (1993). *Tilting the Jar, Spilling the Moon*. Dublin: Dedalus.

Pagels, E. (1979). *The Gnostic Gospels*. London: Weidenfeld & Nicolson.

Pamuk, O. (2005). *Snow*. London: Faber & Faber.

Panikkar, R. (1989). *The Silence of God: The Answer of the Buddha*. Maryknoll, NY: Orbis.

Papanikolaou, A. (2006). *Being with God: Trinity, Apophaticism and Divine-Human Communion*. Notre Dame, IN: University of Notre Dame Press.

Parrott, L. & Parrott, L. (2005). When silence is golden: six times when it's best not to say a word (October 7). At: http://www.christianitytoday.com/mp/2005/001/9.30.html (4/2/2011). Adapted from Parrott, *Love Talk*. Grand Rapids, MI: Zondervan, 2004.

Patel, M. (2003). Silent witnesses: domestic violence and black children. In: Gupta, R. (Ed.), *Homebreakers to Jailbreakers: Southall Black Sisters* (pp. 92–108). London: Zed Press.

Patel, P. (2003). The tricky blue line: policing black women. In: Gupta, R. (Ed.), *Homebreakers to Jailbreakers: Southall Black Sisters* (pp. 160–187). London: Zed Press.

Pearson, R. (2004). *Mallarmé and Circumstance: The Translation of Silence*. Oxford: Oxford University Press.

Penn, W. (1726). *Fruits of a Father's Love: Being the Advice of William Penn to His Children Relating to Their Civil and Religious Conduct*. London: Sowle.

Perloff, M. (1999). The silence that is not silence: Acoustic art in Samuel Beckett's *Embers*. In: Oppenheim, L. (Ed.), *Samuel Beckett and the Arts: Music, Visual Arts and Non-Print Media* (pp. 247–268). New York: Garland.

Petress, K. (2001). The ethics of student classroom silence. *Journal of Instructional Psychology, 28*(2): 104–107.

Philadelphia Museum of Art (2010). *Étant donnés* (Marcel Duchamp). At: http://www.philamuseum.org/collections/permanent/65633.html?mulR=23929 (4/2/2011).

Philips, S. U. (1975). Some sources of cultural variability in the regulation of talk. *Language in Society, 5*(1): 81–95.

Phillips, D. (1994). The functions of silence within the context of teacher training. In: *ELT Journal, 48*(3): 266–271.

Picard, M. (1952). *The World of Silence*. Chicago: Henry Regnery.

Pieper, J. (1957). *The Silence of St Thomas*. New York: Pantheon.

Pindar (1830). [Works of] *Pindar*. C. A. Wheelwright (Trans.). London: Colburn & Bentley.

Pinder, C. & Harlos, K. (2001). Employee silence: quiescence and acquiescence as responses to perceived injustice. *Research in Personnel and Human Resources Management, 20*: 331–369.

Piozzi, H. L. (1826). *Anecdotes of the Late Samuel Johnson, LL.D. During the Last Twenty Years of his Life*. London: Allman.

Plaskow, J. (1990). Beyond egalitarianism. In: Frank, D. H., Leaman, O. & Manekin, C. H. (Eds.), *The Jewish Philosophy Reader* (pp. 519–522). London: Routledge, 2000.

Plutarch (1898). *Morals*. Shilleto, A. R. (Trans). London: George Bell.

Pollak, V. R. (2005). Moore, Plath, Hughes and "The Literary Life". *American Literary History, 17*(1): 95–117.

Pomerius, J. (1947). *The Contemplative Life.* Suelzer, M. J. (Trans.). Westminster, MD: Newman Press, and London: Longmans, Green & Co.

Porter, M. (2002). "All that is necessary for the triumph of evil is that good men do nothing" (or words to that effect): a study of a web quotation. At: http://tartarus.org/~martin/essays/burkequote.html (4/2/2011).

Poulos, C. N. (2004). Disruption, silence, and creation: the search for dialogic civility in the age of anxiety. *Qualitative Inquiry, 10*(4): 534–547.

Price, R. (1994). *A Whole New Life.* New York: Charles Scribner's Sons.

Price, R. (1999). *Letter to a Man in the Fire: Does God Exist and Does He Care?* New York: Charles Scribner's Sons.

Prochnik, G. (2010). *In Pursuit of Silence: Listening for Meaning in a World of Noise.* New York: Doubleday.

Proulx, A. (1994). *The Shipping News.* New York: Charles Scribner's Sons.

Proulx, A. (2006). Blood on the red carpet. London: *The Guardian*, March 11.

Przyłuska, I. (2002). Review of *Silence of the Trembling Hands. Gazeta Malarzy i Poetów, 2* (44). Translated, with photographs of the production, at http://www.ptt-poznan.pl/stronye/72.php (4/2/2011).

Quantrill, M. & Webb, B. (1998) *The Culture of Silence: Architecture's Fifth Dimension.* College Station, TX: TAMU Press.

Rajski, P. (2003). Finding God in the silence: contemplative prayer and therapy. *Journal of religion and health, 42*(3): 181–190.

Ramsay, W. M. (1904). *The Letters to the Seven Churches of Asia and Their Place in the Plan of the Apocalypse.* London: Hodder & Stoughton.

Randall, S. & Koppenhaver, T. (2004). Qualitative data in demography: the sound of silence and other problems. *Demographic Research, 11*(3): 57–93.

Ratzinger, J. (now Pope Benedict XVI) (1995). *"In the Beginning ...": A Catholic Understanding of the Story of Creation and The Fall.* Grand Rapids, MI: Eerdsmans.

Ray, J. (Ed.) (1768). *A Compleat Collection of English Proverbs: Also the Most Celebrated Proverbs of the Scotch, Italian, French, Spanish, and Other Languages, the Whole Methodically Digested and Illustrated with Annotations, and Proper Explications.* 4th ed. London: Otridge & Bladon.

Reik, T. (1926). In the beginning is silence. In: Reik, T. *The Inner Experience of a Psychoanalyst* (pp. 121–127). London: Allen & Unwin, 1949.

Rich, A. (1978). *The Dream of A Common Language: Poems 1974–1977.* New York: W. W. Norton.

Rich, A. (1995). *On Lies, Secrets and Silence: Selected Prose, 1966–1978.* New York: W. W. Norton.

Rich, A. (2002). *The Fact of a Doorframe: Selected Poems 1950–2001.* New York: W. W. Norton.

Richardson, C. C. (Ed.) (1953). *Early Christian Fathers.* London: SCM Press.

Riedweg, C. & Rendall, S. (2005). *Pythagoras: His Life, Teaching, and Influence.* Ithaca, NY: Cornell University Press.

Roberts, A., Donaldson, J. & Cleveland, A. (Eds.) (1885). *Ante-Nicene Fathers, 1.* Buffalo, NY: Christian Literature Publishing.

Robinson, J. M. (Ed.) (1996). *The Nag Hammadi Library in English: The Definitive New Translation of the Gnostic Scriptures, Complete in One Volume.* Leiden, Netherlands: Brill.

Roche, J. J. (Ed.) (1891). *Life of John Boyle O'Reilly, Together with His Complete Poems and Speeches Edited by Mrs. John Boyle O'Reilly.* New York: Cassell Publishing.

Rodek, H. (2005). Review of *Die Grosse Stille* (*The Great Silence*). Berlin: *Die Welt*, September 11. Partly trans. At: http://www.signandsight. com/intodaysfeuilletons/453.html (4/2/2011).

[Frère] Roger (1957). *So Easy to Love.* London: Longmans.

Rossetti, D. G. (1871). "Silent noon". In: Lewis, R. C. (Ed.), *Dante Gabriel Rosetti: The House of Life—A Sonnet Sequence* (p. 73, sonnet 19). Cambridge: Brewer, D. S. 2007.

Rothenberg, J. (1998). "Imagery in the theatre of Nathalie Sarraute". *Neophilologus, 82:* 385–392.

Runcorn, D. (1989). *Silence.* Bramcote, UK: Grove.

Russell, J. B. (1997). *A History of Heaven: The Singing Silence.* Princeton, NJ: Princeton University Press.

Rykner, A. (1996). *L'envers du Théâtre: Dramaturgie du Silence de L'âge Classique à Maeterlinck.* Paris: J. Corti.

Ryrie, A. (1999). *Silent Waiting: The Biblical Roots of Contemplative Spirituality.* Norwich, UK: SCM-Canterbury Press.

Sabath, A. M. (2002). *International Business Etiquette: Asia and The Pacific Rim.* Lincoln, NE: iUniverse.

Sabbadini, A. (1991). Listening to silence. *British Journal of Psychotherapy, 7*(4): 406–415. Reprinted in *British Journal of Psychotherapy, 21*(2): 230–238, 2004.

Sai, Y. (1996). *The Eight Core Values of the Japanese Businessman: Toward an Understanding of Japanese Management.* New York: International Business Press.

Samarin, W. (1965). Language of silence. *Practical Anthropology, 12:* 115–119.

Saville-Troike, M. (1985). The place of silence in an intergrated theory of communication. In: Tannem D. & Saville-Troike, M. (Eds.), *Perspectives on Silence* (pp. 3–18). Norwood, NJ: Ablex.

Schaufler, W. (1995). Interview with Pierre Boulez. Stewart Spencer (Trans.). In: Schoenberg, A., *Moses und Aron*, pp. 13–15 of booklet.

Schlant, E. (1999). *The Language of Silence: West German Literature and the Holocaust*. London: Routledge.

Schnyder, M. (2003). *Topographie des Schweigens: Untersuchungen zum Deutschen Höfischen Roman um 1200*. Historische Semantik 3. Göttingen, Germany: Vandenhoeck & Ruprecht.

Schoenberg, A. (1996). *Moses und Aron*. Pierre Boulez (conductor). Includes 64-page explanatory booklet by various authors. Hamburg: Deutsche Grammophon.

Schwartz, T. F. (2009). Lincoln never said that. At: Illinois Historic Preservation Agency website, http://www.illinoishistory.gov/facsimiles. htm (4/2/2011).

Scollon, R. (1985). The machine stops: silence in the metaphor of malfunction. In: D. Tannen & M. Saville-Troike (Eds.), *Perspectives on Silence* (pp. 21–30). Norwood, NJ: Ablex.

Scollon, R. & Scollon, S. (1981). *Narrative, Literacy and Face in Interethnic Communication*. Norwood, NJ: Ablex.

Scollon, R. & Scollon, S. (2001). *Intercultural Communication*. Oxford: Blackwell.

Scott, V. & Lester, D. (1998). Listening to silence: a column from Befrienders International. *Crisis: Journal of Crisis Intervention and Suicide Prevention, 19*(3): 105–108.

Seiffert, R. (2002). Inarticulacy, identity and silence: Annie Proulx's *The Shipping News*. *Textual Practice, 16*(3): 511–525.

Selden, J. (1689). *Table-Talk: Discourses Relating Especially to Religion and State*. London: Smith.

Seneca the Younger (2004). *Oedipus; Agamemnon; Thyestes; Hercules on Oeta; Octavia*. J. G. Fitch (Trans.). Cambridge, MA: Harvard University Press.

Shambu, G. (2001). Les enfants du paradis. Review at: http://archive. sensesofcinema.com/contents/cteq/01/12/enfants.html (4/2/2011).

Silvas, A. M. (2005). *The Asketikon of St Basil the Great*. Oxford: Oxford University Press.

Silverman, D. (2003). *Ancient Egypt*. Oxford: Oxford University Press.

Sim, S. (2007). *Manifesto for Silence: Confronting the Politics and Culture of Noise*. Edinburgh: Edinburgh University Press.

Simpson, C. (1996). Elisabeth Noelle-Neumann's "Spiral of Silence" and the historical context of communication theory. *Journal of Communications, 46*(3): 149–173.

Simpson, C. (1997). Elisabeth Noelle-Neumann: background documents 1935–1945. At: http://gurukul.ucc.american.edu/radiowave/ noelle/noelle.htm (4/2/2011).

Simpson, J. (1988). *Touching the Void*. London: Vintage.

Singer, T. C. (1998). "Riddles, silence, and wonder: Joyce and Wittgenstein encountering the limits of language". In: Brady, P. & Carens, J. F. (Eds.), *Critical Essays on James Joyce's A Portrait of the Artist as a Young Man* (pp. 243–264). New York: Macmillan..

Smart, J. G. (1970). *The Strange Silence of the Bible in the Church: A Study in Hermeneutics*. London: SCM Press.

Solzhenitsyn, A. (1970). Nobel Prize Lecture (written for Swedish Academy but not delivered as a lecture). At: http://nobelprize. org/literature/laureates/1970/solzhenitsyn-lecture.html (4/2/2011).

Sontag, S. (1970). The aesthetics of silence. In: S. Sontag, *Styles of Radical Will* (pp. 3–34). New York: Delta.

Sourvinou-Inwood, C. (2003). Festival and mystery: aspects of the Eleusinian Cult. In: Cosmopoulos, M. B. (Ed.), *Greek Mysteries: The Archaeology and Ritual of Ancient Greek Secret Cults* (pp. 25–49). London: Routledge.

Spedding, J., Ellis, R. L. & Heath D. D. (Eds.) (1858). *Works of Francis Bacon*. 14 vols. London: Longman.

Spinka, M. (1953). *Advocates of Reform: from Wyclif to Erasmus*. London: SCM Press.

Spregelburd, R. & Sánchez-Colberg, A. (n.d). Tacit borders: on silence, presence and resistance in contemporary Latin American performance. At: http://www.autores.org.ar/spre/Creacion/Adaptaciones/pies/silence.htm (4/2/2011).

Steiner, G. (1967 & revised edition 1985). *Language and Silence: Essays on Language, Literature, and the Inhuman*. London: Faber & Faber.

Stephen, C. (1890). *Quaker Strongholds*. London: Kegan Paul, Trench & Trubner.

Sterb, F. (2001). Subtle silence and its consequences. In: Tewes, H. & Wright, J. (Eds.), *Liberalism, Anti-Semitism, Democracy: Essays in Honour of Peter Pulzer* (pp. 1–10). Oxford: Oxford University Press.

Stern, L. (2003). *The Life and Opinions of Tristram Shandy, Gentleman*. Harmondsworth, UK: Penguin.

Stevenson, B. E. (Ed.) (1948). *The Home Book of Proverbs, Maxims and Familiar Phrases*. New York: Macmillan.

Stevenson. B. E. (Ed.) (1974). *Stevenson's Book of Quotations: Classical and Modern*. 10th ed. London: Cassell.

Stringer, J., Levitt, H. M., Berman, J. S. & Mathews, S. (2010). A study of silent disengagement and distressing emotion in psychotherapy. *Psychotherapy Research, 20*(5): 495–510.

Sukys, J. (2007). *Silence is Death: The Life and Work of Tahar Djaout*. Lincoln, NE: University of Nebraska Press.

Sydney, P. (1999). *The Old Arcadia*. K. Duncan-Jones (Ed.). Oxford: Oxford University Press.

Szabo, L. (2000). The sound of sheer silence: a study in the poetics of Thomas Merton. *Merton Annual*, 13: 208–221.

Tannen, D. (Ed.) (1988). *Linguistics in Context: Connecting Observation and Understanding*. Norwood, NJ: Ablex.

Tannen, D. (2001). The relativity of linguistic strategies: rethinking power and solidarity in gender and dominance. In: Wetherell, M., Taylor, S. & Yates, S. J. (Eds.), *Discourse Theory and Practice* (pp. 150–166). London: Sage.

Tannen, D. & Saville-Troike, M. (Eds.) (1985). *Perspectives on Silence*. Norwood, NJ: Ablex.

Tatar, S. (2005). Why keep silent? The classroom participation experiences of non-native English-speaking students. *Language and Intercultural Communication*, 5(3&4): 284–293.

Tavener, J. (1999). *The Music of Silence: A Composer's Testament*. B. Keeble (Ed.). London: Faber & Faber.

Taylor, C. (Ed.) (1897). *Sayings of the Jewish Fathers, Comprising Pirque Aboth in Hebrew and English with Notes and Excursions*. Cambridge: Cambridge University Press.

Taylor, C. (2009). *The Culture of Confession from Augustine to Foucault: A Genealogy of the "Confessing Animal"*. Abingdon, UK: Routledge.

Teresa of Avila (1976–1985). *The Collected Works of St Theresa of Avila*. Kavanaugh, K. & Rodriguez, O. (Trans.). 3 vols. Washington, DC: ICS Publications.

Terrien, S. (1991). Marianne Moore: poet of secular holiness. *Theology Today*, 47(4): 388–399.

Theodores, D. (2003). *Dancing on the Edge of Europe: Irish Choreographers in Conversation*. Cork, Ireland: Institute for Choreography and Dance.

Thiesmeyer, L. (Ed.) (2003). *Discourse and Silencing: Representation and the Language of Displacement*. Amsterdam: John Benjamins.

Thiselton-Dyer, T. F. (1906). *Folk-lore of Women: As Illustrated by Legendary and Traditionary Tales, Folk-rhymes, Proverbial Sayings, Superstitions, etc.* Chicago: A. C. McClurg, and London: Elliot Stock.

Thomson, J. (1800). A hymn. In: Thomson, J. *The Seasons*. Paris: Louis.

Thoreau, H. D. (1838). Some scraps from an essay on "Sound and Silence" written in the latter half of this month—December 1838. In: Torrey, B. (Ed.), *The Writings of Henry David Thoreau: Journal* (7:64–69). 20 vols. Boston: Houghton Mifflin, 1906.

Thurlow, C. & Jaworski, A. (2010). Silence is golden: the "anti-communicational" linguascaping of super-elite mobility. In:

Jaworski, A. & Thurlow, C. *Semiotic Landscapes: Language, Image, Space* (pp. 187–218). London: Continuum.

Tomkins, C. (1996). *Duchamp: A Biography*. New York: Henry Holt.

Torrey, B. (Ed.). (1906). *The Writings of Henry David Thoreau: Journal*. 20 vols. Boston: Houghton Mifflin.

Tremearne, A. J. N. (1912). Extracts from the diary of the late Rev. John Martin, Wesleyan missionary in West Africa, 1843–48. *Man, 12*: 138–143.

Trevelyan, G. O. (1876). *The Life and Letters of Lord Macaulay*. 2 vols. London: Longmans, Green.

Triplett, W. (2002). Review of *Hamlet ... the Rest is Silence*. Washington, DC: *Washington Post*, April 8.

Tseng, M. (2000). The representation of silence in text: examples from two selected silences. *Dong Hwa Journal of Humanistic Studies, 2*: 103–124.

Tull, H. W. (1989). *The Vedic Origins of Karma: Cosmos as Man in Ancient Indian Myth and Ritual*. Albany, NY: SUNY Press.

Turner, D. (2002). Apophaticism, idolatry and the claims of reason. In: Davies, O. & Turner, D. (Eds.), *Silence and the Word: Negative Theology and Incarnation* (pp. 23–29). Cambridge: Cambridge University Press.

Uekermann, G. (1996). Synopsis. In: Schoenberg, A., *Moses und Aron*, pp. 16–18 of booklet.

Vanier, J. (1970). *Tears of Silence*. Toronto: Griffin House.

Vercors, J. [Bruller, J.] (1944). *The Silence of the Sea*. Connolly, C. (Trans., under the title *Put out the Light*). London: Macmillan.

Vest, N. (1994). *No Moment Too Small: Rhythms of Silence, Prayer and Holy Reading*. Kalamazoo, MI: Cistercian Publications, and Boston, MA: Cowley Publishing.

Vickers, B. (Ed.) (2002). *Francis Bacon: The Major Works*. Oxford: Oxford University Press.

Voegelin, S. (2010). *Listening to Noise and Silence: Toward a Philosophy of Sound Art*. New York: Continuum.

Wagner, G. (1995). Bip se souvient. Interview with Marcel Marceau. At: http://www.guywagner.net/marceau_int.htm (4/2/2011).

Wathen, A. (1973). *Silence: The Meaning of Silence in the Rule of St Benedict*. Washington, DC: Cistercian Publications.

Wechsler, J. (1982). *A Human Comedy: Physiognomy and Caricature in Nineteenth-Century Paris*. London: Thames & Hudson.

Westminster Dictionary of Christian Theology (1983). Richardson, A. & Bowden, J. (Eds.). Philadelphia, PA: Westminster Press.

Wetherell, M., Taylor, S. & Yates, S. (Eds.) (2001). *Discourse Theory and Practice*. London: Sage.

Whitty, K. (2006). Fear and hope [film review of *Tsotsi*]. At: http://entertainment.iafrica.com/movies/topten/879193.htm (4/2/2011).

Wiesel, E. (1986). Speech accepting the Nobel Peace Prize (December 10). At: http://www.pbs.org/eliewiesel/nobel/index.html (4/2/2011).

Wilcox, E. W. (1914). *Poems of Problems*. Chicago: Conkey.

Williams, A. L. (Ed.) (1921). *Tractata Berakoth—Benedictions—Mishna and Tosephta*. London: SPCK.

Williams, D. (1994). *Nobody Nowhere: The Extraordinary Autobiography of an Autistic*. New York: Avon.

Williams, D. (1995). *Somebody Somewhere: Breaking Free From the World of Autism*. Westminster, MD: Times.

Williams, R. (2004). *Silence and Honey Cakes*. Oxford: Lion Hudson.

Willis-Bund, W. & Friswell, J. H. (Eds.) (1898). *Reflections: Or Sentences and Moral Maxims of François Duc de La Rochefoucauld*. London: Sampson Low Marston.

Willnat, L., Waipeng, L. & Detenber, B. H. (2002). Individual-level predictors of public outspokenness: a test of the spiral of silence theory in Singapore. *International Journal of Public Opinion Research*, 14(4): 391–412.

Wilmer, H. A. (1995). Silence: something we rarely hear, which does not exist. *Journal of the American Academy of Psychoanalysis and Dynamic Psychiatry*, 23(4): 723–730.

Winternitz, M. (1927). *A History of Indian Literature*. 2 vols. Calcutta, India: University of Calcutta. Reprinted New Delhi: Oriental Books Reprint Corporation, 1972.

Wittgenstein, L. (1981). *Tractatus Logico-Philosophicus*. Ogden, C. K. (Trans.). London: Routledge.

Woolland, B. (1999). The gift of silence. In: Cave, R., Schafer, E. & Woolland, B. (Eds.), *Ben Johnson and Theatre: Performance, Practice and Theory* (pp. 125–142). London: Routledge.

Wright, W. M. (1997). *Babette's Feast*: a religious film. *Journal of Religion and Film*, 1(2): 1.

Yamada, H. (1997). *Different Games, Different Rules: Why Americans and Japanese Misunderstand Each Other*. Oxford: Oxford University Press.

Yamamoto, H. (1950). Wilshire bus. In: Yamamoto, H. *Seventeen Syllables and Other Stories* (pp. 34–38). Piscataway, NJ: Rutgers University Press, 1998.

Yokouchi, K. (2005). Artist interview. A meeting of Eastern and Western classics: the Noh-staged Shakespeare of Yoshihiro Kurita. The Japan Foundation's "Performing Arts Network Japan" (March 16). At: http://performingarts.jp/E/art_interview/0503/1.html (4/2/2011).

Zarrilli, P. (2006). Senses and silence in actor training and performance. In: Banes, S. & Lepecki, A. (Eds.), *The Senses in Performance* (pp. 47–70). London: Routledge.

Zeligs, M. A. (1961). The psychology of silence. *Journal of the American Psychoanalytic Association, 9*(1): 7–43. Five other authors also write on silence in this issue.

Zerubavel, E. (2006). *The Elephant in the Room: Silence and Denial in Everyday Life.* New York: Oxford University Press.

Zimmerman, M., Rooas, R., Rojas, R. & Navia, P. (1998). *Voices from the Silence: Guatemalan Literature of Resistance.* Athens, OH: Ohio University Press.

Žižek, S. (2006). Burned by the sun. In: Žižek, S. (Ed.), *Lacan: The Silent Partners* (pp. 217–230). Verso: New York.

INDEX